Heritage, Tourism and Society

Edited by
David T. Herbert

PINTER

First published in 1995 by
Mansell Publishing Limited. A Cassell Imprint

Wellington House, 125 Strand, London WC2R 0BB, England
PO Box 605, Herndon, VA 20172, USA

Reprinted in paperback in 1997 by Pinter. A Cassell Imprint

British Library Cataloguing-in-Publication Data
Heritage, Tourism and Society. – (Tourism, Leisure & Recreation Series)
  I. Herbert, David T.   II. Series
  338.4791

ISBN 0–7201–2172–8 (hardback)
ISBN 1–85567–429–7 (paperback)

Library of Congress Cataloging-in-Publication Data
Heritage, tourism and society / edited by David T. Herbert.
     p.   cm.–(Tourism, leisure and recreation series)
    Includes bibliographical references and index.
    ISBN 0–7201–2172–8 (hardback) : $60.00
    ISBN 1–85567–429–7 (paperback)
    1. Historic sites – Conservation and restoration – Social aspects – Great Britain.
  2. Cultural property, Protection of – Social aspects – Great Britain.
  3. Historical museums – Social aspects – Great Britain.   4. Tourist trade – Social
aspects – Great Britain.
  I. Series.
  DA655.H47   1995
  338.4'7914104859–dc20   95–3674
                                           CIP

Typeset by Colset Private Limited, Singapore
Printed and bound in Great Britain by Biddles Ltd, Guildford and King's Lynn

Tourism, Leisure and Recreation Series

Series Editors
Gareth Shaw and Allan Williams

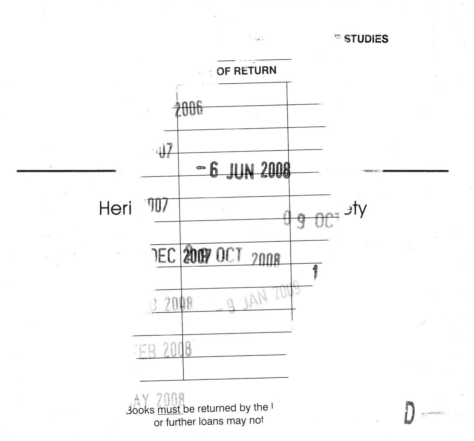

Contents

List of Figures

List of Tables

Contributors

Gregory J. Ashworth   Department of Physical Planning and Demography
Faculty of Spatial Sciences
University of Groningen
Zernikecomplex
Landleven 5, PO Box 800
9700 AV Groningen
The Netherlands

Pyrs Gruffudd   Department of Geography
University of Wales: Swansea
Singleton Park
Swansea SA2 8PP, UK

David T. Herbert   Department of Geography
University of Wales: Swansea
Singleton Park
Swansea SA2 8PP, UK

Peter Johnson   Department of Economics
University of Durham
23/26 Old Elvet
Durham DH1 3HY, UK

Peter J. Larkham   Faculty of the Built Environment
University of Central England in Birmingham
Perry Barr
Birmingham B42 2SU, UK

Duncan Light   Department of Environmental and Biological
Studies
Liverpool Institute of Higher Education
Stand Park Road
Liverpool L16 9JD, UK

Richard C. Prentice   Department of Hospitality and Tourism
                                 Management
                           Queen Margaret College
                           Clerwood Terrace
                           Edinburgh EH12 8TS, UK

Frans F. J. Schouten   Nationale Hogeschool voor Toerisme en Verkeer
                           Sector toerisme en recreatie
                           Sibeliuslaan 13
                           4837 CA Breda
                           The Netherlands

Terry Stevens   Faculty of Leisure, Tourism and Health Care
                                 Studies
                           Swansea Institute
                           Mount Pleasant
                           Swansea SA1 6ED, UK

Barry Thomas   Department of Economics
                           University of Durham
                           23/26 Old Elvet
                           Durham DH1 3HY, UK

Preface

Heritage tourism is now big business. In economic and entrepreneurial terms, it is one of the major success stories of recent years. At a time of declining industrial activity and rising unemployment in Western society, heritage tourism has provided an alternative form of enterprise, creating jobs and generating wealth for local economies. It has capitalized on the growth phenomena of the latter part of the twentieth century – the expansion of leisure time, the emergence of the age of mass tourism, and the many and diverse demands for places to visit. People, as day and weekend visitors or as tourists, need a range of places where they can go not only to relax, to be informed or even educated, but also to be entertained. Heritage, by providing some of these places, has become a component of the tourism industry.

The more problematic aspect of heritage tourism arises from the fact that heritage is a sensitive topic. As a word it has many meanings but most relate to its general interpretation as 'that which is inherited from the past'. The sensitivities arise in part because the inherited past is a fragile concept. Relics, whether they are the ruins of castles or abbeys, works of art or artefacts, are vulnerable to use; they need to be handled with care. The issues of conservation and preservation have emerged in response to these sensitivities and to the responsibilities that have been placed upon one generation to pass on treasured heritage to the next. For those committed to preservation as the overriding priority, heritage tourism is a threat. Greater access has meant greater pressure of visitor numbers, and the demands of an interested, visiting public have to be reconciled with the custodial responsibilities of those who administer a heritage site. Controls of some kind are invariably needed and here the legislative responsibility lies squarely with central and local government, whilst that of good management devolves to the site itself.

The issue of authenticity is another problematic dimension. As heritage tourism has grown, so the notion of the heritage site has changed. Remote sites of crumbling ruins, with occasional curatorship and minimal facilities to help any visitor, have been overtaken by many new forms of heritage attraction. Many of the well-known and heavily visited castles and religious sites have recognized their potential as visitor attractions, and have responded by presenting their heritage in more attractive and legible ways, providing the kinds of facility which visitors expect. Dangers arise because it is relatively easy to invert history and to turn heritage into a marketable product without proper regard for rigour, honesty and factual accuracy in the presentation of heritage. Whereas the bare stones of a ruin may be sufficient for the scholar, they will not attract the tourist unless they are accompanied by displays and commentaries to give them meaning. It is in these situations that questions arise. In what ways and to what extent is it permissible to 'build' a story around these stones in order to provide a heritage attraction? If the presentation is more fantasy than fact, do you need the stones at all? Some of the more scholarly critiques of heritage tourism, such as Lowenthal's *The Past Is a Foreign Country*, revolve around this issue of authenticity and the superficiality of much of what is presented as heritage. The message is unambiguous: 'By changing the relics and records of former times, we change ourselves as well; the revised past in turn alters our own identity' (Lowenthal, 1985, p. 411).

This book, as its title suggests, is centrally concerned with the development of heritage places as attractions for visitors and tourists and with the issues which this raises. It is less concerned with natural heritage than with heritage which has connections with people and events from the past; with sites that bear significant imprints of people upon landscape. The book is concerned with the sites themselves, with the impact they have upon the localities within which they are placed, with the providers and managers who seek to present heritage to a wider public, and with the visitors, for whom heritage may have wide and varying meanings. In a topical field which has stimulated a good deal of debate in recent years, the aim is to add to scholarly understanding rather than to polemic. Most of the major issues that have attracted debate are discussed here. Some are more thinly treated than others, but it is hoped that all are recognized as being part of what has become both a topic for keen academic debate and also a practical issue of increasing relevance to more and more people.

As editor of this book, my thanks to the contributors who have provided extremely interesting and accomplished chapters with admirable punctuality and attention to detail. My thanks also to support staff at the Department of Geography, University of Wales, Swansea, who have helped significantly in the production of this book, particularly to Lynn Muir who 'fixed up' the final versions of manuscripts and Guy Lewis who produced the figures.

David T. Herbert
May 1994

REFERENCE

Lowenthal, D. (1985) *The Past Is a Foreign Country*. Cambridge: Cambridge University Press.

Heritage Places, Leisure and Tourism

David T. Herbert

Heritage, leisure and tourism can all safely be included among the major growth phenomena of the latter part of the twentieth century. Many more people have increased amounts of leisure time and tourism has extended its net to cover many parts of the world and sections of society. For both leisure and tourism, the historical pattern is one of the generalization of a form of behaviour from a small minority to a large majority. What had been the normal components of lifestyle for a privileged few became the common expectation of a much larger number of people. Heritage places are products, or perhaps constructions, of history. They owe their distinctiveness to the past. That distinctiveness remains recognizable but is often used and presented in new ways. Much of this presentation is closely related to the growth of leisure and tourism. Heritage places have been part of the round of leisure-time visitors and tourists.

In common with many key words in the English language, heritage, leisure and tourism are problematic. Part of the problem with both 'heritage' and 'leisure' is that they have different meanings for different people. A historic monument or artefact, judged as valued heritage by one person, may be of no interest to another; one person's chosen leisure activity may be another's involuntary chore. As a term, 'tourism' is traditionally less problematic, though recent academic literature has raised questions about its meanings and implications:

Tourism is not just an aggregate of merely commercial activities; it is also an ideological framing of history, nature and tradition; a framing that has the power to reshape culture and nature to its own needs. (MacCannell, 1992, p. 1)

This view of tourism is very different from that held by those involved in commercial activities, such as hotel owners in Blackpool, St Tropez or Orlando, but it does demonstrate the complex social processes that underpin relatively commonplace forms of behaviour.

Heritage places, leisure and tourism are interrelated, though not necessarily interdependent. Heritage places have autonomous roles as places of formal education, research and conservation, for example, and these roles need not be related to either leisure or tourism. A great deal of leisure time is spent in passive pursuits, such as reading or watching television, and does not involve any tourist activity. Most tourists visit beaches with warm and scenic settings, and visits to heritage places may not figure in their itineraries. Having established the fact that the components of this triad can be autonomous, their interactions can also be noted. Many people, though probably a minority, visit heritage places in their leisure time as tourists. Heritage tourism, a subset of the larger activity, is a recognizable form of tourism in its own right. For both heritage places and tourism, the growth of leisure time, and the uses to which it is put, is the main common theme.

The Idea of Leisure

The idea of leisure is in many ways of relatively modern origin. As Patmore (1983) pointed out, for long periods of time the separation of work and leisure was less a separation of an individual's use of time than the separation of the leisured and working classes. The workers were granted days free of work, but otherwise had no obvious division of time labelled as leisure. Leisure was embedded in life, to a greater or lesser extent, rather than a separate part of it. To some extent this has remained true. Samdahl (1992) argued that leisure occurs in daily routines; it is a common occasion which punctuates our normal lives. These are empirical observations but there have been a number of attempts to define leisure and to isolate 'leisure time'. These can be summarized, but it is worth noting that Horne *et al.* (1987) have argued that there have in fact been very few attempts to construct a 'systematic theory of leisure'.

The most consistent themes in these attempts to define leisure and leisure time have been the recognition of the antithesis between work and leisure and of the fact that leisure must involve choice of activities. Stockdale (1985) recognized three approaches to the definition of leisure. The first of these defined leisure time as that in which choice is the dominant factor; the second classified leisure time as time not required for work or commitments; and the third invoked people's subjective interpretation of leisure: if they regarded an activity as leisure, it could be defined as such and could occur at any time and in any setting. Brook's (1993) features of leisure time included freedom of choice, personal discretion, and 'socio-emotional' involvement in activities. Wearing and Wearing (1992) saw leisure as an escape from commodified time, or time used for materialistic purposes. In their terms, the constructive and positive use of leisure led to a satisfying lifestyle. Definitions such as these are adequate as concepts but falter in detailed application because of the variability of personal interpretations of leisure.

There are other, more discursive attempts to theorize leisure. MacCannell (1976) emphasized the growing significance of leisure and argued that it was displacing work as the centre of social arrangements. Smith (1987) saw leisure as a social-bonding process which provided outlets for relaxation, entertainment and liberation, all of which counteracted some of the stresses of life. Kelly (1991, p. 253) argued that: 'Leisure is important because it is complex, social and contextual, because it is tied to the realities of life rather than confined to movements of rarefied consciousness . . . it is not freedom from a continuing structure but a structured action with a core of self determination.' This statement is of interest because it qualifies the choice assumption of leisure definition; leisure time may contain structures and routines similar to those encountered in the world of work.

Groups in society can be classified by their leisure lifestyles. Age, gender, social class, income, car ownership and education are all strong influences upon leisure activities. Bourdieu (1984) saw leisure tastes as part of a whole range of human activities affected by possession of material and cultural capital. Working-class adults tend to become spectators at sporting events, whereas their middle-class equivalents participate in sports, often involving significant costs, which can be pursued well into retirement. The cultural capital available to professional, middle-class groups makes them more likely to appreciate the arts, visit the theatre or the museum.

A great deal of leisure time is spent at home, and Allan and Crow (1991) found that the extent to which leisure is privatized and home-centred varies not just with social class but also with gender, household composition and housing conditions. For most people, the ideal combination is that of home-based domesticity, family-oriented activities and external social involvement. Again, however, there are group differences. As a generalization, old people and women with young children experience constraints which limit their ability to visit recreational places outside the home. External social involvement will vary in extent and form with tastes and preferences, but is also dependent upon the providers of leisure facilities. Issues of access also become significant – some people will have easy access to leisure facilities but others may experience much more difficulty. Access varies geographically and socially. Rural areas are often relatively disadvantaged and non-car-owners will also suffer access problems. The providers of leisure facilities 'package' the leisure experience and, in so doing, they treat it as a commodity. This commodity is available to those who can afford it and to whom it is accessible. Further, the process of commodification removes choice, promotes conformity and allows fewer opportunities for the exceptional and the individual.

Leisure Trends

The most consistent message from official statistics, such as those recorded in *Social Trends*, is that time spent at work is decreasing and time available for leisure is increasing. A survey in the United Kingdom in 1993 showed that one-third of workers supported the idea of further reductions in working hours (King, 1993, p. 4) and many were prepared to sacrifice wages in return. In their detailed diary study of a set of respondents over the period 1961 to 1984, Gershuny and Jones (1987) produced evidence for reductions in the working week, longer paid holidays, more unemployment, more involuntary leisure time, more early retirement and significant changes in women's access to leisure. Leisure time, defined as residual time after work and time spent with children, showed gains of between 30 and 60 minutes per week for specified groups between 1961 and 1984. *Social Trends* (1993) showed that men in full-time employment had 4.8 hours of free time per weekday compared to 3.3 hours for working women. Retired people with 11.6 hours of free time per day were the most leisured category.

Gender differences in use of leisure time remain strong. Gershuny and Jones (1987) found trends over time showing that more women had jobs, more worked part time, more time was devoted to children but domestic routine work had reduced with improved technology in the home. Women still carried out two to three times the amount of domestic chores compared to men, despite some shift towards redressing the balance. The burden of care also fell unevenly, with greater dependence on women relatives by the elderly and the mentally ill as policies of de-institutionalization are implemented.

Against this background of the changing availability of leisure time are the uses which people make of it. In the winter of 1987, men watched on average 25.5 hours of television per week whilst the figure for women was 30.75 hours. *Social Trends* (1993) suggested that higher-income groups were watching less television, with 18.51 hours for the AB (professional/managerial) group, and 31.56 hours for the DE (semi-skilled/unskilled) groups. Several other home-based activities took up large amounts of leisure time and these included listening to the radio and to music, reading, gardening and DIY. *Social Trends* (1993) estimated 630 million day visits, of which 144 million involved visits to relatives or friends, 66 million were sightseeing trips, and 33 million involved outdoor sports. The Countryside Commission (1985) found that almost 50 per cent of the population made a trip to the countryside at least once a fortnight on average throughout the year, rising to 70 per cent in the summer months. Dower (1965) anticipated this when he wrote about the 'fourth wave', more powerful than its predecessors, which was about to impact upon the country-side. Dower perceived this 'fourth wave' as the outflow of urban dwellers into rural areas in search of recreational space and activities. Of the 630 million day visits, 30 million were specifically to 'heritage places' such as castles, museums and stately homes. Thrift (1989) argued that it was the service class or professional white-collar workers who were the most frequent countryside and heritage visitors. On the provider side, the 1980s were marked by commercial investment in attractions by both the private and the public sectors.

One result of the increased amount of paid holidays has been greater travel, with about two-thirds of adults taking a holiday abroad each year. Despite these foreign excursions and visits to more distant parts of the same country, locality still dominates leisure trips: 'Leisure movements to distant places give deep enjoyment and lasting stimulation, yet most leisure is spent in familiar places, with the constraints as well as the challenges that implies' (Patmore, 1983, p. 234).

A growth in leisure time, then, has been a consistent theme in the second half of the twentieth century. Certainly, all the indicators of shorter working days and more paid holidays point in that direction. Increasing numbers of people are being released from work and household routines and are creating a demand for leisure facilities. Most leisure time occurs at weekends, or at the ends of working days, and may not involve trips outside the home or locality. There are, however, blocks of leisure time, such as annual holidays, which can be set aside for longer excursions that can, more properly, be described as tourism.

Tourism

Whereas leisure is a diffuse concept and leisure activities can take many forms, tourism is more specific and focuses on the idea of trips or excursions away from the normal place of residence, involving at least an overnight stay. Leisure may be an integral part of daily routines, but tourism occurs in specially designated blocks of time. People become tourists when they leave their homes for a significant period of time to visit places, to experience a range of activities, and to enjoy time spent in relaxation or differently from normal routines. It is true that tourism can be interwoven with other activities such as business trips, but it normally and predominantly takes the form of a discrete and single-purpose holiday. Urry (1990) developed the idea of the 'tourist gaze'. People, he argued, go away from home to look at environments with interest and curiosity, they *gaze* at what they encounter. Many tourists are passive visitors: they obtain pleasure from seeing new places and use cameras to capture images which they can re-experience when they return home. Historically, there has always been a broad division between passive and active tourists. The passive tourists may be content to gaze but also to experience the pleasure of being in a place, meeting people, and sampling different lifestyles. The active tourists want to use the landscape as walkers, climbers and skiers. There is no single tourist gaze, nor is there a single tourist experience.

The growth of tourism has been one of the features of the twentieth century. Martin and Mason (1992) showed that, for the United Kingdom between 1979 and 1989, the numbers of adults taking holidays overseas had increased by 65 per cent, short trips within Britain had increased by 31 per cent and there had been a 38 per cent increase in foreign visitors. Statistics of this kind can be replicated in many parts of the world as new areas are opened up to tourism. In the United Kingdom, tourist-related services account for 1.5 million jobs and tourist spending is of the order of £15 billion. For British residents on foreign holidays, long-haul trips showed the most growth, with a trebling of UK visitors to Australia and New Zealand between 1980 and 1990. Whereas the 'internationalization of tourism is a process with long roots' (Shaw and Williams, 1994), it is really a later twentieth-century phenomenon in its scale and range. In 1948 there were 14 million international tourists; in 1989 there were 403 million (World Tourism Organization, 1990).

The origins of tourism are ancient. Urry (1990) suggested that tourism was known in Imperial Rome with the use of seaside 'resorts'; certainly in medieval times pilgrimages to the Holy Land involved pleasure and sightseeing as well as religious duty. As a concept and a reality, the Grand Tour was established by the late seventeenth century as a component of polite society's social round. For the Grand Tour, the guiding texts and the Blue Guides in particular were to assume great significance. Buzard (1993) traced the first dictionary use of the term 'tourist' to the late eighteenth century when it was used as a synonym for 'traveller'. The differences between these two words were to become significant as tourism became generalized beyond the rich and privileged. In the nineteenth century seaside resorts and spa towns were given prosperity by the railway networks' ability to transport large numbers of people at manageable cost. Similar changes opened up foreign travel in the second half of the twentieth century. Buzard (1993) described Thomas Cook as the other 'agent' of change, and certainly the establishment of the means by which ever-wider sections of the population could participate in tourism has been of paramount importance. Along with the massive increase in flows of people has gone the growth in the infrastructure of tourism, which is an essential component.

Urry (1990) has usefully identified the social practices of tourism. In his terms, tourism is a leisure activity typically organized within particular places and occurring for regularized periods of time. Urry was also interested in types of tourist, and the distinction he makes between the romantic and the collective gaze has echoes elsewhere in the literature. The romantic gaze is that of the more aware, the elite group who appreciate magnificent scenery, who value solitude and have the cultural capital to draw meanings from places. The collective gaze belongs to the less discerning majority. It 'necessitates the presence of large numbers of other people. . . . Other people give atmosphere or sense of carnival to a place' (Urry, 1990, pp. 45–46).

In similar terms, Buzard (1993) differentiated between travellers and tourists:

> Travellers sought to distinguish themselves from the 'mere tourists' they saw or imagined around them. Correspondingly, the authentic culture of places – the genius loci – was represented as lurking in secret precincts 'off the beaten track' where it could be discovered only by the sensitive 'traveller', not the vulgar tourist. (Buzard, 1993, p. 6)

The argument has been extended to categories such as that of the 'anti-tourist', which Buzard regarded as equivalent to the practitioner of the romantic gaze. Such people distance themselves from the mass tourist but still require them, as their own identity depends on the contrast which they offer; there is a dialectical relationship. Fussell (1980) recognized the anti-tourists but did not see them as 'travellers'. Their motives, he argued, were not those of genuine enquiry but of self-protection and vanity. Feifer (1986) identified a group which she termed 'post-tourists' who, through the wonders of modern technology, do not have to leave home to experience the tourist gaze, have wide choice and can treat tourism as a game in which issues, such as authenticity, are of no significance.

All the evidence points towards variety amongst the tourist population. Terms such as romantic, collective, anti-tourist and post-tourist are meant to capture this sense of variety, as are more straightforward differences, based on criteria such as age, gender, social class and personal preferences. In all of these studies, the tourist of the collective gaze is seen as in the large majority, the follower of what Buzard (1993) termed the 'beaten track' of touristic space, where all experiences are predictable and repetitive and the fact of being on holiday imposes its own simple routines and conventions. All types of tourist are interested in 'attractions', though by no means the same attractions. At its most basic, the attraction might be the beach, the sun and the local bar; other visitors might be more interested in seeking out a local historic site or the birthplace of some famous former resident.

It is with the relationship between attractions and the tourist that this book is centrally concerned. Leisure time provides the general context, activities outside the home identify the relevant behaviour, and tourism locates the most specific and clear blocks of usable time. The concept of the 'visit' to an attraction will not be restricted, however, to tourism *per se*; many visits are made in 'non-holiday' leisure time and involve local populations. Users of leisure time and tourists constitute the potential demand, or the market, to which the providers of attractions must direct their efforts.

As the entrepreneurs in both the private and local state sectors seek to attract tourists, they enter the role of image-maker. Historically, they have responded to, or have created trends and fashions which have most potential for the increased flows of visitors. The notion of the healthy place or activity, which will enhance physical well-being, is a recurrent theme. Spa towns, health resorts and seaside resorts all had this dimension, combined initially with gracious living in the large hotels and later with the home comforts of boarding-houses. Mountain tourism, especially in the Alps, was initially the preserve of the educated middle-class traveller as active climber, walker or skier, or as appreciative observer of the grandeur of nature. Even as mass tourism developed and the seaside resort became dominant, there were fashionable resorts, such as Deauville in Normandy, which catered for the rich. Health and gracious living were two of the early promotional features. Another was spectacle. Henry James (see Buzard, 1993, p. 155) suggested that 'to travel is, as it were, to go to a play, to attend a spectacle'. Creators of modern attractions have capitalized on this notion. They have sought to draw maximum benefit from attractions where they already exist and to develop them where they do not. Martin and Mason (1992) estimated that around 1000 new sightseeing attractions had opened in England since 1979, one-third of all of those in existence. They include theme parks, country parks, industrial sites such as those associated with Wedgwood and Cadbury, and others such as the Granada Studios and photographic museums. *Social Trends* (1993) cited Blackpool Pleasure Beach with 6.5 million visitors annually as the top British attraction, followed by the British Museum with 5.1 million, and the National Gallery with 4.3 million. Historic sites, museums and galleries rank highly but purpose-built attractions, notably theme parks, have become the hallmark of recent years. Heritage places are part of this range of attractions, part of the providers' smorgasbord to which visitors and tourists are asked to respond. Heritage, the third concept to be discussed, is the main theme of this text.

Heritage

As already indicated, heritage, as a concept, is problematic. Dictionary defini-tions such as 'that which has been or may be inherited' (*OED*, 1983), offer only the most general of guidelines. The 1983 National Heritage Conference defined heritage as: 'That which a past generation has preserved and handed on to the present and which a significant group of population wishes to hand on to the future' (Hewison, 1989, p. 6). This definition indicates culture choice; its focus is on preservation and the fact that *some* people will adopt a conservationist view of heritage. In many ways this was the traditional role of heritage places. Historic sites, usually unmodified ruins, were visited by relatively few people: only by those who had a genuine sense of the past and sufficient education to understand their significance. Such heritage sites were often relatively inaccessible and those who came expected no facilities. As heritage places have become part of the range of visitor attractions, much has changed and the basic conflict between preservation and access has emerged as the dominant issue. It is fairly clear that access is winning. The costs of main-taining historic sites are considerable and public access offers one of the few ways of raising revenue. This fact has had to be faced even by government agencies charged primarily with the role of preservation. Cadw (Welsh Historic Monuments) in defending the fall in attendance at its sites in 1992

Pink Lily 1991

promised that: 'the completion of projects at Oxwich Castle, near Swansea, and Rhuddlan, North Wales, should boost attendances in 1993–94' (*Western Mail*, 16 December 1993).

Organizations such as Cadw are charged with stewardship but have to compromise the preservation ideal with the marketing of their sites (Herbert *et al.*, 1989). These practices bring heritage sites squarely into the range of tourist attractions, but they also raise objections. Lowenthal (1989, p. 213) summed up one position: 'As art-viewing turns into treadmill, heritage has to be protected from public contamination.' In Lowenthal's view, the population of visitors and tourists has lost its cultured, educated capabilities, as it has generalized. As classics have faded from the school curriculum, the elite group, versed in the classical and scriptural past, who visited and understood historic sites, has all but disappeared. Few now understand inherited landscape and heritage; the legacy has become remote. It is a sense of nostalgia, rather than the need to understand, which now makes heritage attractive: 'If the past is a foreign country, nostalgia has made it the foreign country with the healthiest tourist trade of all' (Lowenthal, 1985, p. 4).

Others have passed similar judgements: 'Historic landscapes, suitably sanitised, have become three-dimensional stage sets for tourism' (Cossons, 1988, p. 347).

As heritage has become more closely linked with tourism, the diversity of sites which are described as 'heritage' has increased:

> Essentially in tourism, the term 'heritage' has come to mean not only landscapes, natural history, buildings, artifacts, cultural traditions and the like which are literally or metaphorically passed on from one generation to the other, but those among these things which can be portrayed for promotion as tourism products. (Prentice, 1993, p. 5)

The eclecticism of heritage is reflected by Prentice's (1993) typology of heritage attractions, which comprised 23 subject-types, such as natural history, transport, socio-cultural, theme parks, galleries, seaside resorts and regions. Within each of these subject-types there were many subdivisions. Whereas this range and diversity is real, a number of basic distinctions can be made. One such is the distinction between natural heritage, drawing its qualities from nature, and places which become heritage sites because of their association with people or events. As heritage places are defined and used in this book, they fall into the second of these characterizations. Heritage places include historic buildings or monuments which bear the distinctive imprint of human history. Their interest may derive from architecture or design, from historical significance, or from combinations of these attributes. Heritage places in this sense are linked with people, events, activities and, in a wider sense, with cultures, societies and economies. A religious site may present a magnificent edifice which inspires awe; it will also reflect the cultural history of a people and may retain modern religious significance. Natural and people-made heritage are not mutually exclusive. A ruined castle has historic interest, but its spectacular setting will add significantly to its role as a heritage attraction. A view of the Lake District or the Wye Valley stands in its own right, but is given additional meaning by the link with Wordsworth and his poetry. Alpine mountains, such as the Matterhorn and the Eiger, are imbued with additional meaning by the historical exploits of climbers who have triumphed or failed on their precipices.

As the range has been extended and the 'stock' of heritage places augmented, the question of whether the needs of the tourist industry threaten to contaminate or misuse the concept of heritage has led to an active debate: 'Some of what now purports to be heritage has been antiqued, not only in appearance but, rather more sinisterly, in being presented as if it was significant historically as well as being ennobled by time' (Fowler, 1989, p. 60).

There is then a balance sheet to consider on the question of heritage places as tourist and visitor attractions. On the positive side, favouring the promotion of heritage places as tourist attractions:

1. There is a need to generate funds to allow preservation and conservation; the state will not assume the whole mantle of responsibility.
2. It is desirable to motivate local interest in heritage; groups, often from the 'service class', have key roles in conservation.
3. Public heritage agencies have a conservationist brief and this can ensure a proper balance of access and preservation.
4. Heritage places have assumed economic significance. They can be promoted and developed as projects which generate local employment and wealth. Local authorities have much to gain from the development of heritage. Lumley (1988) estimated that the creation of a job in tourism costs £4000 compared with £32 000 for a manufacturing job. For many cities which have lost their manufacturing base, urban tourism is seen as a major palliative (Robson, 1989). The local state sees advantages in tourism, and these figure strongly in their strategic development plans.

On the negative side of the balance sheet for the case for developing and promoting heritage as a component of the leisure and tourism industries are several broader issues, some of which have already been identified.

1. The first of these issues centres on authenticity. The argument here is that, in the process of attracting visitors, the history of a site is distorted. Fowler's (1989) reference to 'antiquing' is indicative in this context. Lowenthal argued that in interpreting or presenting the past there are constant distortions which distance the reality from that which is seen by modern visitors: 'The managed past may end up not merely segregated but unwittingly destroyed' (Lowenthal, 1985, p. 360). As already suggested, Lowenthal felt that this problem was compounded by the naivety of audiences who did not have the cultural capital to understand heritage.
2. A second negative issue is also related to authenticity. This is the argument that heritage is being less distorted than recreated. Jameson (1984) invoked the idea of a simulacrum, or the identical copy for which no original has ever existed. A similar argument was advanced by Eco (1986) with his concept of hyper-reality, or the ways in which 'the completely real becomes identified with the completely fake'. The transference of this idea into heritage is well described by Hewison (1989, p. 19):

The ultimate logic of the new type of museum is the museum that has no collection, the Heritage Centre, where the original purpose of having a museum, i.e. to preserve and interpret, in a scholarly way, a significant number of objects, has been almost entirely displaced by the desire to give the visitor some kind of more or less pleasurable experience.

This debate on authenticity has prompted different reactions. Boorstin (1985) stated that the contemporary American tourist thrived on 'pseudo-events' and certainly the ubiquitous 'halls of fame' often lack close ties with reality. Oklahoma City's 'Cowboy Hall of Fame' is more representative of the celluloid cowboys of the movie industry than of those who were actually part of the history of the 'West'. MacCannell (1992) regarded Boorstin's view as middle class, simply restating the traveller–tourist dichotomy. For Feifer (1986), the whole post-tourist idea was based on the idea that there were large numbers of visitors or observers who delight in the non-authentic event.

3. The third negative quality concerns selectivity. When developers or presenters of heritage offer their 'goods' to the public, they make a selection and that contains bias. Does heritage include noxious smells, sounds or the hallmarks of suffering and poverty? Places such as Auschwitz are open to visitors: are there ethical questions to be raised about portraying the site of a massacre? Should preserved and presented heritage display the 'down-side' of human history, the events now regarded with shame rather than with pride? At the other end of the scale there is the danger that all heritage will be concerned with stately homes or idyllic scenes and will omit underlying poverty. As Hughes (1992, pp. 37–38) argued in his analysis of the promotion of the Scottish Highlands, 'The characteristic tourist representation of Scotland involves a mix of folk-lore, pastoralism, picturesque scenes', but this portrayal ignores the fact that it is: 'based on a landscape which embodies a history of much human suffering'.

4. The fourth negative impact is upon local people and environments. Development of heritage places may mean invasion of privacy, threat to environment and building fabric, more traffic congestion and so on. Imported ideas on heritage may disrupt local lifestyles and cultures. As Third World societies come into the ambit of tourism, these issues take new forms. What Western observers see as heritage in a country such as Indonesia may in fact be ongoing practices and customs, using normal artefacts, for the local population. Locals are in danger of becoming part of the 'spectacle' of tourism, gazed upon by outsiders who know little or nothing about their culture and society: 'The desire to know on the part of tourists has to be balanced by a desire to tell on the part of the host culture' (Uzzell, 1989a, pp. 7–8).

These are some of the issues surrounding heritage places, leisure and tourism which provide the context for this book and which will be developed in depth in the following chapters. Modern attitudes towards heritage reveal the tensions between the more traditional and elitist positions of preservation and conservation on the one hand, and the thrust to exploitation on the other. Of the older aims, preservation is least fettered by marketing and materialism, and is closer to the aesthetic stance and a 'purist' view of history. Preservation seeks to keep sites as close as possible to their original state, and the guardianship or stewardship roles of organizations such as the National Trust and English Heritage represent this approach. Conservation is a more flexible approach which adopts restorative methods to recreate parts of built heritage. Legislation, such as the Malraux Act of 1962 in France, seeks to improve old built environments and bring them into modern use. Exploitation is the most modern phase: it recognizes the potential for the economic development of heritage sites and is at times prepared to ignore the precepts of preservation and conservation. It is upon this thrust to exploitation that much of the modern 'heritage industry' is founded.

Organization of the Text

The central question of heritage as historical reality provides the focus for a chapter by Frans Schouten, who has interests in psychology and anthropology and has acted as a consultant in the management, presentation and exploitation of heritage. He argues that if the question of *reality* rests on the scientific notion of objective truth and the idea of absolutes, it becomes difficult if not impossible to sustain. Most of the content of heritage – objects, buildings and sites – can be viewed as the tangible remains of some past period but all are transformed, by the subjective gaze of their viewers, into something which is personal and particular. Interpretation plays a part in this process of transformation. It is the intermediary between the object and the observer; it seeks to convey a message or messages, but has no absolute control over the ways in which these are received. Identical events can be presented or interpreted in radically different ways, material can be portrayed so as to ensure that a particular message, either favourable or unfavourable, is conveyed. Among the sources of bias in constructing historical reality is the way in which the historical account has been written, whose view is being represented, some definition of and adherence to 'political correctness', and the durability of material which, in itself, has an impact on what survives and can be represented. An issue of wide significance and debate is that of the so-called 'commodification of history'. For the purposes of presentation and interpretation which have at least some commercial relevance, heritage may become a creation or an adaptation rather than the preservation of what actually exists.

A great deal of our earlier experience of presentation, interpretation and codes of accuracy comes from work with museums. Typically, museums have been factually accurate but boring; their artefacts have been presented in ways which only appeal to a small section of the population. The information made available is often meaningful only to a restricted number of frequent visitors who have the cultural capital to appreciate objects and to place them in their correct historical context. In order to capture the public's imagination and widen the appeal, different approaches to presentation are needed. The distinction between museums, heritage sites and theme parks is becoming more blurred. As museums move towards greater variety in forms of presentation and interpretation, theme parks are showing greater awareness of authenticity. Out of this process of more common goals and the cross-fertilization of ideas, good practice should emerge, but historical reality remains a concept which must be handled with care.

The issue of historical reality and the presentation of heritage is also relevant to David Herbert's chapter on heritage as literary place. Such literary places normally have tangible links with the lives of writers and will attract visitors for that reason. They may also have meaning to visitors as settings for novels, as landscapes occupied by the great characters of fiction. Many writers based their novels in real-world settings, such as Hardy's Wessex and the Brontës' Yorkshire moors, but these settings were occupied by fictional characters such as Bathsheba Everdene or Catherine Earnshaw. Literary places become attractions for tourists as both 'real' and 'imagined' worlds and are part of heritage for both reasons. The route that Tess of the D'Urbervilles followed in her travels around Dorset, the moors where Heathcliff walked, and the streets in London to which Sherlock Holmes was taken by his investigations, have all become attractions to tourists because of their links with imaginary activities. How does one test authenticity or assess historical reality in this context?

The houses in which writers were born, died or wrote a particular novel also acquire meaning. These places fit the normal criteria for heritage. They need to be authentic, to be presented faithfully and to convey the 'atmosphere' in which the writer lived. The house at Chawton, where Jane Austen lived and wrote her novels, and the boat-house at Laugharne, where Dylan Thomas composed some of his works, are part of the itinerary of heritage tourism. Visitors to literary places come for a variety of reasons. Some are genuine 'students' of an author or a text and gain a great deal of pleasure from sight of a writing table or a lock of hair; for such people the visit is experiential and they look at, and feel in awe of, the setting in which they find themselves and the 'meanings' which that place possesses. For others, the visit may have much less meaning. It is pleasurable, relaxing, even entertaining, but it is just one part of the tourist or leisure-time round – a convenient place to spend a little time, with an awareness of the literary connection, but one to which little significance is attached. Literary places have been promoted as tourist attractions, and as much advantage as possible is often sought from connections with writers. Cabourg in Normandy, which has connections with the life of Marcel Proust and also claims to be the setting for the fictional Balbec of his novels, is studied as an example of this kind of literary place.

There are broader purposes for the preservation and presentation of heritage than those of providing an experience for a visitor or tourist. As Pyrs Gruffudd argues, heritage is an all-embracing concept that applies equally to landscapes, customs and narratives of identity. Heritage is an integral part of the concept of nation-building and treasured heritage can become an 'instrument' to create a sense of belonging to a common place. Many nations have used the concepts of common roots, of shared past adversities, and of singular past achievements as part of the process of bonding people together in a common cause. Buildings and monuments often have great symbolic meaning and serve as the icons of an emergent state. The image-builders, or 'spin doctors' of modern parlance, in many ways decide and construct the building blocks from which a sense of national identity can be forged. Authenticity obviously has to be in the forefront as the images created are both highly visible and contestable. Yet there is the view that 'traditions' are often inventions or recycled myths; they rarely have the status of facts.

There are various ways in which the link between heritage and national identity can be explored. Historically, Wales has been typified by 'contested landscapes'. The images which were constructed in the historical past varied over time and differed between sections of society. As Welsh landscapes were assimilated into English narrative and eventually recast by the Welsh, they were idealized and conveyed images of idyllic rural life and of Wales as a land of enchanted castles. Travel literature was the most common means by which such images were created and promoted. Landscape preservation became a central theme for debate, and here the views of the Welsh and non-Welsh often seemed to be in conflict. If the Welsh were unable to appreciate and preserve buildings and landscapes, this could be attributed to a 'visual handicap' and a dearth of material resources. Landscape, language and culture were significant issues which entered the political debate, occasionally with radical outcomes. Landscape in itself, as a physical entity, was insufficient for a growing sense of nationalism in Wales and the notions of culture and 'way of life' as heritage became of central importance. Taking inspiration from elsewhere, the folk museum became a major project to preserve and present Welsh traditions, but it was also conceived as a dynamic link with the past rather than as a sentimental legacy. Landscapes in some parts of Wales reflect the evolution of a 'Welsh' culture, but in others contain all the icons of colonization. Landscapes are palimpsests in which many indicators of the struggle for control and identity can coexist. Museums are also used to display or resurrect particular forms of national identity and can be employed to redefine the past for a particular political purpose. Heritage encapsulates notions of history, politics and identity.

Greg Ashworth develops this theme with his study of the role of heritage as a means of achieving European integration. As the European Community moves towards greater unification, there are arguments for the 'creation' of a common heritage to provide one input to this new, wider sense of place. Within the triad of heritage, political identity and tourism, the arguments for the role of heritage in political terms are explicit. First, the complex legislative moves towards European union have not been matched by any groundswell of popular recognition of the wider geographical unit; emotional attachment has lagged well behind. Secondly, although there are strong links with heritage at the national scale, the translation of these on to a European scale requires significant changes of attitude. In order to achieve progress in both these areas, interventions are needed. Heritage, as an integrating theme, is amenable to goal-directed intervention for which good planning and management are essential. The modern experience of heritage is that it can be produced in the present; this production is demand rather than resource related and, at all stages of the production process, deliberate intervention is explicit.

This is a scenario of 'manufactured heritage' which, at first sight, warrants the worst fears of observers such as Hewison (1987) and which has, in some ways, more sinister overtones. But handled properly, and with proper regard to the issue of authenticity, it is a scenario which makes feasible the creation of a specific European heritage to support the political objectives of unification. Of all the organizations at work in Europe, it is the Council of Europe which has the terms of reference for common heritage and a sense of patrimony among Europeans. Elsewhere, there is a lack of cohesive policies and the most significant developments continue to be at the level of the nation state. The role of tourism in the process of European integration is in itself problematic. Tourism does play a part in the mixing of Europeans and, as it grows, there are more points of contact and opportunities for interaction. Tourism is influential within this role in contradictory ways. It standardizes but also differentiates, it can integrate but also alienate, it can build bridges but also create attitudinal barriers; there is no inevitable cause and effect relationship. Language differences are still critical in Europe, as are differences in customs. The irony, of course, is that these very differences, which are based in historical reality, form many of the attractive qualities of Europe even for Europeans. There is a long road to follow if heritage is to play an integrating role in Europe. The member states have different experiences of European history and will continue to see that history from different perspectives. The more realistic aim might be to identify some of the unambiguous icons of the wider Europe and to associate the union with these but, at the same time, to allow the diversity which is the European reality to flourish. Greg Ashworth raises the question of what should constitute European heritage, and one of his answers is the built environment, especially as it is preserved within the historic cities of Europe. These 'treasured' environments and buildings within cities are of central concern to Peter Larkham in his chapter on heritage as planned and conserved components of the modern city. Peter Larkham writes specifically about the experience of urban conservation in the United Kingdom and argues that heritage planning must involve the three concepts of preservation, conservation and exploitation. There are key decision makers in the heritage planning process and among these the developers and architects can be described as the direct agents of change. Indirect agents include the planning officers, the elected members and the general public. British experience of conservationist legislation has involved several central ideas and procedures. The conservation area concept dates from a Court of Appeal decision in 1964, which ruled that a building could be regarded as having special historical interest if it was part of an assemblage. Such individual buildings or sites could then be seen as contributing to the

overall quality of the group. Subsequent legislation has clarified this area
concept. The listed buildings system was initially part of the 1944 and 1947
Town and Country Planning Acts. Strict guidelines have been developed for
'listing', but they must of necessity be capable of modification to accommodate
change. As the legal standing of conservation areas and listed buildings has
been tested in a series of court cases, new legislation has been introduced to
try to draw together and bring order to the many changes and developments
in conservation planning. Uncertainties continue and there are confusions in
the interpretation of the law. Whereas the United Kingdom cannot be held up
as a model of conservation planning, the principle has been enshrined within
the legal system since 1882 and, despite losses, much has been achieved in the
conservation of historic parts of the built urban environment.

The next two chapters consider the relationships between heritage and
education. What roles can heritage places play in the general education of
visitors? How do visitors react to information which is presented to them
at heritage sites? Duncan Light examines these questions with reference to
informal processes of education, and ways in which the general public reacts
to interpretation. Freeman Tilden remains the resonant voice in the literature
of interpretation and although his principles were designed for national parks
in the United States, they have lasting generality. As early as the sixteenth
century, the idea of historic sites as learning experiences had been established
as part of the incipient idea of the Grand Tour which was enjoyed by the
privileged classes in English society. By the late nineteenth century there was
clearly an expanding interest in travelling and learning, and historic places
were part of that itinerary. During the twentieth century this pattern has
become generalized across social classes and the role of interpretation has been
established with the purposes of informing, educating and promoting interest
in heritage sites. Interpretation passes messages, which usually have a conservation agenda, from presenter to visitor. Interpretation is increasingly aimed
at wider audiences, though visitors to historic sites are still drawn predominantly from the higher social class groups. It can be employed in all kinds
of places: rural or urban environments, museums or theme parks. Evidence
suggests that the majority of visitors wish to learn or to be informed, and
surveys of museums in particular indicate that frequent visitors are those with
more specific, dedicated interests. This type of visitor, usually of higher social
class, seems in some ways to be seeking to assert social status and to demonstrate a need to accumulate cultural capital. The practice of interpretation
should, and usually does, reflect the needs of different types of visitor; as
major investments are made in 'heritage places', there are much stronger
proactive roles to be adopted than have previously been common.

The actual process of conveying knowledge has been influenced by ideas
from various sources, including that of cognitive psychology. 'Learning in a
leisure environment' provides a new set of parameters to be understood and
catered for. As seen elsewhere in this chapter, this process carries dangers. The

media may *become* the message and the authenticity question is again to the fore. Interpretation is now the *sine qua non* of heritage but its growth threatens to loosen the ties with the fine principles of effective communication, revelation, provocation, learning and understanding. Attempts to measure the effectiveness of interpretation at heritage sites are still comparatively rare, but evidence is now being assembled which at least sets the research agenda.

As informal education can be regarded as integral to the idea of heritage places, so in a way can formal education. School parties visiting the ruins of an abbey or castle, and educational tours to the classical world, are indicators of that role. The ruins at an historic site provide the catalyst for the development of an educational story; the children's presence at that site makes the story much more meaningful and memorable for them. Richard Prentice recognizes fieldwork and projects as established components of subjects such as geography and history. As the National Curriculum for schools in England and Wales has been developed, it has retained these components. By and large, the 'providers' of heritage have welcomed school links by developing special facilities at sites and publications or materials aimed at a school audience. As this is formal education and part of the curriculum, the issue of effectiveness is again of central importance. How much do children learn? Surveys by Prentice in south-west Wales show that the most popular venues for school visits were the countryside, museums, theatres, castles and technology centres. Visits were generally subject-specific and the majority view was that the introduction of a National Curriculum justified more visits of this kind.

Another of Prentice's surveys showed that students in higher education regarded fieldwork and visits as important parts of the learning process. Investigation of the ways in which they took in information at sites suggested that traditional interpretive media, such as display boards with text, had limited effectiveness. Built heritage registered less strongly than environmental concerns. Tests of acquired knowledge from the visit showed many wrong answers and misunderstandings. Although care must be taken in generalizing from case studies, there is evidence of a lack of real understanding of the educational market by heritage managers. As today's pupils are tomorrow's taxpayers who need to be convinced of the value of heritage, this is a conclusion which calls for action.

Chap. 9 As many of the themes already discussed have implied, heritage is a business and sites are being developed with commercial and marketing considerations in mind. Peter Johnson and Barry Thomas focus on these issues. A production process, which creates a value-added component, is applied to heritage. There are questions about activities which increase or maintain the heritage stock; about the extent to which heritage represents a renewable resource; and about the relative costs involved in conservation and exploitation. As the heritage industry grows, the problems of accounting increase. What are the dimensions of the heritage resource? How can it be classified, costed and funded? How do we measure consumption: by numbers of visitors, entrance fees paid, or sales at sites? Many aspects of heritage production and consumption can be addressed under standard economic headings such as supply and demand. Marketing similarly applies a set of economic and business principles to the management of heritage. Heritage uses resources and produces an output which has a value to society. There are policy issues and government has a significant role to play in controlling development and in safeguarding both quality and basic principles. There is a balance to be maintained between the amount of heritage, the amount of conservation and access. The principles of the unfettered, free market may not be sufficient and those of trust, guardianship and public stewardship must be accommodated.

Practitioners, as the providers within the heritage market, form the focus of the chapter by Terry Stevens. They constitute the decision makers, in both public and private sectors, who determine the nature of the product. If a heritage feature is to become a 'visitor attraction', in whole or in part, there are key questions of product identification, accessibility, marketing and management to be resolved. Whereas there is a general awareness of the special meaning of heritage, the private sector in particular is almost invariably consumer oriented and is inclined to produce heritage attractions with the market in mind. Some counterbalance for this comes from public agencies and legislation. It is reassuring that despite some spectacular, large-scale projects, such as the Jorvik Centre, preservation has remained the strong ethic. It is now clear that heritage attractions, as a means of generating tourist income, are often central to local authority plans. Tourist boards also have their potential strongly in mind, and regional authorities are providing the frameworks within which local projects can develop. Individual providers still have important roles as decision makers. They determine the style and amount of interpretation, pricing policies, facilities and constraints on use such as closed seasons. As the leisure day-trip market becomes more competitive, the balance between conservation and enhancement of a site is always under consideration by the provider. Quality control and concern for the fabric of a site must always be in the best interest of providers and consumers; the providers need to be, or need access to, efficient professionals who can plan, design and manage their sites.

References

Allan, G. and Crow, G. (1991) Privatisation, home centredness and leisure. *Leisure Studies*, 10, 19–32.

Boorstin, D. (1985) *The Image: A Guide to Pseudo Events in America*. New York: Atheneum Press.

Bourdieu, P. (1984) *Distinction: A Social Critique of the Judgement of Taste*. Cambridge, Mass.: Harvard University Press.

Brook, J. A. (1993) Leisure meanings and comparisons with work. *Leisure Studies*, 12, 149–162.

Buzard, J. (1993) *The Beaten Track: European Tourism, Literature and the Ways to Culture, 1800–1918.* New York: Oxford University Press.

Cossons, N. (1988) Postlude. In *Proceedings of the First World Congress on Heritage Presentation and Interpretation, Edmonton, Alberta. Culture and Multi-culturalism,* pp. 343–349.

Countryside Commission (1985) *National Countryside Recreation Survey, 1984.* Cheltenham: Countryside Commission.

Dower, M. (1965) *The Challenge of Leisure.* London: Civic Trust.

Eco, U. (1986) *Travels in Hyper-Reality.* London: Picador.

Feifer, M. (1986) *Tourism in History: From Imperial Rome to the Present.* New York: Stein and Day.

Fowler, P. (1989) Heritage: a post-modern perspective. In D. L. Uzzell (ed.) *Heritage Interpretation: The Natural and Built Environment.* London: Belhaven, 57–63.

Fussell, P. (1980) *Abroad: British Literary Travelling between the Wars.* New York: Oxford University Press.

Gershuny, J. and Jones, S. (1987) The changing work–leisure balance in Britain: 1961–1984. In J. Horne, D. Jary and A. Tomlinson (eds) *Sport, Leisure and Social Relations.* London: Routledge, 9–50.

Herbert, D. T., Prentice, R. C. and Thomas, C. J. (eds) (1989) *Heritage Sites: Strategies for Marketing and Development.* Aldershot: Avebury.

Hewison, R. (1987) *The Heritage Industry: Britain in a Climate of Decline.* London: Methuen.

Hewison, R. (1989) Heritage: an interpretation. In D. L. Uzzell (ed.) *Heritage Interpretation: The Natural and Built Environment.* London: Belhaven, 15–22.

Horne, J., Jary, D. and Tomlinson A. (eds) (1987) *Sport, Leisure and Social Relations.* London: Routledge.

Hughes, G. (1992) Tourism and the geographical imagination. *Leisure Studies,* **11,** 31–42.

Jameson, F. (1984) Post-modernism or the cultural logic of late capitalism. *New Left Review,* **146,** 53–92.

Kelly, J. R. (1991) Counterpoints in the sociology of leisure. *Leisure Sciences,* **14,** 247–253.

King, A. (1993) One in three workers wants a cut in hours. *Daily Telegraph,* 2 August, 4.

Lowenthal, D. (1985) *The Past Is a Foreign Country.* Cambridge: Cambridge University Press.

Lowenthal, D. (1989) Heritage and its interpretation. In *Proceedings of the First World Congress on Heritage Presentation and Interpretation, Edmonton, Alberta. Culture and Multi-culturalism,* pp. 7–28.

Lumley, R. (1988) *The Museum Time Machine: Putting Cultures on Display.* London: Routledge.

MacCannell, D. (1976) *The Tourist: A New Theory of the Leisure Class.* New York: Schocken Books.

MacCannell, D. (1992) *Empty Meeting Grounds: The Tourist Papers.* London: Routledge.

Martin, B. and Mason, S. (1992) Current trends in leisure: the changing face of leisure provision. *Leisure Studies,* **11,** 81–86.

Patmore, J. A. (1983) *Recreation and Resources: Leisure Patterns and Leisure Places.* Oxford: Blackwell.

Prentice, R. C. (1993) *Tourism and Heritage Places.* London: Routledge.

Robson, B. T. (1989) Social and economic futures for the large city. In

D. T. Herbert and D. M. Smith (eds) *Social Problems and the City: New Perspectives*. Oxford: Oxford University Press, 17–31.

Samdahl, D. M. (1992) Leisure in our lives: exploring the common leisure occasion. *Journal of Leisure Research*, **24**, 19–32.

Shaw, G. and Williams, A. M. (1994) *Critical Issues in Tourism: A Geographical Perspective*. Oxford: Blackwell.

Smith, J. (1987) Men and women at play: gender, life-cycle and leisure. In J. Horne, D. Jary and A. Tomlinson (eds) *Sport, Leisure and Social Relations*. London: Routledge, pp. 51–85.

Social Trends (1993) London: HMSO.

Stockdale, J. E. (1985) *What Is Leisure?: An Empirical Analysis of the Concept of Leisure and the Role of Leisure in People's Lives*. London: Sports Council/ESRC.

Thrift, N. (1989) Images of change. In C. Hamnett, L. McDowell and P. Sarre (eds) *The Changing Social Structure*. London: Sage, pp. 12–42.

Urry, J. (1990) *The Tourist Gaze: Leisure and Travel in Contemporary Societies*. London: Sage.

Uzzell, D. L. (ed.) (1989a) *Heritage Interpretation*: Vol. 1: *The Natural and Built Environment*. London: Belhaven.

Uzzell, D. L. (ed.) (1989b) *Heritage Interpretation*: Vol. 2: *The Visitor Experience*. London: Belhaven.

Wearing, B. and Wearing, S. (1992) Identity and the commodification of leisure. *Leisure Studies*, **11**, 3–18.

World Tourism Organization (1990) *Current Travel and Tourism Indicators*. Madrid: World Tourism Organization.

2

Heritage as Historical Reality

Frans F. J. Schouten

But the real truth, no one knows
nor will he be able to know it ever: not about the gods.
Neither about anything I speak about.
And if by accident he will express
the perfect truth, he would not know.
For everything is nothing but a web woven of guesses.

Xenophanes

There is a preoccupation in science with the word 'evidence'. Once I parti-
cipated in a tour around Hadrian's Wall headed by an archaeologist, and the
only reply we got to our active participation and our efforts to create an image
of that period was, 'Interesting idea, but there is no archaeological evidence
for it.' If there is one thing to demotivate your visitors, it is this phrase. From
the scientific point of view, the archaeologist was correct: there were no hard
facts for my projections. Yet he failed as a communicator for he unwillingly
reduced an interesting site into 'just another heap of stones', as my son
used to say on our holidays. Visitors are not primarily looking for scientific
historical evidence.

They may even be only partly interested in the historical reality as such.
Visitors to historic sites are looking for an experience, a new reality based on
the tangible remains of the past. For them, this is the very essence of the
heritage experience. Heritage is not the same as history. Heritage is history
processed through mythology, ideology, nationalism, local pride, romantic
ideas or just plain marketing, into a commodity. A good example of this
process is the observation of Washington Irving on the Alhambra in Granada:

'The peculiar charm of this old dreamy palace is its power of calling up vague reveries and picturings of the past and thus clothing naked realities with the illusion of the memory and the imagination' (quoted by Trevelyan, 1985, p. 8).

The past is to most visitors not an aim in itself, but a starting point from which they depart on a discovery tour. A journey that will tell them as much about themselves as it will about history, provided, that is, they are prepared to listen and look carefully, and provided the story is communicated properly, giving the facts, but leaving space for imagination, wonder and curiosity.

When we talk about 'heritage as historical reality' we refer to the scientific notion that there is some kind of objective truth, and to the idea of absolutes. That idea leads us to saying that there is or is not any 'scientific evidence'. But how real is 'real'? Can we really know for sure? When history has been processed into heritage, scientific evidence has lost its case, for 'heritage' creates its own reality. Without going any further into a discussion about epistemology, I will allow the above quotation from Xenophanes, about which I feel comfortable, to convey my position.

Reality is also often used as a word to denote the tangible world outside ourselves. This applies to 'historical reality' as it is perceived by visitors to museums and historic sites. The physical remains of the past are out there, they are literally 'objective' but at the same time subject to our 'subjective' experience. We all experience this reality as a quality of ourselves and of the world outside. As anyone with some understanding of psychology knows, both aspects are virtually inseparable. The world becomes real in its relationship with us, and on to the world outside we project our hopes and fears, our dreams and expectations.

Imagination and understanding of reality are always linked. As John Barlow, lyricist for the Grateful Dead, once stated:

> History is what you remember, and if you do not believe it is reviewed all the time, you have not paid enough attention to your own memory. When you remember something you do not remember the thing itself, you only remember the last time you remembered it. (quoted in Calvin, 1989, p. 2)

The 'historical reality' is not an independent identity, because it is subject to interpretation, both scientifically and psychologically. The interpretation provided by heritage professionals in museums and on sites is only one of the manifold interpretations our visitors carry around in themselves. We all have an image of the world around us, and this image guides our perception of the world (Schouten, 1987). New information is always related to our own concept of the world – sociologists talk of our 'frame of reference', and psychologists call it the 'cognitive structure'. These images of the world have a very important characteristic. According to Gestalt psychology, it is a complete image, and all new information should be stored within this complete, and sometimes false, image. If new information fits in with the cognitive structure of the visitors, it will be easily assimilated. But the more remote the new information is from the cognitive structure, the more easily it will be rejected by the visitors. If information does not correspond with the way we perceive the world, it will be neglected, changed, ignored or even not perceived at all. The more subtle the cognitive structure, the more easily we can adopt new information, and integrate it into a new or enriched image of the world, so that we see things in a different way. Younger people do not have a fixed image of the world and are consequently more open towards adding to their cognitive structures. Curiosity could be described as an open image of the world, rendering a person more receptive to new information. Good interpretation is based upon making connections with ideas and experiences with which we are already familiar, and upon raising curiosity in our visitors.

The Perception of the Presented Historical Reality

Visitors to a reconstructed village of peat cutters in the eastern part of Holland have a particular interpretation of the 'historical evidence' presented to them. Although the presenters tried to convey a message about the hardship of making a living in such conditions, most of the visitors do not see the poverty, but only their own poetic projections. It reminds them of times when life was simple and easy, for which they have a longing, living quietly 'in the country', far away from frustrations, responsibilities and hectic lives. Their reactions, as noted in field observations, are likewise: 'Look, how cute', and 'Isn't it funny?' Visitor reactions can be even more awkward: the Dutch art historian Pierre Jansen once told a group in front of Van Gogh's *Aardappel eters* (The Potato Eaters) about the poor living conditions in those days. One of them retorted, 'It cannot have been so hard. Look, they even had an antique oil-lamp above the table!'

Realities are largely constructions

David Lowenthal (1985) wrote a book entitled *The Past Is a Foreign Country* (the phrase is originally by H. E. Bates), and that is exactly the right expression. 'Reality', whether historical or in the present, is not a static, but a dynamic, quality. History is not fixed in time, but changing within the present. The past is merely our conception of it and does not have an unchanging identity of its own:

> Objects have not a single past but an unbroken sequence of past times leading backward from the present moment. Moreover there is no ideal spot on the temporal continuum that inherently deserves emphasis. . . . In elevating or admiring one piece of the past we tend to ignore and devalue others. One reality lives at the expense of countless others. (Crew and Sims, 1991, p. 160)

When the Wall was still separating East and West Berlin, people interested in history had the opportunity to visit two exhibitions separated by half a mile but using the same language, expressing two different 'historical evidences'. The Museum of German History in the Eastern sector and the exhibition in the Reichstag in the West presented the same historical reality with virtually the same objects, and yet told totally different stories. On the Eastern side of the border the Weimar Republic was depicted as an instrument of reactionary bourgeois forces; on the Western side, Weimar was shown as being weakened by communist agitation.

Some may say, 'Yes, of course, we told the truth, and the communists were bloody liars', but it is never that easy. History has always been written by the winners and not by the losers, and winning in itself does not provide historical truth. This sounds like a simplified statement, but when you look around our historical presentations you will find many examples of twisting the available data.

The Spanish will put more emphasis on the bad weather conditions when they present the defeat of their 'Great Armada', and the British on the determination of their commanders and their superior skills as sailors. Another good example of this phenomenon can be found at the Airborne Museum near Arnhem in Holland, which commemorates the Battle of Arnhem in 1944 in which an Allied task-force was defeated by the German defenders. It is full of heroics, of the glory of battle, everything of the kind you can imagine. But it does not touch upon the question of why these soldiers were defeated and least of all does it consider the lack of coordination among the Allied chiefs of staff and their stupid quarrels about competence and dominance.

The sources of bias in constructing the historical reality

When we look into the predominant representation of history in the West, it is not difficult to show that it is less 'objective' than is claimed. There is enough material to show its bias. Notwithstanding our 'objective views', 'historical evidence' and any other kind of qualification we attach to our interpretations, there will always be someone to challenge these.

Feminists will point to the mis- and under-representation of women in the displays. Ecologists will focus on the lack of information on the deforestation of Europe and northern Africa by the Romans as the price nature has to pay for their success. Protestants complain about the absence of information on the Crusade against the Cathars in French history museums. Catholics could do the same with the Dutch, who pay little attention to the movement against holy icons in the mid-sixteenth century.

Name it and you will have no difficulty in finding a group who is not pleased or who is even offended by the representation or non-representation. This type of bias has to do with what can be called 'canonical history': the way history has been written and interpreted by previous generations, and the way we often take that interpretation for granted until it is challenged by new arguments.

A second bias, closely related to the historical canon, is what nowadays is called 'political correctness'. It may have started as an honest attempt to undo the existing bias in the historical canon, but in its extreme forms it is best described as twisting the facts to help the truth. The phenomenon is not new, however, and we should not forget that – from a technical point of view – the first successful didactic exhibition in history was 'Entartete Kunst' in Nazi Germany. In the near future, museums and heritage sites have to face this ideological challenge. Not because of 'objective facts', 'scientific evidence' or any other such phrase, but simply to keep an open mind and to raise the appropriate questions.

The third source of bias has little to do with people making decisions on what to portray, but is the result of the durability of material, the ravages of time, wars, neglect and a lack of conservation. The simple fact that not everything from history survives the historical process is a source of bias. Castles, palaces and cathedrals have a longer lifespan than the dwellings of ordinary people. The same applies to the furnishings and other contents of these premises. In a town like Leyden in Holland which was, in the seventeenth century, occupied by approximately the same number of people as live in that town today, the inhabitants lived within the walled town, an area more than five times smaller than modern Leyden. In most of the houses several families lived together in circumstances beyond our imagination. In museums, however, the visitors only find fine period rooms giving an image of the lifestyle of the upper class of that era. No wonder people who stroll around exhibitions are filled with nostalgia; the evidence in the museums shows that life used to be so much better in those days. The whole idea that the past was a better time in which to live is induced by this bias in its representation in museums and heritage centres.

Among many of the custodians of the past there is a growing awareness of this bias and there is now a move to preserve the ordinary and redress the balance. There is an increasing interest in social history, in particular through collections from the late nineteenth and early twentieth centuries, which still can be put together. Interest in industrial archaeology is also a good expression of this change in attitude. Wigan's pier, the Liverpool Science Museum and the City Museum of York are good examples of this development. The appeal of the Jorvik Centre is partly based on the sense the audience can get of the lives of ordinary people in the early Middle Ages.

Heritage as a Commodity

History, as the interpretation of the past, is – like any other phenomenon – subject to change and even to fashion. The way historians in the past looked at history tells us nowadays as much about them and their place in society as it tells us about history itself.

The same applies to heritage, which is often too simplistically defined as the tangible remains of the historical process. Heritage is 'objective' in the sense that it is there – outside – in a physical form. But at the same time heritage 'has a quite specific meaning which is not the same as conserved relict historical resources' (Ashworth, 1992, p. 99). Ashworth argues that heritage is the product of a commodification process in which selection is central:

> heritage conservation is creation and not preservation of what already exists. . . . The nature of the final product (as heritage) is not determined by the resource endowment, nor can it reflect any supposedly accurate factual record of the past. (Ashworth, 1992, p. 97)

Heritage is a product and, as a product, it is as subject to differences in validation and interpretation as the historical process itself. Heritage changes over time in the way it is presented and also in the ways in which the public reacts to its presentation.

These developments have to do not so much with scientific evidence – although they may be based on thorough research – but with the creation of new realities which are both recognizable and understandable to a public who can relate them to daily experiences. The proposition can even be put that in order to make everything in heritage 'more real', historical reality must be increasingly violated. In museums, period rooms and historical reconstructions, we may have to help reality a little to make it more real. So we depict the *Pithecanthropus erectus* in an Indonesian museum with Malay facial features, not because there is any evidence of them, but because that is the way Indonesians perceive humans. In the Museum of Natural History in Washington, DC, the Neanderthal man is shown giving a dominant gesture over his wife. We actually have no clue whether this was the case and the presentation tells us a lot more about our way of perceiving the world around us than it does about our ancestors.

This process is most obvious in movies based on historical themes. King Arthur is presented as a knight in magnificently shining armour which was unknown in his day. But as this is the image imposed on the audience by movies, television, novels and comic books on knights, it has to be presented that way. Otherwise, the image presented to the public would not be perceived as reliable. The picture of this era in history painted in *Monty Python and the Holy Grail* is probably much more accurate, but less popular and less acceptable.

But the process also works in reverse: the influence of the mass media in forming the images of the past held by visitors to museums and heritage sites cannot be underestimated. They can shape the ways in which history and heritage are seen by the public. Furthermore, because of the impact of television, there is a generation of young people for whom reading is a secondary means of collecting information. Their learning attitude is primarily focused on the visual impact and they are used to having these images very well staged. For those used to watching television and film, the staging of information in museums is not only poor, but often incomprehensible. The impact of television is staggering: in the United Kingdom people spend 25 to 30 hours per week in front of the screen (Herbert, 1989, p. 6); and a series like *Dallas* is seen in 98 countries, *Sesame Street* in 84 countries (Naisbitt and Aburdene, 1990, p. 136). From the classical point of view, one could say that there is a growing intellectual deprivation among the public, the rise of a new kind of illiteracy. There is less detailed background knowledge than there used to be and likewise there is less demand for detailed information. At the same time, visitors carry around much more sophisticated images of their surrounding world and there is a need for more coherence in these images. Visitors are more critical of what is presented to them and are much more outspoken in their opinions. Museums and heritage sites will have to adjust to these changes in attitude if they want to survive in the competitive leisure market.

The Typical Museum Experience

David Lowenthal (1985, p. 244) observed: 'Although it is now evident that artifacts are as easily altered as chronicles, public faith in their veracity endures; a tangible relic seems *ipso facto* real.' This conviction is rooted in the nineteenth century and the first half of this century when science was supposed to be objective and value free. This is reflected strongly in the museum displays of those days. Museums used to look – and some still do – much like storage-rooms of objects, packed together in showcases. Good for scholars who want to study the subtle differences in design but not for the ordinary visitor, to whom it all looks alike. Hardly any explanation is given:

Mahawairocona of the Nganjuk Mandala,
bronze, appr. last quarter 10th cent.
or first half 11th cent. Majapahit;
East-Java; cat.no. A 1706/BD/2354.

This kind of information dates back to the times when the museum was the exclusive domain of the scientific researcher. But it does not make any sense to a lay person who is not familiar with Mahawairocona or the Nganjuk Mandala, who may have a quite different interpretation of a mandala, who knows nothing about the Majapahit kingdom and is not interested in the catalogue number (cat.no.) at all. Such a person must not be regarded as stupid or uneducated. Maybe he or she has a degree in economics from Cambridge. But in the specific field involved – Indology – most of us are just starters, interested – that is why we visit the museum – but innocent beginners.

Museum professionals should not be surprised when people leave the museum after half an hour. They just have had enough of looking at objects that more or less look the same, have an incomprehensible explanation and say no more than people can see for themselves.

Most Heritage Interpretation Is One-Dimensional

When Patrick Süskind in his novel *Perfume* describes the stench of a city like Paris in the seventeenth century, he is probably very accurate:

> It was a mixture of human and animal smells, of water and stone and ashes and leather, of soap and fresh-baked bread and eggs boiled in vinegar, of noodles and smoothly polished brass, of sage and ale and tears, of grease and soggy straw and dry straw. Thousands upon thousands of odours formed an invisible gruel that filled the street ravines, only seldom evaporating above the rooftops and never from the ground below. (Süskind, 1986, p. 35)

Kenneth Hudson wrote similarly about this subject:

> Smells distinguish one culture and one country from another more thoroughly and effectively than any other characteristic (unfashionable as it may be to say this) but, with very rare exceptions, museums do not deal in smells. (Hudson, 1991, p. 461)

Although it is done at some sites, like the Jorvik Centre, it seems to be difficult to add this 'historical evidence' to our displays. Besides, a lot of heritage professionals are horrified by the idea, which in their opinion would interfere in the interaction between the objects and the viewer. In their view, looking is obviously the only activity you are supposed to do in a museum – but why not also hearing, touching, tasting and smelling? We do have more senses than the eye to perceive the world around us. Reducing the importance of the other senses is a reduction of the image of the world to a one-dimensional experience. It reduces objects in a showcase to pictures in a book.

Changes in the way the heritage is presented

Nowadays we have a different attitude towards our heritage and the way it should be presented. When you compare the Museum of London with the Musée Carnavalet in Paris, both dealing with the history of their respective cities, the difference is obvious. Carnavalet looks like a picture gallery in fully furnished period rooms, whereas the Museum of London provides an historical environment. But the Museum of London, compared to the newest developments, is already old-fashioned in its presentation. Today the key word in heritage display is experience, the more exciting the better and, if possible, involving all the senses.

A good example of this approach is the Jorvik Centre. The Museum of the Moving Image and the World War I experience in the Imperial War Museum are already the second generation in this development. In the United States this tendency emerged much earlier: Williamsburg has been a prototype for many new heritage developments. On heritage sites the re-enactment of historical events is increasingly popular. Nobody can predict where this process will end, but soon enough we will encounter virtual-reality devices in the heritage trade that will provide visitors with a vivid image of the historical period of their own choice in which they themselves can act as if they were part of that historical environment. These developments can be criticized (Hewison, 1987; Lumley, 1988) as an intolerable vulgarization. We may agree with this evaluation but their comments reflect a vision of heritage that differs from that of the public. Martin and Mason in their article 'The future of attractions' observe that 'Disneyfication' has become a pejorative term when applied to the use of historic topics in theme parks and similar locations. The success of many such venues suggests that the public does not share these critical views. However, greater authenticity and 'real' experiences could well be what the new 'thoughtful consumer' wants.

According to Martin and Mason (1993, p. 39), the potential visitor in the near future will have more or less the following characteristics. He or she will be:

older than we are presently accustomed to, more likely to be middle aged; able to spend more;
more demanding in terms of quality of the places visited and the services and experiences provided;
more critical of ways in which available time and money should be spent;
looking for physical and mental challenges, as well as the opportunity to participate and to learn, and to have fun and be entertained.

The sharp distinction between museums and heritage sites on the one hand and theme parks on the other is gradually evaporating. They already borrow ideas and concepts from one another. Museums have adopted story-lines for exhibitions, sites have accepted 'theming' as a relevant tool, and theme parks are moving towards more authenticity and research-based presentations, as well as responding more to public demands for a 'green' approach which offers visitors closer contact with wildlife and the natural surroundings. The new developments in zoos are illustrative in this respect: no more animals in cages, but in open spaces as 'ecosystems', either in the open air or in enormous greenhouses as in the jungle and desert environments in Burgers' Zoo near Arnhem in Holland. This trend was set in Europe some ten years ago by the famous 'Noorderdierenpark' in Emmen, the Netherlands, and is still considered by Kenneth Hudson in *Museums of Influence* (1987) to be one of the major developments in the presentation of natural history in the twentieth century.

Martin and Mason also observe that the visitors seek to explore aspects of everyday work and life, today and tomorrow, as well as to learn about their past heritage. In 'Theme parks: playgrounds or agents of social and cultural development', Terry Stevens notes a change in theme parks which he calls 'reality versus fantasy'. He says: 'Herein lies perhaps the biggest challenge facing theme park managers globally. Can rides, themes, and storylines be harnessed to communicate societal issues and contribute to public awareness of environmental, political, and economic concerns?' (Stevens, 1993, p. 69). This challenge comes quite close to that faced by traditionally more serious institutions.

This development is neither good nor bad, it is the way the market develops. Museums and heritage sites have a special role to fulfil, which cannot be replaced by theme parks. But at the same time they have to be aware that they are in a very competitive environment: visitors make choices on how and where to spend their free time. As calculating citizens, they also seek value for money.

Heritage and museum experts do not have to invent stories and recreate historical environments to attract the visitors; their assets are already in place. The only thing the experts in the field of museums and historic sites must ensure is that the exhibits they create for the heritage experience are based on artefacts and the historical facts as we now know them, and that they are presented in an attractive way.

I do not think it will be possible to develop standards of presentation. Every theme or site will have its own challenges, requirements, problems and solutions in developing its storyline and presentation. The main thing is to keep on being critical about one's own work and the work of others and never avoid professional discussion. This is the only way to improve the quality of our performance. The only thing we know for sure is that the proper link between the objects and what we know of the historical facts is in a heritage experience called authenticity. According to Martin and Mason (1993), a new 'thoughtful consumer' will emerge in the near future for whom authenticity is more important. But authenticity is like perfection: you can only strive for it, without ever having the illusion of reaching it.

The Heritage Interpreter

Heritage as a historical reality can only exist by virtue of interpretation. But that interpretation is – like the study of history itself – subject to fashion, taste, ideology and, last but not least, personal preferences. This sometimes puts those professionally engaged in the art of interpretation in a difficult position. They have to navigate between the Scylla and Charybdis of 'evidence' and 'attractiveness', the more so because nowadays there is an increasing emphasis in the heritage industry on income-generating activities.

There is, however, one compensating thought for the interpreters: if they do not provide the interpretation, the visitors will do so for themselves, based on their own ideas, misconceptions and prejudgements, and no matter how exciting the result may be, it will contain a lot more bias than the educated presentations of the professionals.

Historical reality does not pop up from the remains of the past; it has to be created. This paradox is similar to that in the quotation from Oscar Wilde, who described a book on Italian literature as showing 'a lack of knowledge which can only be the result of years of study'. This is the trap which heritage interpretation has to avoid and here we are back where we started, with the 'scientific evidence' for interpretation. History and historical reality are black boxes: we do not know what they contain, but with an input of imagination and good research, the output can be marvellous. Interpretation is the art that makes history 'real'. Artists, especially painters, have known this for ages. Degas stated: 'As a painter you have to transfer the idea of the truth by means of the untrue.' Picasso put it even more precisely: 'Art is a lie that convinces us of the truth' (quoted in Hughes and Brecht, 1978).

References

Ashworth, G. J. (1992) Heritage and tourism: an argument, two problems and three solutions. In C. A. M. Fleischer van Rooijen (ed.) *Spatial Implications of Tourism*. Groningen: Geo Pers, 95–104.

Calvin, W. H. (1989) *The Cerebral Symphony: Seashore Reflections on the Structure of Consciousness*. New York: Bantam Books.

Crew, S. and Sims, J. (1991) Locating authenticity: fragments of a dialogue. In I. Karp and S. Lawine (eds) *Exhibiting Cultures: The Poetics and Politics of a Museum Display*. Washington, DC: Smithsonian Institute.

Herbert, D. T. (1989) Leisure trends and the heritage market. In D. T. Herbert, R. C. Prentice and C. J. Thomas (eds) *Heritage Sites. Strategies for Marketing and Development*. Aldershot: Avebury, pp. 1–14.

Hewison, R. (1987) *The Heritage Industry*. London: Methuen.

Hudson, K. (1987) *Museums of Influence*. Cambridge: Cambridge University Press.

Hudson, K. (1991) How misleading does an ethnographical museum have to be? In I. Karp and S. Lawine (eds) *Exhibiting Cultures: The Poetics and Politics of a Museum Display*. Washington, DC: Smithsonian Institute, pp. 457–464.

Hughes, P. and Brecht, G. (1978) *Vicious Circles and Infinity*. London: Penguin Books.

Lowenthal, D. (1985) *The Past Is a Foreign Country*. Cambridge: Cambridge University Press.

Lumley, R. (ed.) (1988) *The Museum Time Machine: Putting Cultures on Display*. London: Routledge.

Martin, W. and Mason, S. (1993) The future of attractions: meeting the needs of the new consumers. *Tourism Management*, February, 34–40.

Naisbitt, J. and Aburdene, P. (1990) *Megatrends 2000*. New York: Morrow.

Schouten, F. (1987) Psychology and exhibit design: a note. *International Journal of Museum Management and Curatorship*, 6, 259–262.

Stevens, T. (1993) Theme parks: playgrounds or agents of social and cultural development. In *Annual Review of Travel*. New York: American Express, pp. 61–72.

Süskind, P. (1986) *Perfume*. London: Penguin Books.

Trevelyan, R. (1985) *Shades of the Alhambra*. London: Secker and Warburg.

3

Heritage as Literary Place

David T. Herbert

Both heritage and tourism have always been strongly connected with places. Historically, places with special qualities of the natural environment served as attractions for tourists and visitors. Mountainous areas, such as the Alps in Europe, offered spectacle and the grandeur of nature to capture the 'tourist gaze' (Urry, 1990). Water – rivers, lakes, waterfalls and the seashore – had considerable appeal and the combination of landscape with favourable climate assumed paramount importance as the age of 'mass tourism' dawned. Even in the historical sites which attracted visitors, the emphasis was on the spectacular, and the great monuments of the ancient world, such as the Parthenon and Colosseum, were standard features of the tourist route. Tourists and visitors were not of course all of one kind and the distinctions made between travellers and tourists (Buzard, 1993), or between the *romantic* and those of the *collective gaze* (Urry, 1990), are valuable. These are gross classifications but they do point to the fact that visitors may not be seeking the same kind of experience, even when they are visiting the same places. Further, and perhaps more significantly, there are types of heritage place which appeal to different 'segments' of the market. The idea of marketing places has long been an integral part of the tourism industry but more recent is the broadening of the perceived range of places which can be marketed. This range now extends beyond places with more obvious environmental qualities to others with claims as heritage attractions which rest on their connections with people and events rather than on the intrinsic qualities of the place.

A number of places have assumed heritage significance because of this kind of connection. They include sites of battles, speeches or declarations, foundations of movements and so on, where the event or the individual gives meaning to the place. This chapter explores the roles of 'literary places'.

By this term is meant both those places associated with writers in their real lives and those which provided the settings for their novels. Great works of imaginative literature are often set in the real world of the writer's experience: there is an interaction of real and imagined worlds which is of central importance. This mixture of fact and fiction, of the real and the metaphorical, finds expression in Hardy's description of Wessex as a 'partly real, partly dream' world (Birch, 1981). Current thinking in cultural geography stresses this interrelationship of real and imagined rather than their separateness. For Daniels and Rycroft (1993, p. 461), novels, poems, travel guides, maps and regional monographs all belong together as components of the field of textual genres. There are connections, overlaps and different degrees of 'objectivity', but the role of portraying place is shared. Something of this, 'the worldliness of literary texts' (Daniels and Rycroft, 1993, p. 461), is brought out in an observation on the writing of Hardy:

> Hardy observed and described the smallest details of soil, contour, crop and vegetation, and he adds to this knowledge an antiquarian interest in topography and a poet's use of language . . . he could . . . tell each tree from the distinctive rustling of its leaves. His novels contain the most precise and informed descriptions of country tasks, and of man's relation to the land. (Drabble, 1979, p. 91)

Literary places are the fusion of the real worlds in which the writers lived with the worlds portrayed in the novels. Any distinction is unlikely to be made in the minds of visitors. Haworth, for example, is the landscape in which the Brontës lived, but is also that occupied by the characters in their novels. The writer infuses the novel with a sense of place but the novel in turn adds meaning to place. As literary places enter the itineraries of visitor attractions, these are the special qualities which are emphasized. This sense of a symbiosis between writer, novel and place was well expressed by Melvyn Bragg in his foreword to a study of writers and their homes:

> In these places a visitor can still today walk out of a house and into landscapes which have barely changed since the writer drew breath from them and breathed literature into them.
>
> We walk in our writers' footsteps and see through their eyes when we enter these spaces. (Marsh, 1993, pp. xi, xv)

Some Issues on Heritage as Literary Place

Several general issues affecting heritage tourism are raised when considering literary places. The issue of authenticity is particularly relevant. Heritage tourism based on literary places can use both the real lives of the writers and the worlds created in their novels. Visitors can be attracted to houses where writers lived and worked and also to the landscapes which provided the settings for their novels. The lines blur as imagined worlds vie with real-life experiences. An analogy is perhaps offered by studies of religious pilgrims

(Eade, 1992), where the issue of 'real' and 'imagined' is also very relevant. The issue of authenticity affects both kinds of visitor experience, but is more acute where it is a landscape or landmark from a novel to which special meaning is being attributed. Pocock (1987, 1992) studied visitors to the Brontë country as promoted by the Bradford Metropolitan District in Yorkshire, and also to the Catherine Cookson country, designated by South Tyneside Metropolitan District. In both places the visitors are encouraged to encounter the worlds of the novels and those of the writers. Pocock (1992) noted that the trail through Catherine Cookson country included not only locations relevant to the life of the author, but also places associated with her characters. Key elements of the trail, including the birthplace of the writer and a house where she lived for some years, had disappeared, but the gaps were filled in the promotional literature to ensure the complete visitor experience. These questions on the issue of authenticity take on additional dimensions in relation to literary places. They apply to the actual houses or sites associated with the writer and also to the landscapes of their novels; how can the guidelines of authenticity be applied to places where real worlds and dream worlds are so closely intertwined?

Another issue of some importance is that of the kinds of visitor who come to literary places. Rationally, it would be expected that we are dealing with travellers rather than tourists, with the romantic rather than the collective gaze. Pocock (1992) used the term 'literary pilgrim' on the assumption that this type of visitor is seeking to learn and be educated in a discerning way. Squire (1993) described the reactions of visitors to Hill Top Farm, the former home of Beatrix Potter, in the English Lake District. Visitors were attracted by literary influences, but also found the visit to this particular place, with all its connotations of childhood, Englishness, preservation, and rural nostalgia, as a 'medium through which a range of cultural meanings and values can be communicated'.

Research of this kind suggests that visitors to literary places are more purposeful and have more specific reasons for making their visit, but there remain questions to explore. What do visitors seek and expect to find when they visit a literary place, and how much prior knowledge of writers and their works do they bring with them? Is a particular type of visitor drawn to literary places, or is there a mixture within the visitor group?

There are also questions relating to the ways in which literary places can be seen as part of the heritage industry. To what extent and in what ways are they being developed and promoted with the aims of attracting visitors? There is clear evidence that various agencies, in both the public and private sectors, have realized the potential of the literary connection in attracting tourists and visitors, and are promoting the images of literary places. Examples, such as the promotion of Brontë and Catherine Cookson country by local authorities, have already been cited. In addition to the proactive marketing and publication of promotional material, there are also more academic guides which are designed for other purposes, but nonetheless add to the process of identifying literary places. Daiches and Flower (1979) and Drabble (1979) have written accessible and popular books on the theme of landscape and literature within the British Isles. Marsh (1993) has published a detailed guide to the former residences of some fifty or so British and Irish authors. In this guide, a modern writer has contributed a short essay on each of the houses and there is a gazetteer which lists facilities, hours of opening and such details and, in effect, acts as a visitors' guide. All but one of the houses included are open to the public. These publications can be viewed as part of a general strategy to bring literary places to the attention of potential visitors.

Jane Austen and Marcel Proust

This discussion of heritage as literary place will draw upon two surveys of visitors to places associated with particular writers. The writers, Jane Austen and Marcel Proust, belong to different centuries, different countries and occupy very different places in the history of literature. Jane Austen (1775–1817) was among the earlier women writers and her novels, which revolve around close studies of social relationships, have had a wide and sustained popular appeal. Books such as *Emma* have become standard texts in the school curriculum, and others, such as *Pride and Prejudice*, have also been popularized by film and television. Her works belong with the 'classics' of English literature, yet she is a popular author who is accessible to a wide range of people. She was born into a large family, the seventh child and second daughter of the Reverend George Austen, an Oxford-educated clergyman of modest means. Her mother was Cassandra Leigh, whose family had aristocratic connections. She was niece of the Master of Balliol College, Oxford. Jane Austen was born at Steventon, Hampshire, and lived there until 1801; she lived in Bath from 1801 to 1806, then in Southampton until 1809, and in Chawton, Hampshire, from 1809 to 1817. She died in Winchester and was buried in the Cathedral there. She attended schools at Oxford and Reading and her travels were confined to the Home Counties, such as Kent and Surrey, and to parts of the West Country, principally Somerset, Devon and Dorset. The main settings of her novels – *Emma* (Surrey), *Sense and Sensibility* (Devon), *Pride and Prejudice* (Hertfordshire), *Persuasion* (Somerset), *Northanger Abbey* (Wiltshire) and, a little eccentrically, *Mansfield Park* (Northamptonshire) – reflect her experiences.

Marcel Proust (1871–1922), who lived a century later than Jane Austen, was a French writer of major stature. His principal work, *A la Recherche du temps perdu* (literally 'In Search of Lost Time'), translated under the title *Remembrance of Things Past*, occupied much of his life and is a major landmark in French literature. It is a work for the serious student of literature. It does not possess the accessibility of the novels of Jane Austen, its length is daunting, its language dense and its plots require careful attention. Whereas Marcel Proust is widely known and there have, for example, been films based on his life, he is much less widely read. Proust's art has been analysed in many ways: as the search for truth, for the reality which lies behind the appearance of everyday things (Fowlie, 1967), and as the exploration of memories, recapturing both conscious and subconscious, in an almost autobiographical context. Marcel Proust was born in Paris, where he also died and where he is buried in Père Lachaise cemetery. His childhood was mostly spent in four places: Paris, where he lived at his parents' home; Illiers, where family holidays were spent; Auteuil (Paris), where he stayed at the home of an uncle; and resorts, principally Cabourg, on the Channel coasts of Normandy and Brittany. Proust suffered from ill-health for much of his life; he was nine years old when his illness, in the form of an asthmatic attack, first caught up with him (Levin, 1963). He travelled occasionally in France and also to Italy and the Netherlands, and served in the infantry at Orléans. Fowlie (1967) stated that Proust travelled little but succeeded in making Faubourg Saint-Germain in Paris the microcosm of the world. His father was a doctor and the family had sufficient wealth to assure Marcel a comfortable style of life. Maurois (1960) found many parallels between Proust's own life and the characters and places in his novels. Elisabeth de Gramont was a model for the Princesse des Laumes, Charles Haas for Swann, and la Comtesse Greffuhle for the Princesse de Guermantes. None of these models was exact and, similarly, Proust integrated fragments from different parts of the real world to form his fictional places. Locations in the novels are often imprecise. His description of Balbec, for example, does not place it on the Côte Fleurie but further west, whilst his placing of invading armies in Combray would locate it further east than Illiers, which is in the Beauce region of France. Painter (1965) suggested that Proust moved the known landscape of Illiers to give it the 'kaleidoscopic' quality of a dream, but for Ardagh (1989), the details of the remembered landscape remain precise so that tracing the borderline between vision and reality is 'a fascinating task for the Proustian tourist'. Both Clébert (1990), who described the Proustian geography as a major puzzle, the pieces of which had never been convincingly assembled, and Fowlie (1967), who regarded the fictional towns of the novel as having been formed from many borrowings and deft, patient, artistic creations, shared the view that Proust reconstructed places in composite ways.

Jane Austen's house at Chawton, Hampshire

The literary place chosen in relation to Jane Austen was her residence at Chawton, Hampshire, where, after the death of her father, she lived with her family, from 1809 to 1817, in a cottage on the estate of her brother, Edward Knight. The cottage was divided after 1845 and what survives is not a carefully constructed period home but a small museum (James, 1993). There are memorabilia of Jane Austen and her family and items of original furnishings, and the arrangement of rooms is basically unaltered. The house is now owned and administered by the Jane Austen Memorial Trust. For those interested in Jane Austen, Chawton is the clearest literary place. The rectory where she was born at Steventon no longer exists, and the house where she died in Winchester is part of a college and inaccessible, though her burial place in Winchester Cathedral is clearly marked. It was at Chawton that Jane Austen wrote or completed several of her novels and the house is set in the type of English landscape with which her work is associated.

A study of visitors to Jane Austen's house was conducted during the summer of 1993, and 223 completed interviews were obtained. Interviewers worked throughout the summer and included both weekdays and weekends in their schedule. The sample population proved to be a mixture of local visitors and tourists, with just under 50 per cent stating that they were on holiday in the area: 56.1 per cent had travelled from other parts of Hampshire that day, and just under 80 per cent from Hampshire, Surrey and London; 18.9 per cent of the sample were overseas visitors. This visitor sample was composed largely of professional and business people (60 per cent). Adding a further 30 per cent, who were classified as students, retirees or housewives, it is clear that bluecollar and less-skilled workers were very under-represented in the visitors to Chawton. This profile is reasonably typical of visitors to heritage sites (Herbert *et al.*, 1989). The age range of visitors was wide, with 23.4 per cent under the age of 35, and 36.1 per cent over the age of 55.

The first issue addressed concerned the kinds of people who visited Chawton. Were they 'general' tourists who happened to call at the site, or were they more focused literary tourists who had identified Chawton because of its specific associations with a writer? One strategy was to examine visitor awareness of other literary places in Britain. Visitors were asked to identify up to five British places which they linked with specific writers. Only eleven of the respondents failed to identify any such places and several claimed that there were too many to mention. Dickens, mentioned by 40 per cent of respondents and usually linked with London, was the most frequent citation, followed by the Brontës (Haworth or Yorkshire) and Shakespeare (Stratford), both with 35 per cent, and Hardy (Dorset) and Wordsworth (Lake District), both with 20 per cent. In total, around 120 different places and writers were mentioned, with a range from classical (Shakespeare) to modern (Pratchett) literature. Levels of detail shown were often impressive, with names of houses, such as Monk's House (Virginia Woolf) and Lamb House (Henry James) being cited. Dylan Thomas was identified with Swansea, Llanelli and Wales, but also with Cornwall, scene of his marriage in 1937. Although there were some obvious errors, the question elicited a large number of answers and was indicative of a high level of literary awareness among the sample of visitors. This evidence was indicative but not conclusive. Writer–place connections such as Shakespeare–Stratford and Dickens–London tend to be common knowledge.

Respondents were also asked questions designed to test knowledge about Jane Austen and her novels. Out of the 223 people interviewed, 30 (13.5 per cent) had read none of her novels. On the other hand, 28.2 per cent had read six or more of her novels, and over 60 per cent had read three or more. Of the individual novels, *Pride and Prejudice* was the most widely read (80.3 per cent), followed by *Sense and Sensibility* (58.3 per cent) and *Emma* (56.5 per cent). The least read novel was *Persuasion*, but this still scored 40.8 per cent and there were 42 mentions of 'other works', such as the unfinished *Sanditon*. This evidence confirms the literary awareness of the sample.

In addition to the questions about the novels, there were also questions on the life of Jane Austen and the segment of society to which she belonged. This topic is well covered in the literature (Herbert, 1991) and it has also been argued that she wrote about her own 'narrow segment' of society. Jane Austen belonged to the gentry in the lower part of the middle classes, but had access to the leisured middle classes and moved easily in those circles; her brother inherited property, and Honan (1987) has suggested that she inherited a fine sense of class from her mother. Her novels reflect these influences: 'She restricted her material to a narrow range of society and events: a prosperous middle-class circle in provincial surroundings' (Wynne-Davies, 1989, p. 332). Servants tend to be shadowy, mute figures, the working classes rarely have any significant presence, people with 'new' money are treated with some disdain, and the real aristocracy with a sense of irony. Fifty-one per cent of the visitors placed Jane Austen in a class termed 'gentry', and a further 23.8 per cent in a group called 'leisured classes'; both can be regarded as accurate assessments and this again offers a positive indication of the awareness of visitors. The caveat is that these could be judgements based upon experience of the house at Chawton rather than on a reading of the novels or a knowledge of Jane Austen.

A set of questions was designed to investigate visitors' knowledge of Jane Austen's novels. Respondents were presented with a list of ten topics or features and asked which of these they would think of in relation to Jane Austen's novels. About 90 per cent of respondents identified qualities of 'romantic relationships', 'proper behaviour', 'good manners', and the 'place of women in society'. About two-thirds of those interviewed identified 'wealth' and 'southern England', but 'politics', 'economic matters', 'changing times' and 'poverty' were identified by only one-third or less. By and large, these responses confirm the idea of a well-read and knowledgeable group of visitors who are able to identify the features most commonly associated with Jane Austen. There are nuances and hidden meanings in the writing of Jane Austen, as with any author, as she was bound by the conventions of her time and her awareness of what publishers would find acceptable. Said (1989) found evidence of an attitude towards colonialism in *Mansfield Park*, which he summarized (p. 158) as 'the importance of empire to the situation at home', whilst Tanner (1986) stressed Jane Austen's sensitivities to social change and her reactions to it. These are some of the issues for literary debate, but the survey showed good visitor awareness of some of the main features of Jane Austen's novels.

The evidence so far suggests that visitors to Chawton are knowledgeable about Jane Austen and her novels and have a good level of general literary awareness. There were also direct questions on reasons for the visit; 56.9 per cent said that they had come to be informed or to be educated rather than to be entertained or to relax. This does give some clear insight into the nature of the sample of visitors as this majority belongs to the more discerning category of tourists, in Urry's (1990) terms, the 'romantic gaze'. Pressed for more specific reasons, 31.8 per cent said that they were 'fans' of Jane Austen, and this was the first-ranked reason for the visit. If first- and second-ranked reasons are taken, 46.1 per cent are 'fans' of the writer. Additionally, 38.1 per cent identified the wish to learn more about Jane Austen as a first- or second-ranked reason. Taken together, these responses show a high level of genuine interest in Jane Austen. Among other reasons mentioned, 32.8 per cent had come just to have a day out, or had noticed the sign when passing. Others cited reasons of convenience, favourable weather for a trip, or the fact that they were on holiday in the locality.

Most visitors were motivated by a genuine literary interest but the visitor sample was not uniform in its composition. A significant minority viewed the visit to Chawton as a leisure rather than as a literary experience. Spending a few hours in a relaxing, pleasant environment may have been as important as achieving some empathy with the author and her works. If there is a dichotomy, however, its edges may well be blurred. There was a widely held 'interest' in the literary connotations of Chawton. For some visitors this was the specific motivation for being there; for others it was much more peripheral. Many were able to combine interest and relaxation in acceptable ways: these were not mutually exclusive features of the visit. This interpretation was partly confirmed by other evidence. Over 80 per cent were first-time visitors to Chawton and 85 per cent had visited other historic or more 'general interest' places in the vicinity. Winchester, Salisbury and Stonehenge were the most frequently mentioned places also visited, though specific houses, such as that linked with Gilbert White, were often cited. These are the kinds of visitor who patronize heritage sites in general and see literary places as part of that experience.

Having established some of the characteristics of the visitors, the issue of whether they were drawn to Chawton to explore the real life of Jane Austen or to have contact with the worlds of her novels was examined. Questions of authenticity affect both areas. Was this the small table at which Jane Austen wrote? Is her room as she saw it almost 200 years ago? Can any of her characters be placed in these settings? As already suggested, there is a strong supposition that real and imagined worlds fuse in the minds of the visitors. A study of visitors to Brontë country found that visitors were affected by a powerful image of the moors as a bleak, isolated and windswept place but the experience of crossing the moors was suffused 'less with the excitement of treading in the Brontës' steps, than with the thought that Heathcliff might appear' (Pocock, 1987, p. 138).

Chawton itself is not likely to generate such images, as the house and its setting have no obvious place in her novels. But there are real places in the novels: Box Hill where Emma spent time with her party and the Cobb at Lyme Regis where Louisa had her accident in *Persuasion* might serve similar purposes. Jane Austen's characters, however, lack the drama of a Heathcliff and her places are less imbued with incident and emotion. For example, while she used the Cobb as a setting for incidents in *Persuasion*, a visitor today looking down the Cobb is much more likely to have an image of Sarah Woodruff, in *The French Lieutenant's Woman* (Fowles, 1969), as a figure who inhabits that place.

The suggestion that the visitor group at Chawton had good literary awareness was supported by their responses to a question on which features of the house they had found of most interest. Sixty-six items were mentioned, ranging from the 'atmosphere of the place' to the 'creaking door' which warned Jane Austen that she should put her work to one side. Most responses were linked to Jane Austen herself rather than to any characters in her novels. Over half of the items mentioned were personal things such as letters, a lock of hair, her own room and details of her illness; many others referred to her family and to the house. Clearly, those who visited the house at Chawton were drawn there because of the links with Jane Austen and her family, but they also found the house of intrinsic historical interest. Hampshire and Chawton have no part in the writings of Jane Austen, there is no door here which opens to lead visitors into the imagined world of her novels. This view was confirmed when visitors were questioned on what they had learned most about during the visit: 91.1 per cent felt they had learned at least something about Jane Austen, her family and their lifestyle; 40.4 per cent felt they had learned nothing about the settings for her novels, and 32.3 per cent nothing about Jane Austen as an author.

There were questions to test awareness of places where Jane Austen had lived, and also about places that appear in her novels. Responses to both were thin and unconvincing: 68.6 per cent connected her with Winchester Cathedral; 37.2 per cent with the house in College Street, Winchester; 52.5 per cent with Bath; and 36.3 per cent with Lyme Regis. These are the more obvious connections but only 5.8 per cent identified Steventon as a place associated with Jane Austen, although it was her birthplace and she spent much of her life there. When visitors were questioned on places associated with the Austen novels, Bath, which features in *Persuasion* and *Northanger Abbey*, was prominent, being identified by 76.2 per cent, but thereafter the highest scores were Hampshire (71.7 per cent), which is basically incorrect as it is not a setting for the novels, and London (37.7 per cent), which features in several novels, though never prominently. More appropriate were Lyme Regis (36.3 per cent), in *Persuasion,* and Box Hill (19.7 per cent) in *Emma.* Other key places, such as Northamptonshire (11.2 per cent) in *Mansfield Park,* and Derbyshire (1 person), Darcy's home in *Pride and Prejudice,* are clearly not at all well known or remembered.

All the evidence tends to point in the same direction: a visit to Chawton is a visit to the former home of Jane Austen and her family and not to the world of her novels. Visitors to Chawton had, at a detailed level, limited awareness of the world of the novels, or even of the places linked with Jane Austen. The low response on Steventon was revealing, as was the absence of any mention of Great Bookham, a possible model for Highbury, or of the Darcy home, 'Pemberley', in Derbyshire, which Nicolson (1991) believed was modelled on Godmersham in Kent. These omissions may reflect the nature of Jane Austen's writing, with its lack of descriptive detail of places and settings, and also the nature of her settings which are attractive but subdued landscapes in which events unfold with little or only a rare sense of drama or traces of violence or sudden change.

Marcel Proust and Cabourg, Normandy

Several places in Paris are associated with the life of Marcel Proust. The house where he was born, in rue La Fontaine, Auteuil, no longer exists, but he lived with his family in boulevard Malesherbes and, after their deaths, in boulevard Haussmann, rue Laurent-Pichat and rue Hamelin. For some time he frequented several salons in Paris. Although most of his life was spent in Paris, he has not left his mark on the city in the form of Proustian literary places. His associations are much more strongly felt to be with Illiers, the small town in Beauce where he spent his childhood holidays at the home of his aunt and uncle. Illiers, as the imagined place called Combray, features as a setting for significant parts of his writing and the municipality decided to change its name to Illiers-Combray in recognition of this fact. The family house on rue du St Esprit, Illiers, is now a museum, maintained by the Société des Amis de Marcel Proust. It has been refurbished in the style of the 1870s, with original windows and wall panelling and 'is full of Proustian ghosts' (Ardagh, 1989). Modern writers on French literature tend to transpose imagined and real worlds when describing the life of Marcel Proust. Fowlie (1967) wrote that at the house in Illiers visitors can still walk in the garden where the family (in the novel) 'used to listen for the ringing of the bell which announced Swann's arrival' (p. 191). Ardagh (1989) saw the walks taken by Marcel Proust and his family as the equivalents of the 'Swann's Way' and the 'Guermantes Way' of the novels, and Clébert (1990), in his survey of French literary places, devoted at least as much space to the places of the novels as to the real places of Proust's life. The assumption that these places are the same, and that *A la recherche du temps perdu* was strongly autobiographical, is clearly there.

One line of explanation for the lack of connections between Paris and Proust is that the Parisian places identified in his novels, such as the Champs-Elysées and the Bois de Boulogne, do not belong solely to Proust; they are too overladen with other images.

The fictional town of Balbec is an important literary place in the writings of Proust. It is a composite of memories, from places such as Trouville, Deauville, Houlgate, Honfleur and Cabourg, gleaned from his holidays on the Normandy coast. One of the problems in disentangling real life and imagination in the work of Marcel Proust is that the principal character and narrator in the novel is also called Marcel.

> Then she would find her tongue and say: 'My . . .' or 'My darling . . .' followed by my Christian name, which, if we give the narrator the same name as the author of this book, would be 'My Marcel', or 'My darling Marcel'. (Proust, 1989, Vol. 3, p. 69)

Critics such as Levin (1963) have overcome the difficulty by referring to the author as Proust or Marcel Proust and to the character as Marcel. Proust spent several summer holidays at Cabourg between 1881 and 1914. He first came, as a child, with his grandmother and stayed at the Grand Hôtel. On later visits as an adult, he also stayed at the Grand Hôtel. Marcel, in the novel, stays at the Grand Hôtel de la Plage in Balbec. It is here that Marcel meets Albertine, with whom he had one of the great romantic relationships of his life. Balbec is a 'composite' of several places but it is with Cabourg that it is most easily and persistently associated. Certainly, of the Proustian places, Cabourg most energetically promotes the connection: the Grand Hôtel serves *petites madeleines*, the small cakes given to Marcel by his mother which evoked strong memories of Combray, where his Aunt Léonie many years before had often given him a little piece of *madeleine*, 'dipping it first in her own cup of tea or tisane' (Proust, 1989, Vol. 1, p. 50). The hotel has a Marcel Proust room, a restaurant called Le Balbec, and a casino bar called Du Côté de Chez Swann. 'If sleepy, provincial Illiers largely ignores its great heritage, assertive, touristy Cabourg certainly does not' (Ardagh, 1989, p. 101).

It is clear that Cabourg has made an attempt to develop the Proust connection as part of its image for visitors. Tourist literature available at the Information Centre states that 'Marcel Proust immortalised Cabourg as the town of Balbec in his book *A l'ombre des jeunes filles en fleurs* (*Within a Budding Grove*) which he wrote looking out to sea from his room in the Grand Hôtel.' The municipality of Cabourg instituted a Marcel Proust Literary Prize in 1972 and has identified tourist trails which explore 'Marcel Proust's Normandy'. There is a promenade Marcel Proust, a place Marcel Proust and display boards outside the Information Centre contain quotations from the novel *A l'ombre des jeunes filles en fleurs*. The Grand Hôtel itself, perhaps the pivot of Proustian Cabourg, is replete with reminders of his former presence.

The Cabourg survey was conducted over part of a day in late September 1993 at various locations in the town. In total 151 people were interviewed though some of these, about 15 per cent, were local people who regarded their visit as a normal trip to see family or friends or to transact business. Information on occupations suggested a much wider range of social class types than had been evident at Chawton, though lower-income, working-class groups were still under-represented. Professional, business and white-collar workers accounted for 35.4 per cent of the sample, blue-collar workers for 15.6 per cent and the unskilled and unemployed for 3.5 per cent. There was a significant number of retired people – 26.4 per cent – and the remainder comprised housewives and students. All age groups were represented with 31.5 per cent between the ages of 15 and 34; 32.2 per cent between 35 and 54; and 23.5 per cent over the age of 64. Most of those interviewed (70 per cent) had travelled from within the *département* of Calvados that day, 15 per cent had come from Paris, 6.6 per cent from Seine-Maritime, and 5 per cent from either Eure or Loire et Cher. Many were on holiday and came from other parts of France. About one-quarter came from Paris and another quarter were from overseas, with the United Kingdom being the largest single overseas source (16.6 per cent).

It became clear on analysing the responses to the questionnaires that, whereas there was a Proust connection which was very meaningful to some of the visitors, the majority had been drawn to Cabourg by its attractiveness as a tourist resort in much more general terms. Most visitors had not come to a literary place but to an attractive seaside town at which they could spend some time relaxing. It is difficult to isolate the Proust connection as a separate effect, though it was probably a very significant factor for a small minority, a pleasant adjunct to their visit for many, and a fact of little or no interest for a large number of visitors.

Fewer than 5 per cent of those interviewed said that they had specifically come to Cabourg because of the Proust connection. The most frequent reason was that they had wanted a day out and Cabourg was an attractive place; just under half of those questioned replied in these terms. Another 20 per cent were on holiday in the area and Cabourg was a convenient place to visit; about 15 per cent were on shopping or business trips and just over 10 per cent were visiting family or friends. Asked about the more general purposes of their visit, 90 per cent said they had come to relax, and only 6.5 per cent wanted to be educated or informed by their visit. This set of questions did not convey any impression of a set of 'literary pilgrims'; the Proust connection was usually a background factor for a group of 'tourists'.

In response to a question on whether the connection with Proust had influenced their visit, 40.4 per cent of the total sample said they had been influenced either a great deal or a little by this consideration; 50.3 per cent said the factor had no influence at all and the rest were unsure; 23.8 per cent intended to visit parts of Cabourg which had links with Proust; 40.4 per cent did not; and 35.7 per cent did not know. Just over half of those responding to the questions had read the tourist literature and intended to visit the Grand Hôtel. Over 90 per cent were going to admire the views and about three-quarters said they would enjoy a day out. Asked which features of the town they had found most interesting, 46.1 per cent mentioned the beach and the sea, 24.3 per cent the town itself with its buildings, architecture and layout, and 10.7 per cent the general atmosphere or ambience of the place. Just under 10 per cent specified features which were linked with Proust.

Asked if they had read any of Proust's novels, 6.6 per cent said a lot, 43.0 per cent said a little, 47.7 per cent said none at all, and 2.6 per cent were unsure. Although the 'hard core' of people very familiar with Proust's work is small, about half of those asked had some awareness of his novels, though these figures are still far less impressive than those found in the Chawton sample where, for example, only 13.5 per cent had not read any of Jane Austen's novels. The suggestion of limited real knowledge of Proust and his work was confirmed by responses to other questions. When asked which places in France they would associate with Proust, 18 named Paris, 11 named Normandy and 8 identified Illiers-Combray. There were other suggestions, including Dieppe, Chartres and 'Guermantes'. The latter is a prominent family name in the novels and does reveal awareness of the text but, at best, about one-quarter of the sample could offer a place in France they would connect with Proust. Asked which parts of Cabourg they would link with Proust, 25 (16.6 per cent) mentioned the Grand Hôtel, and 14 the promenade or seashore; this latter figure included two mentions of the girls, one of whom was Albertine, who are first introduced in the novel as they come down the promenade: 'a little band, progressing down the esplanade like a luminous comet' (Proust, Vol. 1, 1989, p. 848). Mention was made of streets in the town, mainly those named after Proust, and more general references were to the countryside, town and ambience. Overall, about 30 per cent identified places in Cabourg which had connections with Proust.

On the more general question of places in France associated with writers, 45.7 per cent named such places, though not all of these could identify both writers and places, and some included artists rather than writers. There was a very wide spread of both places and writers, with nothing like the levels of consensus apparent in Chawton. Paris and Normandy, including Honfleur and Rouen, were the places most frequently mentioned. Victor Hugo was mentioned nine times and was linked with places such as Paris, the place des Vosges, Jersey, Guernsey, Villequier and Aisnes. Hugo had many homes in Paris, including one in the place des Vosges where there is now a Victor Hugo museum; he was exiled to the Channel Islands, and his daughter drowned in the Seine at Villequier, where there is also a small museum. Maupassant was mentioned nine times and is linked with places in Normandy, such as Rouen, Étretat and Fécamp. For the rest, there are fewer mentions and authors range widely from the classical (Rousseau) to the modern (Pagnol).

Although knowledge of Proust and awareness of French literary figures were not overly impressive, visitors were supportive of Cabourg's policy of developing the link between the town and the writer: 78.8 per cent supported the idea, 12.6 per cent were against, and 8.7 per cent were unsure or did not answer; 29.1 per cent were strongly in favour of similar policies being developed for other places, and a further 55 per cent were moderately in favour; a large majority therefore had some support for policies of this kind. Asked what they would like to see as the main components of such a policy, 70.7 per cent of those offering an opinion supported the idea of guided tours, 79.4 per cent were in favour of museums, 80.9 per cent of exhibitions or displays, 71.1 per cent of tourist pamphlets or similar literature, and 90 per cent supported measures to conserve the heritage of places such as Cabourg. Overall, the evidence for Cabourg suggests a 'generalist' group of visitors. A small minority had been drawn to the town because of the Proust connection, but for most of the visitors the more obvious attractions of Cabourg as a seaside resort were dominant.

Conclusions

This chapter has raised several broad issues in relation to the theme of heritage as literary place and has examined these with reference to studies of two contrasted locations. The contrast between Chawton and Cabourg is of great importance and affects all the findings which have emerged. Whereas Chawton is a specific site dedicated to a writer, Cabourg is a town for which the literary connection is but one part of a wider set of tourist attractions. The issue of authenticity is of particular interest in the study of literary places for reasons which have been identified. If visitors seek an experience from their visit which is meaningful to them in relation to a writer and his/her fiction, should we be concerned whether that experience draws upon fact or reality, or whether the two can be distinguished? The answer to that question is 'probably not'. If the experience is authentic to the visitor, that is sufficient.

Some visitors, though probably a small minority, are extremely interested in the authenticity of the site and are likely to be disappointed if things are not 'real'. Some visitors to Chawton expressed disquiet that items contained in the house might not be genuine. As suggested, this is almost certainly a minority view and careful reconstruction is normally acceptable to visitors when originals are not available. At Cabourg, the issue could not arise in such a detailed form as, apart from hotel and promenade, there was little by way of material objects which could be linked to the author in real life. Proust certainly spent significant amounts of time at Cabourg but his personal, lived-in environments are not visible. It is the spirit of his former presence which is invoked, the chance to occupy similar spaces to the writer, and to look out upon those sights – seashore and promenade with their activities – which might have inspired his work. At Chawton, it is the life of Jane Austen which is portrayed: the table at which she wrote, the room in which she slept and the lock of her hair. Chawton does not invoke her characters as they do not really belong there; her imagined places have their touching points elsewhere. Visitors to Chawton have no imperative to look out on to the street and see Emma Woodhouse in their mind's eye; at Cabourg, however, there is the feeling that they might envisage Albertine as they look down the promenade: 'a girl with brilliant, laughing eyes and plump, matt cheeks' (Proust, 1989, Vol. 1, p. 850). None of this is of course real, these people never existed except in the pages of a book, but the power of the novel combined with the place evokes such images. It is in this sense that authenticity in its conventional form becomes a questionable issue. One could verify the authenticity of the table or the lock of hair, and that would be important for some people, but the authenticity of the experience of people and events at literary places is of a different order. If visitors gain a meaningful experience, that is authentic whatever its grounding in reality. In some ways this is a Proustian type of argument. Proust believed that true reality resided in the object and its symbolism and *within* the characters; his question was often: 'which is true, which is the truth?' (Levin, 1963, p. 385).

The question regarding the kinds of visitor who will be attracted to literary places is going to be answered in different ways for different places. Here the contrast between Chawton and Cabourg is evident. A visit to Chawton is focused and people come with the knowledge that it was a writer's home. By and large, these were visitors of the *romantic gaze*, more discerning and less general, who wished to learn more about a particular writer. Whether they could be regarded as single-minded 'literary tourists' is more questionable. Most had a wider interest in heritage, and literary places were one part of an itinerary which included places with quite different historical interests. Many came to learn and follow up their interests but combined these purposes with relaxing in their leisure time. Cabourg was a different situation. Proust was one element in a tourist resort of many attractions. Only a small minority were purposeful, Proustian tourists; the rest were tourists or visitors of the *collective gaze*.

The final question is whether the literary connection can be promoted as a part of heritage. Clearly it can. Its significance will vary from one location to another but the basic appeal is evident. Visitors look for a variety of experiences and many of these can be provided by heritage sites, of which literary places are a part. This message was clear at Chawton, where the Jane Austen House was part of the heritage round. At Cabourg, considerable efforts were being made to promote the literary connection in a resort which has a range of attractions to offer. This marketing may add a segment to the visitor trade, and it also helps create the image which the town wishes to convey to the outside world. Many visitors to Cabourg have little awareness of Proust and come for different reasons, but the connection can be used to promote special events, such as the occasion of the award of the literary prize, which attracts different types of visitor at particular times of year and also to set Cabourg apart from other resorts on the Normandy coast. Of interest was the very widespread support for the Cabourg initiatives and for policies for interpretation at other literary places. These literary places are part of heritage and can be used to attract visitors. In many ways they pose challenges of presentation and interpretation which are exceptional and, as yet, scarcely explored. People's expectations and experiences will vary but literary places can form significant components of the heritage industry.

References

Ardagh, J. (1989) *Writers' France: A Regional Panorama*. London: Hamish Hamilton.

Birch, B. P. (1981) Wessex, Hardy and the nature novelists. *Transactions, Institute of British Geographers*, 6, 348–358.

Buzard, J. (1993) *The Beaten Track: European Tourism, Literature and the Ways to Culture, 1800–1918*. Oxford: Clarendon Press.

Clébert, J.-P. (1990) *Les Hauts Lieux de la littérature en France*. Paris: Bordas.

Daiches, D. and Flower, J. (1979) *Literary Landscapes of the British Isles*. London: Bell and Hyman.

Daniels, S. and Rycroft, S. (1993) Mapping the modern city: Alan Sillitoe's Nottingham novels. *Transactions, Institute of British Geographers*, 18, 460–480.

Drabble, M. (1979) *A Writer's Britain: Landscape and Literature*. London: Thames and Hudson.

Eade, J. (1992) Pilgrimage and tourism at Lourdes, France. *Annals of Tourism Research*, 19, 18–32.

Fowles, J. (1969) *The French Lieutenant's Woman*. London: Cape.

Fowlie, W. (1967) *A Reading of Proust*. London: Dennis Dobson.

Herbert, D. T. (1991) Place and society in Jane Austen's England. *Geography*, 76, 193–208.

Herbert, D. T., Prentice, R. C. and Thomas, C. J. (1989) *Heritage Sites: Strategies for Marketing and Development*. Aldershot: Avebury.

Honan, P. (1987) *Jane Austen: Her Life*. London: Weidenfeld and Nicolson.

James, P. D. (1993) Jane Austen, Chawton, Hampshire. In K. Marsh (ed.) *Writers and Their Houses*. London: Hamish Hamilton, pp. 3–11.

Levin, H. (1963) *The Gates of Horn*. New York: Oxford University Press.

Marsh, K. (ed.) (1993) *Writers and Their Houses*. London: Hamish Hamilton.

Maurois, A. (1960) *Le Monde de Marcel Proust*. Paris: Librairie Hachette.

Nicolson, N. (1991) *The World of Jane Austen*. London: Weidenfeld and Nicolson.

Painter, G. D. (1965) *Marcel Proust: A Biography*. London: Chatto and Windus.

Pocock, D. C. D. (1987) Haworth: the experience of a literary place. In W. E. Mallory and P. Simpson-Housley (eds) *Geography and Literature*. Syracuse, NY: Syracuse University Press, pp. 135–142.

Pocock, D. C. D. (1992) Catherine Cookson country: tourist expectation and experience. *Geography*, 77, 236–243.

Proust, M. (1989) *Remembrance of Things Past*. London: Penguin Books, 3 vols. (First published 1954, Paris: La Pléiade Gallimard.)

Said, E. W. (1989) Jane Austen and empire. In T. Eagleton (ed.) *Essays for Raymond Williams*. Cambridge: Polity Press, pp. 150–164.

Squire, S. J. (1993) Valuing countryside: reflections on Beatrix Potter tourism. *Area*, **24**, 5–10.

Tanner, T. (1986) *Jane Austen*. London: Macmillan.

Urry, J. (1990) *The Tourist Gaze: Leisure and Travel in Contemporary Societies*. London: Sage.

Wynne-Davies, M. (ed.) (1989) *Bloomsbury Guide to English Literature*. London: Bloomsbury.

4

Heritage as National Identity: Histories and Prospects of the National Pasts

Pyrs Gruffudd

The concept of the nation has, in recent years, become problematic. Nations are increasingly seen as being shot through with fluid, contextual and contested discourses (e.g. Bhabha, 1990; Parker *et al.*, 1992). No longer, therefore, can we talk of fixed national identities or of stable definitions of 'the national heritage'. Anderson's (1991) influential study of the rise of nationalism defined nations as 'imagined communities' made up of individuals who, though they may never meet, identify with their compatriots and believe themselves to hold certain values, myths and outlooks in common. At the core of this process of identification is the cultural and historical imagination – a profoundly fickle and fluid construct. Whilst Anderson's analysis is best known for its comments on the role of novels and newspapers in psychologically unifying diverse peoples, it also offers an eloquent commentary on the messages embodied in the archaeological reconstruction and the museum. Smith (1986, 1991) has similarly argued that a sense of ethnic history and of mythology underlies the contemporary nation state, and that 'a rich ethnohistory can be a significant source of cultural power and a focus of cultural politicization' (Smith, 1991, p. 164). However, it must be realized that, as Hobsbawm and Ranger (1983) have pointed out, ethno-histories – encoded as 'traditions' – are frequently inventions or recycled myths. Rarely can they have the status of fact.

History, commemoration and conservation are all, therefore, implicitly political. What a self-defined group or a nation seeks to preserve, and to represent to others, allows us to understand something of what a particular 'imagined community' thinks it is. As I write, for instance, a multi-layered debate rages in Britain over the form and function of D-Day commemorations. Similarly, the arena of 'heritage' or the 'heritage industry' has been embroiled in political trauma. For Hewison (1987), the heritage industry – by which he meant the theme parks and museums that were opening, in his opinion, at a frightening rate in 1980s Britain – was emblematic of a culture in decline and rapidly losing the ability to challenge that decline:

> At best, the heritage industry only draws a screen between ourselves and our true past. I criticize the heritage industry not simply because so many of its products are fantasies of a world that never was; not simply because at a deeper level it involves the preservation, indeed reassertion, of social values that the democratic progress of the twentieth century seemed to be doing away with, but because, far from ameliorating the climate of decline, it is actually worsening it. (Hewison, 1987, p. 10)

There is much of value in Hewison's argument, particularly the ironic political resonances struck by industrial museums opening in an age of industrial depression. But irony can only carry an argument so far; in asserting the importance, indeed existence, of a 'true past', Hewison failed to engage with the notion that all national pasts are essentially fantasies.

Wright (1985) offered what is perhaps a subtler, and consequently more engaging, reading of the role of the national past. On returning to England after five years in North America, Wright realized that he 'had come back to a country which was full of precious and imperilled traces – a closely held iconography of what it is to be English – all of them appealing in one covertly projective way or another to the historical and sacrosanct identity of the nation' (p. 2). But for Wright it was not a simple opposition of modern and nostalgic, good and bad, but the weaving together of a number of discourses of identity, politics and culture. Rather than the past obscuring the present, as Hewison seemed to suggest, Wright's past and present feed off each other. Historical narratives reveal contemporary anxieties, and contemporary desires are fulfilled in the preservation of the past: 'The national past is above all a *modern* past and . . . it is defined not just in relation to the general disappointment of earlier historical expectation, but also and more pointedly around the leading tensions of the contemporary political situation' (ibid.).

The argument in this chapter is that we should aim at a broad understanding of the concept of heritage. It demands a subtler definition than that conventionally allowed in texts on the subject. Heritage does not only reside in those sanctioned sites, fenced off and ticketed, under the auspices of Cadw (Welsh Historic Monuments) or English Heritage. It is about how we mediate our relationship with 'our past'. Heritage is an all-embracing concept that applies equally to landscapes, customs and narratives of identity. In this chapter I will attempt to develop this sense of heritage by discussing some of the ways in which Welsh identity has been negotiated around the general themes of history and preservation. In many ways, such an analysis could apply to most nations, but it can be argued that such debates have been, and remain, particularly important in Wales. Wales has lacked full political recognition since the Act of Union of 1536 incorporated it into English political structures and it has long been, therefore, confined to the status of an 'imagined nation' (e.g. Curtis, 1986). In such a nation, history and historiography become ingredients of a radical political agenda. This was the case during the Romantic period of the eighteenth and nineteenth centuries (Morgan, 1983, 1986) and the later nineteenth-century 'national revival' (Morgan, 1982), when a new economic, cultural and political confidence manifested itself in Wales. This carried through into growing opposition to British centralism in the first half of this century, expressed in one way by the formation of Plaid Cymru, the Welsh Nationalist Party, in 1925 (Davies, 1983).

This chapter focuses on Welsh debates on heritage and identity in the first half of the twentieth century. It begins by examining the way in which contemporary political and social debates came to be implicated in landscape preservation and the work of a nascent planning movement in Wales. This movement was challenged by readings of landscape which claimed cultural 'authenticity' and legitimation. The chapter then considers how such notions of 'authenticity' came to be encoded in a Welsh national folk museum, and it highlights the political role of this institution. It ends by speculating on the present and future roles of the national past. Indeed, the contemporary role of the past is central to the argument throughout. In Wales, the national past is enlisted as dynamic legitimation or as a blueprint for the future. To quote Wright (1985) again, the national past is a *modern* past.

Landscapes and Legends

The invention of national traditions often draws heavily on territorial myths. As Anderson (1988, p. 18) claimed, nations are not simply located in space:

> rather they explicitly claim particular territories and derive distinctiveness from them. Indeed nationalists typically over-emphasize the particular uniqueness of their own territory and history.

Smith (1986) noted how 'legends and landscapes' intersect to give space ethnicity. Landscapes, and their representation in painting, texts and so on, are powerful components in the construction of national identity (see Daniels, 1993; *Landscape Research*, 1991). Their preservation can therefore assume wider symbolic significance.

The landscapes of Wales have always been contested. Morgan's work (1983) on the Romantics' 'discovery' of Wales in the late eighteenth century vividly outlined how the uplands were assimilated into a particular English narrative, and the way in which that narrative was recast by the Welsh for their own purposes. Early eighteenth-century English tastes were far from sympathetic to the rugged terrain of Wales; one writer suggested that Wales looked 'like the fag End of Creation; the very Rubbish of *Noah's* Flood' (quoted in Andrews, 1989, p. 109). But from receiving no mentions in the *Gentleman's*

Magazine for most of the century, an article on Wales appeared in every issue in the 1780s and 1790s (Zaring, 1977). This change can be partly attributed to hostilities with France which forced the abandonment of the Grand Tour, on which privileged males had hitherto embarked in a quest for education amidst the landscapes and antiquities of the classical world. Attention turned inwards to the landscapes of Britain and this encouraged the development of a new aesthetic – the 'Picturesque'. Artists came to find value in the asymmetry and irregularity of the rugged and unkempt landscapes and buildings of places like Wales, Scotland, the Lake District, and the rustic landscapes of lowland England. This aesthetic taste was codified into the routes and discourses of the Picturesque Tour. In 1798, one writer noted that an excursion amidst the picturesque beauties of the Wye Valley had 'become an essential part of the education . . . of all who aspire to the reputation of elegance, taste, and fashion' (quoted in Wordsworth *et al.*, 1987, p. 96). The search for the picturesque was created by and mediated through the emerging genre of the travel book; through the descriptions of writers like William Gilpin and the Welshman Thomas Pennant, the charms of particular districts were added to the rigorously structured itinerary of the Picturesque Tour and to the scenic heritage. Pennant's *Tour in Wales*, published in 1778, was part of a great outpouring of topographical literature aimed at an educated and privileged readership. About 50 books recording tours through Wales were published between 1770 and 1800, written by scientists, antiquarians, genealogists and – increasingly – those for whom travel and aesthetic appreciation itself was the sole purpose. Whilst some writers, like Pennant, were members of the native but Anglicized gentry, many of these books were written by and for the English and served to construct for Wales a particular heritage narrative for external consumption. Thus, landscapes were viewed through the lens of Picturesque aesthetic theory; the simple, noble, rural life of the peasantry was idealized and landscape features like abbeys, castles and great houses became re-enchanted by myth.

As Wales was being 'discovered' by English aesthetes, its meanings were also being reworked by the Welsh. Morgan (1983) argued that the Welsh were slow to appreciate the beauties of their own land, and that much of the inspiration for the revival of their heritage came from exiles: 'It was the London Welsh throughout the eighteenth century who gave the lead in things Welsh, and it was they, the exiles long separated from the reality of things at home in Wales, who most readily turned to an invented Wales, a Wales of the imagination which they then gave to their native land' (Morgan, 1986, p. 29). A series of cultural revivals by 'patriot propagandists' was aimed at making the Welsh common people – the *gwerin* – think of themselves as a nation. Landscape and the built heritage played a part in this imaginative process. By the mid-nineteenth century the Welsh had come:

> to see their hills not as a punishment from the Almighty who had driven them from the lush lowlands of England, but as a fastness or fortress for the

nation ... *Gwlad y Bryniau* (Mountain Land) soon became a Welsh cliché, even for those living in lowland Wales. ... As the Welsh became more and more industrialized, so they came to cherish the image of the Welshman as a sturdy tough hillman, free as mountain air. (Morgan, 1983, pp. 88–89)

Wales is characterized, according to Williams (1985) by two competing discourses – the rural *gwerin* and the industrial working class – and in the cultural politics of the national revival we find an adoption of the former in opposition to the Anglicized latter. But whilst the romantic mythologizing of Wales appears to connect this native sense of heritage to that propagated by travellers, it contained a greater emphasis on myth and its contemporary resonance. Its writers engaged with the lives and concerns of the natives in opposition to the more disengaged and aestheticized 'monarch of all I survey' (Pratt, 1992) stance of the English traveller. Wales was reconstructed in the image of contemporary discourses and not simply as a dehistoricized and generalized 'heritage'. Thus in the nineteenth century, landscape and heritage intersected as a politically engaged commentary on the present.

The preservation of rural Wales

Landscape was equally a focus for ideas of heritage and national identity in the inter-war period. The scenic heritage of Britain was defined in innumerable texts – popular and quasi-academic – of the period. Whilst much of that heritage was located firmly in the villages and gentle downland of southern England (see Wiener, 1981; Howkins, 1986) Wales was, as in the eighteenth century, subjected to this gaze. Published tours played a great part in disseminating received wisdom on landscapes and buildings of worth to a growing market amongst the middle classes. Books like Edward Thomas's *Wales* (1983, originally published in 1905) and H. V. Morton's (1932) *In Search of Wales* defined itineraries for the educated and historically minded traveller. Didactic texts from Batsford's 'British Heritage' and the 'Face of Britain' series were similarly resonant with narrative and myth. As late as 1949 Eiluned and Peter Lewis (1949, pp. 1–2) warned the reader, in *The Land of Wales*, that 'The traveller who buys a ticket at Paddington or Euston should be warned that he is about to travel backwards as well as westwards, for Wales is a storehouse of the past.'

Yet this heritage was under threat. Throughout Britain groups railed against the despoliation of the countryside and the planless sprawl of the cities and suburbs. The Council for the Preservation of Rural England (CPRE) noted that:

Our scenery is a heritage from a number of sources, some generous, some ungenerous; their gifts in some part rich and beautiful; in other parts, but dross. ... If, taking this wide view of our scenery, we balance beauty against ugliness the scales are heavily weighted in favour of beauty. The beauty is in great measure natural; in some measure, man-made. All of the ugliness is man-made. (Howarth, 1937, p. 1)

The scenic heritage of Britain, built up organically over the centuries, was threatened by a new scale of change. In a CPRE promotional cartoon issued in 1928, St George 'fights the spread of an urban and brashly commercial culture, the pollution of the factory, the invasion of the country by the petrol engine and its attendants of garage and hoarding' (Matless, 1990, p. 180). By contrast, St George protects the family who shelter behind him and the English village which clusters organically around a church in the middle distance. This was the familiar scripting of conservation culture in the inter-war years.

But tensions emerged in early twentieth-century Wales around the idea of landscape preservation. The Council for the Preservation of Rural Wales (CPRW) was formed in 1928 as a sister organization to the CPRE. Whilst its core of members and officers came from what might loosely be called professional and 'society' circles, the initial appeal was to a broader national sentiment. The idea of the CPRW was launched at the Holyhead National Eisteddfod of 1927, a festival which was itself part of the Romantic remaking of Welsh heritage and identity (Morgan, 1983) and which the Council doubt-less hoped could be enlisted as a forum for this latest remaking. Wales's particular scenic heritage of scattered cottages and wild hill-lands was invoked as an inheritance passed down from earlier generations. Landscape preserva-tion through the agencies of town and country planning, therefore, became a patriotic duty for the Welsh. Lord Boston (quoted in Abercrombie, 1928, p. 169) urged the Welsh to avoid the charge 'that we of this generation failed, through inaction or indifference, to do our level best to safeguard those scenic, artistic and historical features of our country, which constitute not only a national asset, but a priceless heritage'. This did not, however, constitute a bar on all development. At the same meeting the prominent planner Patrick Abercrombie weighed and measured the relative demands of tradition and modernity: 'It is no longer necessary to labour the need for preserving the beauties and seemliness of Wales. Everyone is agreed that while it is essential that nothing shall interfere with the legitimate development of the resources of Wales, the wanton destruction of beauty, which is invariably unnecessary, must be stopped' (Abercrombie, 1928, p. 156). Abercrombie was sensitive to history and tradition and argued that no one could 'plan for the future without understanding how the background has been built up in historical stages' (Abercrombie, 1938, p. 4). In an earlier address to the National Eisteddfod he had highlighted the particular aesthetic qualities of the Welsh countryside and shown a profound awareness of the nation's ancient and more recent history (Abercrombie, 1924). Abercrombie's form of regional planning stressed an evolutionary continuity between tradition and modernity.

The CPRWs first pamphlet, *Three Questions and an Answer* (CPRW, 1928), defined what ought to be preserved in terms both aesthetic and historical. Landscape was understood in an anthropological sense as a record of society's intersection with nature:

The cottages of Britain, the manor houses, the bridges, the winding ways with their bordering trees, the villages and little towns, all grew as it were out of the soil, having been created of local materials by local craftsmen. The buildings showed details of structure distinctive of their district, and each racial or political area of the country thus possessed a recognisable individuality. In Wales this individuality is still very marked. (CPRW, 1928, p. 3)

In addition to this organic, evolving sense of landscape there was also a more assertive notion of heritage and of drama: 'there are preserved to our time ... structures of great historical interest; and ... a variety of unspoilt sites whereon took place critical actions in the history of the nation' (ibid.). Together, such features constituted a 'spiritual heritage', but one that was being neglected or destroyed. Natural landscapes were being despoiled by commercial pressures and the spread of urban and industrial tendencies and aesthetics to the countryside. Furthermore, there existed a 'lack of appreciation of the value to the nation of the structures and sites which illustrate its chequered history, and of the dwelling-places of its notable sons and daughters' (ibid., p. 4).

In the Council's opinion, the harm done to old buildings, to natural beauty, or to the historical associations of either of these 'is a harm done to the soul of the nation, not measurable in terms of money' (ibid., p. 5). So, in essence, the CPRW represented a fusion of antiquarian, archaeological and aesthetic concerns with a more thoroughly modernist desire, amongst the Council's avant-garde, for the rationality and order offered by planning legislation. As in England (see Matless, 1990), landscape preservation was woven into discourses on national identity and its dependence upon the symbolic power of 'the heritage'.

The 'visual handicap'

However, tensions emerged in discourses around planning and preservation, with Anglicized amenity campaigners – as well as a number of Welsh sympathizers – accusing the native Welsh of being insensitive to questions of aesthetic beauty and, by implication, to their heritage. There was nothing new in this criticism. Lord has argued that the 'visual handicap' has long featured in the historiography of Wales with most art intellectuals espousing, by the beginning of this century, the view 'that what they perceived as the failure of art in Wales was the consequence of a national soul not suited to visual expression' (Lord, 1992, p. 18). Lord labelled this view fraudulent but shows it to have been widely held. It was a view that served to marginalize the Welsh capacity for producing a rich cultural heritage, as defined within the Western high art tradition. As the geographer H. J. Fleure put it in 1916, the Welsh express their idealism 'in music, poetry, literature and religion rather than in architecture, painting and plastic arts generally. They rarely have a sufficiency of material resources for the latter activities' (Fleure and James, 1916, p. 42).

Not only was the Welsh capacity to produce a 'true' artistic heritage apparently impaired; so too was the nation's ability to preserve its cultural inheritance of landscape. A leading figure in the fight for planning and preservation was the architect Clough Williams-Ellis. His highly influential polemic *England and the Octopus* attacked the general absence of aesthetic appreciation amongst the British populace and the resulting despoliation which 'will leave indelible scars upon this physical world of ours that will outlast humanity itself' (Williams-Ellis, 1928, p. 14). As Chairman of the CPRW, Williams-Ellis led campaigns to define and preserve Wales's scenic heritage, but felt that his efforts were impaired by a lack of aesthetic awareness amongst the Welsh. He vehemently attacked 'the poverty of the Celtic races in the visual arts generally and architecture in particular' (Williams-Ellis, 1939, p. 63). More seriously, 'landscape' itself was a concept seemingly lost on the Welsh. An early CPRW pamphlet – *Land of My Fathers (and of My Children): Why Only Sing about It?* (CPRW, 1930) – mocked the Welsh national anthem's praise of homeland in the light of apathy on matters aesthetic. 'What right', Williams-Ellis asked, 'have we to sing "Land of My Fathers" so sanctimoniously, when we respect that land so little in what we do or suffer to be done?' (quoted in CPRW, 1930, p. 3). Whilst the CPRW had – in keeping with the view of Wales established by eighteenth-century travellers – stressed an easy and depoliticized resonance between landscape and myth, the Welsh, according to Williams-Ellis, were culturally imbalanced in failing to recognize that their 'heritage' was all-encompassing:

> After the green hillock named in honour of some fabled princess has been crowned with a cafe [the Welsh] will sing about the lady's exploits just as melodiously and movingly as before such an outrage occurred. Archaeology, hagiology and ancestor-worship are not enough. (Williams-Ellis, 1939, p. 62)

According to Williams-Ellis, and other CPRW members, a pride in Welsh culture and tradition was naive when it did not inspire a concern for the look of the land. By implication, patriotism and concern for an aesthetically defined heritage were weakened by the Welsh 'visual handicap'.

Landscape and Welshness

Not surprisingly, perhaps, this definition of Wales's heritage was vehemently challenged, in particular by an emerging nationalist movement which made the control and planning of Welsh territory a prominent issue, and which stressed the maintenance of cultural continuity in the rural areas of north and west Wales which were the heartlands of the Welsh language (Gruffudd, 1995). Plaid Cymru, the Welsh nationalist party founded in 1925, attempted to reconcile the Welsh awareness of the past with modern town and country planning, but they defined the past they sought to preserve in a much more dynamic fashion than the CPRW. In essence, they implicated the preservation of landscape in contemporary political debates on the maintenance of cultural continuity. Plaid Cymru launched direct attacks on the CPRW's failure to understand that landscape was a dynamic record of cultural change and was thus an arena for political action, rather than simply a neutral record. This heritage was an evolving rather than a fixed concept. According to the then President of Plaid Cymru, Saunders Lewis:

> Before the beauty of . . . the land of Wales may be preserved or increased, one must love Wales, must love and know her history and her past, one must understand the people who built the houses on her land, must understand their literature, must partake in their experiences. (Lewis, 1930, p. 5)

In this way, the heritage – in the form of landscape – became explicitly politicized in a way which directly challenged the CPRW's somewhat gentler and more superficial reading of history and society.

This distinction in the readings of landscape was highlighted dramatically by the case of a proposed Royal Air Force training camp at Porth Neigwl on the Llŷn Peninsula (Gruffudd, 1995). The CPRW, satisfied that the camp would be well planned and probably less unsightly than a sporadic tourist development, did not oppose the plan. Iorwerth Peate – a student of H. J. Fleure, an expert on folk culture at the National Museum of Wales and a former member of Plaid Cymru – opposed this incursion into what he theorized as an unspoilt peasant community. For Peate, changes to the landscape of Wales were to be read in cultural and political context. He argued that the declining standard of architecture, and in particular the introduction of standardized house types, represented the inroads made by English-language culture into the hitherto organically Welsh rural community (Peate, 1944a). He challenged the CPRW's reading of such changes as simply signifying a vulgarization of taste. For Peate, the Llŷn Peninsula was 'virgin ground almost completely unaffected by modern building and the effects of tourist and English influences' (Peate, 1935b) and this made its protection imperative. He recognized that the CPRW's definition of landscape heritage did not extend to the cultural milieux, but challenged the Council to recognize 'that to preserve rural Wales you have also to preserve its rural culture which includes its language' (Peate, 1935a). This line of argument was developed by Saunders Lewis, who resigned from the CPRW over the affair, charging the Council with failing to understand that which they sought to preserve and with promoting an Anglicized, 'outsiders' stance by stressing landscape aesthetics. Lewis and two compatriots were later jailed for an arson attack on the camp, an event which has assumed immense significance in Welsh nationalist history.

These frequently conflicting readings of Wales's landscape and heritage have continued beyond the inter-war period. The politicization of landscape remains as part of the territorial impulse behind Welsh nationalism. But debates have also, in part, hinged on the tension between tradition and modernity – the desire to preserve the past, but to allow for the future. In

Wales, the countryside has been viewed as a dynamic repository of Welsh identity rather than as a narrowly conceived amenity area. This has frequently meant compromising conventional landscape aesthetics in order to allow for rural development and, therefore, the continuity of national identity. This tension was highlighted by Iorwerth Peate in a trenchant reading of the Scott Report, *Land Utilisation in Rural Areas*, published in 1942. Peate (1943) disagreed with the report's division between town and country and its sense of the latter as an amenity area for residents of the former, with the concomitant need for scenic preservation. This was a sentimental and fundamentally immoral division, Peate claimed, having no application in Wales. Wales had traditionally been characterized by the dual foundation of agriculture and industry and to apply the Anglicized aesthetic values of the preservation movement to rural Wales was to stifle its dynamic contribution to Welsh national identity:

> We must face these facts rather than live in a sentimental mist and be content with the persistent feebleness of the countryside. There are dynamic foundations to true beauty. (Peate, 1943, p. 14)

Peate advocated the wholesale redevelopment of rural Wales on new technological foundations like hydro-electricity and mobile industries such as plastics alongside agriculture and the crafts (Gruffudd, 1990). In this way, the old diversified social order and the network of largely self-sufficient organic communities would be renewed and propelled into the future – a vision labelled 'techno-arcadianism' by Luckin (1990) – and Welsh culture would maintain its distinctiveness.

Peate, in common with many pre- and postwar nationalist politicians and intellectuals, saw Wales's rural heritage as a dynamic foundation for a future political culture. National salvation lay in going 'back to the land' (Gruffudd, 1994). In this way, the rural ceased to be a stable, anthropological entity that needed to be preserved, and became a dynamic, evolving environment that was seen as holding in trust qualities that were decreed to be significant. Preservation on the grounds of 'alien' aesthetic criteria could challenge that dynamism. Modernization – often to the detriment of conservationist landscape aesthetics – was seen as being more attuned to the role of the rural in the manufacture of a Welsh national identity than any narrow sense of conserving the 'heritage' for the sake of the historical record. In 1970 the prominent nationalist Dafydd Iwan outlined what he – and, by implication, the nationalist movement – understood by conservation. It was a classic restatement of the debates we have seen outlined between the wars. The predominant interpretation of environmental protection was, he said, superficial – 'like designing a colour scheme for a house whose foundations are cracking' (Iwan, 1970, p. 21). In Wales, the environment

> is considerably more than clean air and soil, far more than picturesque mountains, valleys and moorland, and an inspiring coastline. We have a people, a

way of life, a long cultural tradition, an intricate network of rural communities, and, above and basic to all these, we have a language. . . . Just as our physical environment is being eroded, so is our cultural environment, and of the two, the latter is of more fundamental and lasting importance. (Iwan, 1970, pp. 21–22)

Similar arguments are currently being advanced in mid-Wales where conflicts between 'conserver' incomers and locals over such issues as wind farms can be understood as conflicts between a metropolitan and aesthetic definition of heritage on the one hand and an indigenous one on the other, which stresses sustainability and rural dynamism above all else. Landscape offers both a rooted territorial and anthropological identity and an evolutionary sense of rural heritage.

Archiving Culture

It has been argued that for some Welsh academics and politicians debates on landscape preservation intersected with studies of cultural change and with challenges to folk culture. But in the same way as landscapes became emblems of national identity so too did the *gwerin* (the folk) that lived amongst them. Iorwerth Peate was part of a broad group of Welsh intellectuals and politicians who idealized the *gwerin* and hailed their continuing role in modern Welsh society. He depicted Wales as a resilient refuge from the continual modernization of the lowlands and as the kind of organically evolving society seen as typical of the 'Highlands' in Cyril Fox's (1932) *The Personality of Britain*. According to Peate, in west Wales could be found 'folk songs, superstitions, crafts, the gentle bearing of the poor, and a host of other things which are as pieces of dreams lost in the uproar of the juggernaut of Industry' (1931, p. 2).

In this sense, Peate's representation of the rural west of Wales echoed those in other European countries, where geographically marginal areas and their folk were imagined as being culturally central (see Shields, 1991). In Ireland, for instance, the Gaelic-speaking far west, the Gaeltacht, served as a cornerstone in the manufacture of Irish national identity and as a focus for a politics of culture (Johnson, 1993; Nash, 1993a, 1993b). And in Denmark the study of agrarian history and folk life was perceived to be of great contemporary importance (Fleure, 1943).

Peate worked in the National Museum of Wales, then under Cyril Fox's directorship, where he concentrated on folk culture, particularly the crafts, and established a sub-department of Folk Culture and Industries in 1932. There still remained, in Peate's opinion, a large tract of the Welsh countryside reasonably unaffected by modern industrial development and in these areas old traditions of craftsmanship and building lingered. But change threatened this organic heritage. The *gwerin's* existence, and by implication that of Welsh rural culture, hung in the balance. Modern mass production and the mechanization of labour threatened the crafts industries of rural Wales and so also threatened to destroy the rural polity:

The shoddy furniture of the cities and the short-lived manufactures of the mass-production firms have found their way into the countryside, and the result is not only a deterioration of the common necessities of life, but a disintegration also of rural society. (Peate, 1928, p. 103)

The folk museum

It was in this context that Peate identified the need for a sterner defence of the heritage than that advanced by groups like the CPRW. The future of rural Wales lay, in Peate's opinion, with education in the value of tradition and its development for present social needs. Peate advocated a dynamic role for tradition and suggested that it might be reconciled with modernity in a new version of social progress. Indeed, he argued that the study of folk life had a critical role in defending civilization from an 'upthrust into barbarism' (Peate, 1959, p. 109). His task was to awaken in the folk's conscience an appreciation for its own culture, thus creating fertile soil for a sense of identity to re-emerge. In this, Peate drew on the work of his mentor H. J. Fleure. For Fleure, awareness of locality through regional survey – the systematic study of all aspects of the life of the regional unit – brought past, present and future into evolutionary dialogue. If teachers, for instance, could: 'stir up a community to celebrate its tradition, they may be unconsciously working towards the re-birth of a Folk Drama and a Folk Literature, as well as other evidences of a growth of taste and appreciation' (Fleure, 1915, p. 5). A centre promoting such work could then become 'a centre of civic reference, a training ground for citizenship, a means of raising local government out of its political ditches' (Fleure, 1915, p. 6).

Peate had long argued the case for a Welsh Folk Museum where 'the culture of the Welsh nation in its varied aspects can be given adequate representation' (Peate, 1932, p. 296). He looked enviously to other nations, and especially Scandinavia, where folk culture had attained credible status. The Swedes had established the first open-air museum in 1891, rebuilding traditional structures and illustrating the old way of life. Norway followed suit in 1894 and Denmark in 1909. Peate nurtured his Scandinavian links and a visit there in 1930 by Cyril Fox earned support for a Welsh Folk Museum. Other links were also cultivated; in 1935, Peate was the only British delegate at the opening of the German National Museum of Folk Culture (see Peate, 1935c). For Peate, the folk museum represented a dynamic engagement with the past rather than any sentimental longing for earlier certainties. He claimed in 1948, that

Too often we all think of museums as storehouses of dead things. And not without reason, for, during many generations, museums were considered to be places where curios and old-fashioned objects were collected. (Peate, 1948, p. 9)

However, the museum had now assumed an educational function, a role in awakening the national spirit and in reviving social life. The museum was to use 'the past to link up with the present to provide a strong foundation and a healthy environment for the future of their people: and so to show clearly the unity of all life and of all human activity, yesterday, to-day and to-morrow' (Peate, 1948, p. 13). This vision underlay the formation of the Welsh Folk Museum at Sain Ffagan in 1946 with Peate as its first curator.

In practical terms, the preservation of arts, industries and customs gave a firm foundation for the national life of the future, and Peate advocated a role for folk museums in postwar reconstruction proposals. A survey of local traditional building styles, for instance, would rescue for the future an inspirational heritage of localism in design. Peate suggested (1944a, p. 5) that such education in the value of tradition 'and in the methods of developing it to suit present social needs will provide the only solution for the present "desecration of the countryside" which many deplore but which some only criticize unintelligently'.

As outlined above, the identification and analysis of the traditional industrial structure of the countryside by such an institution, and the subsequent dissemination of knowledge and planning advice, offered a blueprint for rural revival on the foundation of new technologies. Even Henry Ford, Peate (1932) argued, believed that this diversified and self-sufficient industrial structure was the answer to economic malaise in the modern world and, significantly, Ford was himself responsible for one of the first open-air museums in the United States (Bennett, 1988). More generally, the museum would offer an intelligent commentary on change, and would become the wellspring of a new 'folk', reunited with their heritage but building a new, modern nation on its foundation. Such museums would be living community centres, not memorials of a dead culture; each would be 'the fountainhead of new cultural energy' (Peate, 1948, p. 33). In Peate's open-air museums – a chain of which he wished to see established throughout rural Wales – the Welsh might walk through centuries of cultural history. The effect would be inspirational and dynamic:

> Such a museum would focus cultural aspirations in a unique way. By this means, a national museum does indeed become the living heart of a nation, where people can forgather not only for instruction and inspiration but for festivals and conferences too. (Peate, 1944b, p. 126)

As the above quotation suggests though, the folk museum had a political as well as a more broadly conceived sociological function. According to Horne (1984) the observation of the peasantry by ethnographers, their representation by Romantic artists, and the construction of folk museums are all part of the process of national imagination that he sees at the core of self-definition through heritage tourism:

> As the old peasant life began to drain away at the end of the nineteenth century, relics of it became not only significant collectors' items but also important symbols of nationalism. For conservatives in established nations, the peasants

could be presented as breathing the true spirit that held a regime together: for those trying to establish the uniqueness of 'new nations' against imperial occupiers, the peculiar customs of the peasantry could be made to seem 'proof' of the unique culture of the nation, and of its long history. (Horne, 1984, pp.172–173)

Lord (1992) added to Horne's theorization of folk museums by suggesting that the critique which generated open-air folk museums in Scandinavia was one that both recognized and celebrated the marginality of these nations to imperial political and economic power. Peate certainly praised Sweden's healthy regional democracy and concern with social values – a state of affairs, he suggested, that other small nations like Wales might aspire to. In retrieving a heritage of rural crafts, such museums also celebrated the creativity of the vernacular as a direct challenge to conventional high-art definitions of artistic value (Lord, 1992).

It appears that Peate's vision of the folk museum also emerged from this anti-imperialist discourse. As noted above, Peate was an early member of Plaid Cymru and he used the party's paper, *Y Ddraig Goch*, as a vehicle for his ideas on the centrality of folk culture in Wales. He was a socialist, but one who felt that the notion of a denationalized proletariat was a threat to the continuity of Welsh culture. Offered a choice between the two competing discourses of the *gwerin* and the working class, Peate was certain that his role was to educate the latter to recognize their roots in the former while campaigning for the mechanisms of social justice. Peate's version of Welsh history stressed a classless and self-sustaining Welsh folk liberated from the tyranny of nineteenth-century industrialism by a new, utopian social and economic order.

For Peate, the museum was part of the recovery of what he considered to be the 'authentic' national past. Still a cultural nationalist, he sought to define both the history and the future of the Welsh nation. He argued that folk museums should appeal to a broadly conceived patriotism, founded on an empirical and systematic understanding of heritage. Through the museum the folk was to be reunited with its tradition – expressed through building, crafts, costume and folklore – and also with its identity in a revitalized Wales. The museum was to be assembled by the donations of groups and individuals so that it might 'grow naturally out of the living Welsh society' (Peate, 1948, p. 61). Peate affirmed the importance of expressing the 'national character' or 'national spirit' through such a museum and the displays' consequent effects on the 'soul of the nation'. In such a museum, Peate argued (quoting the words of an earlier campaigner), 'a self-knowledge of the nation is concentrated, and from it there is breathed the inspiration of a truer patriotism' (Peate, 1948, p. 13). But the museum was also to be a museum *of* Wales and not simply *for* Wales. It was to present, to both the Welsh and to others, as comprehensive a picture of the nation and its positive potential contribution to world culture as possible. Peate summarized the museum's role thus:

To it will come school-children for tuition, architects, artists and craftsmen for inspiration, country men and women 'to cross the bridge of memories', colliers and quarrymen to view anew their wider heritage, and townsfolk to discover the permanence of Welsh life. Here too will come men and women from the four corners of the earth, merely to know Wales. Who can measure the influence of such an institution? It will . . . 'teach the world about Wales and the Welsh people about their own fatherland': it will strengthen and deepen the best in our national life so that we may attain new standards in our life and culture and serve civilization yet again for long centuries to come as a small nation which is conscious of its part in a larger world. (Peate, 1948, pp. 61, 63)

The museum was, therefore, to be a dynamic repository of knowledge and not simply a nostalgic evocation of a declining rural society. In this sense it mirrored the nationalists' evocation of rural landscape in the face of the preservationists' manifestos and served to disseminate the academic research that contributed to the proposed remaking of rural Wales. The museum served also to define the nation; its appeal was to a classless version of the nation – the *gwerin* – united by having its 'authentic' heritage revealed to it. As Peate put it, 'To equate "folk life" with "lower class" is a fundamental misconception' (quoted in Lord, 1992, p. 38). Finally, the museum served to define the nation as a recognizable cultural and political entity following a different path to the industrial and imperial powers, but taking its place within the community of nations. Whilst presenting itself as apolitical, therefore, the project that underlay the folk museum was deeply ideological in its understanding and use of the past. Although it professed 'authenticity' in its detailed empirical construction of knowledge about rural Wales, it nonetheless contributed to the remaking and reactivation of certain myths about Welshness.

Conclusion – The Future of the Past

Whilst I have argued that Welsh discourses on heritage and preservation have been characterized by a dynamic engagement with the present, Lord has suggested that an element of closure has crept into the debate. The Welsh Folk Museum, he argued:

locks Wales into a perpetual rural past and as the general western fashion for 'heritage' grows in strength, the ghetto-ization of Wales as a narrowly defined folk culture becomes an increasingly potent force acting against the living culture. There seem to be few implications for now in what is presented and certainly no organic development into now. Wales has come to an end at some indeterminate point in the nineteenth century, a passive nation existing in a time warp. It is a concluded story. (Lord, 1992, p. 40)

If this is true – although Lord himself suggested that a degree of dynamism has returned – then the museum has lost contact with its founding vision and has lost the sense that heritage speaks to the present and, indeed, *of* the present. This loss of vision would indeed be ironic, for there are signs of a growing critical awareness of the power of the past to define what is termed 'national' or even 'natural'. There is a growing willingness to see the past as constructed and ideological.

Few events in recent years have raised such questions about British (or, probably, English) definitions of identity and 'heritage' as the Windsor Castle fire in November 1992. Initial reports proclaimed a grave threat to the misty notion of heritage; more than a mere building, the essence of identity was threatened by the flames. But what characterized this event most, it could be argued, was the reaction against traditional, conservative definitions of the nation expressed by guardians of the heritage – either official, like the Heritage Secretary Peter Brooke, or self-appointed like Patrick Cormack, MP (author of the 1970s anti-Labour text, *Heritage in Danger*). The backlash against what was being presented as 'our heritage' served to open debates both on the role of a modern monarchy – Ruritania versus Sweden, as it came to be characterized – and on the future of the national past. The *Independent* (24 November 1992) argued that 'this country is too keen on the preservation and creation of a national heritage' and others regularly pointed to the failure to overcome deference for heritage and 'decrepit' institutions.

In part the debate crystallized around the issue of conservation policy and architectural style, echoing Peate's recognition of the issue's potency. The fire revealed that St George's Hall had been remodelled several times since its original construction in 1363 and this layering, therefore, raised questions of 'authenticity'. Didn't the unmasking of this pastiche building cause stable ideas about history to become unstable? Was this not, consequently, an opportunity to make a modernizing statement? The Royal Institute of British Architects called for an architectural competition to rebuild Windsor Castle in a contemporary, rather than antiquarian, style. In *The Times* (28 November 1992), Simon Jenkins called for a modern layer to be added to the 'medley' of royal history, the paper illustrating his piece with a cartoon placing a Louvre pyramid, guarded by Beefeaters, inside the castle's ramparts. According to Deyan Sudjic in the *Guardian* (7 December 1992), 'One of the more unexpected results of the Windsor fire was the blow it dealt to the deep-rooted assumption that new always means worse.' Windsor set in train once more the battle which Wright (1991) has typified as being between 'Brideshead and the tower blocks', between the sandstone patina of aristocratic England and the concrete certainties of the welfare state:

> on one side stands Brideshead – a countervailing and predominantly rural world based on private values and culturally sanctioned hierarchy, where history is venerated as tradition and culture is based on ancestry and descent. On the other side . . . lies the wreckage of 1945 piled up under the sign of the urban tower block: the commitment to public as opposed to private values, the anti-hierarchical egalitarianism, the hope that history could be made through the progressive works of an expert and newly enlightened State, the idea of a society based more on consent than descent. (Wright, 1991, p. 94)

As if to confirm Wright's point, the *Daily Telegraph* (Moore, 1993) entitled a more recent article on the first-ever listing of a postwar tower block 'This is your heritage – OFFICIAL', a title which suggested both that ridicule was the appropriate reaction to such a listing and that worrying evidence of Big Brother could be discerned.

The Windsor debate served to highlight the dynamic understanding of heritage that I have tried to outline in inter-war Wales. A cartoon in the Welsh-language magazine *Golwg* (26 November 1992) comically blamed the fire on Welsh holiday-home arsonists Meibion Glyndwr, further attesting to the potential symbolic power of the past! This satire highlighted the complexity of defining a 'British' heritage, but also acknowledged that heritage is a potent political target. Whilst in this case the acknowledgement was made for primarily humorous reasons, the bombers of the Uffizi Gallery in Florence essentially made the same statement. The concept of heritage, and its attendant policies like conservation and 'museumification', embodies notions of politics and identity that speak across the centuries. Heritage is at its most potent when it recognizes this and uses its undoubted power to engage with and to enliven contemporary debates. It is at its most dangerous when it seeks to obscure this power and attempts to codify a hegemonic version of history.

References

Abercrombie, P. (1924) Wales: a study in the contrast of country and town. *Transactions of the Honourable Society of Cymmrodorion*, 1923 Session, pp. 175–192.

Abercrombie, P. (1928) The preservation of rural Wales. *Transactions of the Honourable Society of Cymmrodorion*, 1926–1927 Session, pp. 156–169.

Abercrombie, P. (1938) Geography: the basis of planning. *Geography*, **23**, 1–8.

Anderson, B. (1991) *Imagined Communities: Reflections on the Origins and Spread of Nationalism*. London: Verso.

Anderson, J. (1988) Nationalist ideology and territory. In R. J. Johnston, D. B. Knight and E. Kofman (eds) *Nationalism, Self-determination and Political Geography*. London: Croom Helm.

Andrews, M. (1989) *The Search for the Picturesque: Landscape Aesthetics and Tourism 1760–1800*. Aldershot: Scolar Press.

Bennett, T. (1988) Museums and 'the people'. In R. Lumley (ed.) *The Museum Time Machine: Putting Cultures on Display*. London: Routledge, pp. 63–85.

Bhabha, H. K. (ed.) (1990) *Nation and Narration*. London: Routledge.

CPRW (1928) *Three Questions and an Answer*. Letchworth: Garden City Press.

CPRW (1930) *Land of My Fathers (and of My Children): Why Only Sing About It?* London: CPRW.

Curtis, T. (ed.) (1986) *Wales: The Imagined Nation. Essays in Cultural and National Identity*. Bridgend: Poetry Wales Press.

Daniels, S. (1993) *Fields of Vision: Landscape Imagery and National Identity in England and the United States*. Cambridge: Polity Press.

Davies, D. H. (1983) *The Welsh Nationalist Party 1925–45. A Call to Nationhood*. Cardiff: University of Wales Press.

Fleure, H. J. (1915) *Regional Surveys in Relation to Geography.* Oxford: Holywell Press.

Fleure, H. J. (1943) Peasants in Europe. *Geography,* **28,** 55–61.

Fleure, H. J. and James, T. C. (1916) Geographical distribution of anthropological types in Wales. *Journal of the Royal Anthropological Institute,* **46,** 35–153.

Fox, C. (1932) *The Personality of Britain: Its Influence on Inhabitant and Invader in Prehistoric and Early Historic Times.* Cardiff: National Museum of Wales.

Gruffudd, P. (1990) 'Uncivil engineering': nature, nationalism and hydro-electrics in north Wales. In D. Cosgrove and G. Petts (eds) *Water, Engineering and Landscape.* London: Belhaven, pp. 159–173.

Gruffudd, P. (1994) Back to the land: historiography, rurality and the nation in inter-war Wales. *Transactions of the Institute of British Geographers,* **19,** 61–77.

Gruffudd, P. (1995) Remaking Wales: nation-building and the geographical imagination. *Political Geography,* forthcoming.

Hewison, R. (1987) *The Heritage Industry: Britain in a Climate of Decline.* London: Methuen.

Hobsbawm, E. and Ranger, T. (eds) (1983) *The Invention of Tradition.* Cambridge: Cambridge University Press.

Horne, D. (1984) *The Great Museum: The Re-presentation of History.* London: Pluto Press.

Howarth, O. J. R. (1937) *The Scenic Heritage of England and Wales.* London: Sir Isaac Pitman and Sons.

Howkins, A. (1986) The discovery of rural England. In R. Colls and P. Dodd (eds) *Englishness: Politics and Culture 1880–1920.* London: Croom Helm.

Iwan, D. (1970) What I understand by conservation. *Planet,* **1,** 21–26.

Jenkins, S. (1992) Crowning the castle's glory. *The Times,* 28 November.

Johnson, N. C. (1993) Building a nation: an examination of the Irish Gaeltacht Commission Report of 1926. *Journal of Historical Geography,* **19,** 157–168.

Landscape Research (1991) Theme issue on 'Landscape and national identity', **16** (2).

Lewis, E. and Lewis, P. (1949) *The Land of Wales.* London: Batsford. (First published 1937.)

Lewis, S. (1930) Cadw harddwch Cymru. *Y Ddraig Goch,* **5** (1), 5.

Lord, P. (1992) *The Aesthetics of Relevance.* Llandysul: Gomer.

Luckin, B. (1990) *Questions of Power: Electricity and Environment in Inter-war Britain.* Manchester: Manchester University Press.

Matless, D. (1990) Definitions of England, 1928–89: preservation, modernism and the nature of the nation. *Built Environment,* **16,** 179–191.

Moore, R. (1993) This is your heritage – OFFICIAL. *Daily Telegraph,* 26 November.

Morgan, K. O. (1982) *Rebirth of a Nation: Wales 1880–1980.* Oxford: Oxford University Press.

Morgan, P. (1983) From a death to a view: the hunt for the Welsh past in the romantic period. In E. Hobsbawm and T. Ranger (eds) *The Invention of Tradition.* Cambridge: Cambridge University Press, pp. 43–100.

Morgan, P. (1986) Keeping the legends alive. In T. Curtis (ed.) *Wales: the Imagined Nation. Studies in Cultural and National Identity.* Bridgend: Poetry Wales Press, pp. 17–41.

Morton, H. V. (1932) *In Search of Wales.* London: Methuen.

Nash, C. (1993a) Remapping and renaming: new cartographies of identity, gender and landscape in Ireland. *Feminist Review,* **44,** 39–57.

Nash, C. (1993b) 'Embodying the nation': the West of Ireland landscape and Irish identity. In B. O'Connor and M. Cronin (eds) *Tourism in Ireland: a Critical Analysis.* Cork: Cork University Press, pp. 86–112.

Parker, A., Russo, M., Sommer, D. and Yaeger, P. (eds) (1992) *Nationalisms and Sexualities*. London: Routledge.

Peate, I. (1928) The social organization of rural industries. In *Welsh Housing and Development Yearbook 1928*. Cardiff: Welsh Housing and Development Association.

Peate, I. (1931) *Cymru a'i Phobl*. Cardiff: Gwasg Prifysgol Cymru.

Peate, I. (1932) Welsh folk culture. *The Welsh Outlook*, 19, 294–297.

Peate, I. (1935a) Letter to J. D. K. Lloyd, 20 June 1935, *CPRW Papers 9/19*. National Library of Wales, Aberystwyth.

Peate, I. (1935b) Contained in letter to J. D. K. Lloyd, 27 July 1935, *CPRW Papers 9/19*. National Library of Wales, Aberystwyth.

Peate, I. (1935c) The German National Museum of Folk Culture. *Museums Journal*, 35, 329–332.

Peate, I. (1943) Yr ardaloedd gwledig a'u dyfodol. *Y Llenor*, 22, 10–18.

Peate, I. (1944a) *The Welsh House: A Study in Folk Culture*. Liverpool: Hugh Evans & Son/Brython Press.

Peate, I. (1944b) Museums and the community. *Montgomeryshire Collections*, 48, 124–130.

Peate, I. (1948) *Amgueddfeydd gwerin – Folk Museums*. Cardiff: University of Wales Press.

Peate, I. (1959) The study of folk life: and its part in the defence of civilization. *Gwerin*, 2, 97–109.

Pratt, M. L. (1992) *Imperial Eyes: Travel Writing and Transculturation*. London: Routledge.

Shields, R. (1991) *Places on the Margin: Alternative Geographies of Modernity*. London: Routledge.

Smith, A. D. (1986) *The Ethnic Origins of Nations*. Oxford: Basil Blackwell.

Smith, A. D. (1991) *National Identity*. Harmondsworth: Penguin Books.

Sudjic, D. (1992) Restoration dramas. *Guardian*, 7 December.

Thomas, E. (1983) *Wales*. Oxford: Oxford University Press. (First published 1905.)

Wiener, M. J. (1981) *English Culture and the Decline of the Industrial Spirit 1880–1980*. Cambridge: Cambridge University Press.

Williams, G. A. (1985) *When Was Wales? A History of the Welsh*. Harmondsworth: Penguin Books.

Williams-Ellis, C. (1928) *England and the Octopus*. London: Geoffrey Bles.

Williams-Ellis, C. (1939) Snowdonia. *Geographical Magazine*, 9, 59–72.

Wordsworth, J., Jaye, M. C., Woof, R. and Funnell, P. (1987) *William Wordsworth and the Age of English Romanticism*. New Brunswick, NJ, and London: Rutgers University Press.

Wright, P. (1985) *On Living in an Old Country: The National Past in Contemporary Britain*. London: Verso.

Wright, P. (1991) *A Journey through Ruins: The Last Days of London*. London: Radius.

Zaring, J. (1977) The romantic face of Wales. *Annals of the Association of American Geographers*, 67, 397–418.

5

Heritage, Tourism and Europe: a European Future for a European Past?

Gregory J. Ashworth

The Triptych

This chapter brings together three fields or topics and examines the relationships between them to allow a new line of argument to be opened up. These are:

- the evolution of the idea of heritage from the preservation of aspects of a past;
- the growth of a leisure activity, heritage tourism, based upon the resources of a preserved past;
- the uses of the remembered past for furthering the identification of individuals with particular places or specific political jurisdictions.

These themes are of central interest to this book as a whole, but the task here is to examine the links between all three constituents of the triad and then to discuss the extent to which they can be manipulated to achieve a political purpose.

The links can be expressed in a simple triangular diagram (Figure 5.1) in which the apices are related through the following propositions:

- Heritage contributes towards political identity.
- Heritage supports heritage tourism.
- Tourism in general and heritage tourism in particular contribute towards the individual's appreciation of places and thus political identification. This idea is assumed in the educational and socialization functions of heritage.

The system sketched above is not closed: each of the apices has different sets of links with wider systems of which they are integral parts. Heritage has been created for a variety of reasons; heritage tourism is only one form of tourism and many factors contribute to a sense of political identity with places. Figure 5.1 shows a simple system which is very much open to influences from outside.

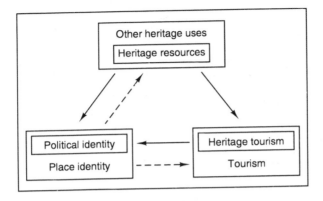

Figure 5.1 Heritage, place identity and tourism: components of a triangle.

The Specific Political Argument

The specific reasons for focusing on the relationships within this triad are both interventionist and overtly political; they can be expressed in a set of propositions:

1. The nation states of Europe are in the process of attempting to create a form of continental, political unit and have proceeded over the past 40 years to establish, by means of a series of legislative and organizational instruments, some form of supranational jurisdiction which it is widely assumed, whether in hope or fear, will further evolve. However, the transformation of various administrative and bureaucratic procedures into a social, cultural or political unit requires a consensus of popular identification with such a supranational entity. This basis of support in popular sentiment is currently weak and an intellectual or political assent is not matched by an emotional attachment or identity.

2. The European nation state was sustained and legitimized by the creation and propagation of a largely *national* heritage. Historically it is no coincidence that the timing of the popular awakening and official sanctioning of interest in the conservation and promotion of national histories, national museum collections and even conserved national architectures and landscapes in the latter half of the nineteenth century, coincided in Europe with the consolidation of the nation state as the dominant form of political entity (Lumley, 1988). The only issue is whether nation states created national heritage, or the reverse. Equally it has become clear in the post-Maastricht discussions in Europe that the obituaries to the nation state, written by the supporters of a new post-nationalist Europe, were, to say the least, premature. National identity based on an awareness of a national history is still a vital force in the countries of Western Europe, where it had lain somewhat dormant in the years of the postwar settlement and cold war confrontation of the supra-national ideologies. In addition, the collapse of Soviet hegemony in Central and Eastern Europe is releasing new, or at least previously suppressed, and conflicting nationalisms based upon a rediscovery of national histories with their claims and counterclaims.

3. The previous two propositions are in conflict. If continental unity and identity
    is to be achieved, then national identity must make some concessions to
    accommodate the wider scale. In short, a new Europe will require a new
    heritage. Heritage tourism may have a role in linking European heritage and a
    European identity. There are wider questions about the delimitation, nature
    and desirability of this 'new Europe', but here it is the possible role in its
    shaping that could be, or has been, played by heritage in general and heritage
    tourism in particular that will be discussed.

The whole argument developed here is permeated with the idea of deliberate,
goal-directed intervention. The relations between the three elements provides
the opportunity for manipulation in pursuit of specified objectives. The question, 'What is happening?' is only a necessary preliminary to the much more
important and interesting questions of 'What do we want?' 'How do we achieve
it?' and 'Who are "we" anyway?'

There is also an assumption in this line of argument that, in the triad,
heritage is the active component, which contributes *directly* to European place
identity. Heritage also fulfils an *indirect* role as it supports European place-
identity through heritage tourism (see Figure 5.1). In terms of the argument
developed here, both of these roles – the direct and the indirect contributions
of heritage – provide opportunities for political intervention. As Figure 5.1
indicates, however, there are possible reversals in causality. Changes may
occur in European identity and these may, in turn, lead to changes in the
nature of both heritage itself and in the activity of heritage tourism.

The relevance of these questions needs to be validated and there are two
widely held, but contrasting, sets of assumptions on the relationship between
heritage and its various users that pre-empt further discussion because they
render managed intervention superfluous. Both sets of assumptions are
labelled 'naive' in the sense that they oversimplify the relationships and then
draw conclusions that foreclose the argument. Both assume absolute but
opposite relationships from the fact that the same heritage resources have
multiple uses: one assumes harmony and the other conflict. The first renders
intervention unnecessary, because the objectives will anyway be attained,
while the second renders it fruitless because it cannot succeed.

The Naive Assumptions of Harmony

The assumption here is that heritage can freely contribute to both of the other
components of the model without difficulty; indeed that there is an automatic
and self-evident symbiosis in the multi-use of the same resources for quite
different purposes and an equally harmonious symmetry in the dependency
relationship between the two elements. Equally, no reverse relationship occurs
between the two uses and the resource they are using in such a way that the
use of the heritage resource for any one purpose changes its nature so as to
preclude or hinder its use for the other.

The argument is often expressed that the evolution of tourism and the development of an active concern for the preservation and presentation of surviving aspects of the past, have been more or less synchronous over the last two centuries. It is therefore not difficult to trace at least a coincidental relationship between the two. The dependence of the eighteenth-century Enlightenment in Western Europe on a rediscovery through travel of a classical world, to which nineteenth-century Romanticism added the medieval 'Gothic', provided an influential constituency of support for both preservation and reconstruction as well as the first-hand experience of the Grand Tour.

The details of the link between the conception of the idea of a common heritage of the civilized world and the visiting of such heritage have been traced by many (for example Ross, 1991). The idea has been taken much further, however, by reversing cause and effect and assuming that travel, for whatever motive, will enlarge and enhance the idea and appeal of heritage. Such a process can be assumed to be continuous with world heritage and world tourism feeding mutually from each other in an ever-growing and influential lobby. This can become manifest in powerful crusades, which find expression in such worldwide popular reactions to threats to that heritage, as demonstrated, for example, by the 'Save Venice' movement after the 1966 floods or the spectacular Abu Simbel rescue operation of UNESCO in the 1960s.

It is small wonder then that an assumption of harmony has developed based upon an idea of mutual justification. Tourism makes use of the conserved artefacts of the past, thereby acquiring a patina of artistic patronage and educational worth, while the conservation lobby acquires justification and political support, as well as the possibility of a much-needed financial contribution, directly or indirectly from an economic use of its conserved fabric (College of Europe, 1993).

Similarly the uses, in this case commercial tourism and political identity, are harmoniously related to each other, usually in one of two ways. There is the 'turnstile model' which argues that from the point of view of the facility it matters little who uses heritage and why it is being used. The presence of users is justification enough. The second argument is the 'windfall gain model' in which heritage created initially or principally for one of the major uses is assumed to be capable of being exploited by the other at no extra cost and without modification. Usually in the Western world, it is tourism that is seen as the fortunate by-product of a local or national heritage industry that already exists in the service of other, often political, purposes. Occasionally, local political objectives are seen as reaping the windfall gain from heritage development for tourism. In either circumstance, appropriate resources are viewed as being freely available to, and unaffected by, uses additional to those originally intended.

The objection to both arguments is of course that different uses will require and therefore create different products, and to view it otherwise misunderstands what is actually occurring. Both arguments reveal an attitude to resources which assumes free availability, appropriateness and invulnerability to any category of use, all of which are questionable.

If the conserved past is treated as a resource which is neither inexhaustible nor instantly renewable, then various choices have to be made and the assumption of harmony contains no intrinsic mechanism by which this can be achieved. Similarly, the relationship of the heritage tourism industry with conservation may be asymmetrical in that heritage tourism has an absolute need for the resources provided by conservation and could not exist otherwise, whereas conservation does not actually need tourism for its justification. A parasitical dependence would be an apposite description if the allocation of economic costs and benefits are not in harmony. In economic terms, tourism treats the past as a zero-priced, public good in inexhaustible supply whose existence within the production process is not reliant on payments to it. The result is therefore likely to be reckless overuse untempered by internal economic constraints.

The term 'naive' therefore must be applied to an assumption which provides no means of even appreciating the existence of these possibilities let alone finding management solutions for the problems they may cause. It must be rejected as unhelpful, while recognizing that it is a widespread and influential view.

The Naive Assumption of Conflict

The assumption of conflict takes the opposite and equally naive position that because there are demonstrably different uses of heritage, by users whose motives and behaviour are predictably quite different, then conflict is continuous and inevitable. The same heritage just cannot be used as a resource for a commercial tourism industry and also as the basis for popular identification with a political unit. The only possible management reactions are thus either prioritization in favour of one of the categories of use or a strict segregation of uses. This reaction frequently merges into a more widely based attack either on all political uses of heritage as a somehow undesirable perversion of an ideologically neutral revelation of the past, or conversely on all tourism uses of heritage as a commercialization and, by implication, trivialization of the past. Underlying both are more substantial ideas contained in the 'dominant ideology thesis' (applied in Abercrombie et al., 1980) which, as refined by Bourdieu (1977), regards all cultural production, including heritage, as national 'capital' to be 'captured' and subsequently exploited to legitimize the dominance of particular social or political groups. Also relevant is the 'destructive tourist thesis' which sees tourism flows as composed of barbaric hordes to be at worst tolerated with ill grace and defensive planning policies, and at best kept at bay in the name of cultural consumers deemed more worthy.

It is argued here, as in the case of 'naive harmony', that the set of assumptions is not tenable. Multi-use is not in itself a sufficient cause of conflict. The potential for friction exists only if those uses not only conflict, but cannot for various reasons be served separately. On the contrary, heritage is especially amenable to goal-directed intervention. Each of the two major categories of use is dependent upon resources which, compared with resources required in most activities, are effectively ubiquitous, often reproducible and frequently physically robust: they are flexible rather than immutable and often highly mobile. Few products or activities are so amenable to intervention in order to avoid conflict or mitigate its consequences. The question is: how can this be achieved through planning and management, while in pursuit of the political objective? First, however, a model of what is actually happening when heritage is created, for whatever purpose, must be established.

Pasts, Histories and Heritages

The process of commodification, through which the past becomes heritage, has been described at length elsewhere (Ashworth, 1991). It is necessary, however, to stress some of the implications of such models derived from marketing, as a precondition for seeking verification of the initial propositions in contemporary Europe (and also in practice as a device for avoiding irrelevant and distracting objections based on quite different models of history or heritage). In particular such models define the relationship between resources, products and markets, allowing each of these elements to be identified. The conserved or remembered past provides a set of potential resources which are converted into heritage products through a process of interpretation. History, in the sense of the remembered and related past, is not the only contributor to the broader concept of heritage which also draws upon mythologies, folklores and products of creative imaginations. This interpretation is a highly selective assembly process creating heritage products for specific markets. Three general consequences of this model are critical for the argument of this chapter. First, heritage is a contemporary product created in the present to serve perceived needs of the present; secondly, the production process is demand not resource driven; thirdly, deliberate intervention is implicit at all phases of the process from resource selection to market targeting.

These consequences render feasible the creation of a specific European heritage in support of the predetermined political objective. Europe's rich past experiences provide an almost inexhaustible quarry of potential resources, capable of being used in an equally wide selection of heritage products for many different markets. Planning and market management are not only possible, they are inevitable in one form or another as decisions about which pasts, which products and which markets will be made with or without deliberate intervention in pursuit of particular political goals.

Towards a European Heritage Tourism

If, as argued above, heritage is a deliberately created contemporary product capable of serving a number of specific contemporary needs, then the possibility of one of these providing support for a new European political entity can now be examined in more detail with a view to establishing the preconditions for appropriate policies. Each of the three sets of links in the triangle (Figure 5.1) must be examined, although with unequal attention. The link between heritage and a European identity is the most relevant relationship and the one which has received most practical recognition and support from official agencies. The role of tourism in general, and heritage tourism in particular, in contributing to an idea of a European identity has frequently been invoked but with little practical substance. The third link, between heritage resources and heritage tourism, is a field of study of only indirect relevance.

Heritage and Europe

The attraction of using the urban heritage to support a popular identification with the idea of Europe is simply that the built environment of the cities is experienced daily by most Europeans. It is highly influential in terms of popular place identification, and its architecture and urban morphology form a free, permanent, visible display of cultural expression needing no linguistic intermediary. Governments in all European countries have long assumed major legislative, administrative and financial responsibilities for what has very largely become official public heritage: public, both in the sense of general accessibility and also through being part of the public administrative domain. How and why these responsibilities were acquired over time has been discussed *inter alia* by Dobby (1978), Kain (1981) and Burtenshaw *et al.* (1991).

The list of international organizations, pressure groups, official coordinating bodies and the like, operating at least partially in Europe in urban architectural conservation, is long and authoritative. Their achievements, if these are measured by declarations, conventions and prestigious official publications, are also impressive. Bodies such as UNESCO have been effective in orchestrating and coordinating international expressions of concern and action; the International Council of Museums (ICOM) and the International Council of Monuments and Sites (ICOMOS) are professional coordinating bodies whose main functions in practice can be summarized as a mixture of emergency rescue and information exchange. The rescue function, involving the identification and revelation of heritage 'at risk', has been the most obvious initiative and has led to the conclusion that 'European conservation policies have only emerged when the problem has reached a crisis' (Matthew *et al.*, 1972, p. 13). The transfer of techniques, experiences and current conventional thinking has been furthered by numerous international conventions and by both political and professional organizations.

Specifically on the European scale, only the Council of Europe has both a continent-wide coverage and terms of reference that include a stated concern for 'safeguarding the common heritage' as the 'patrimony of all Europeans' (Council of Europe, 1992). It is, however, an association of sovereign states and has always operated through national systems on the principle of encouragement. It achieves this by both promoting 'best practice' cases suitable for imitation, and encouraging a 'levelling up' of national systems that are lagging behind the European average. Its long-standing efforts, beginning in 1954, to draw up inventories of the existing national conservation systems were not completed until 1979 (Council of Europe, 1979) and remain a compendium that demonstrates the existing variety in legislative approaches, organizational scales of operation, balance of public and private involvement and criteria for heritage selection, rather than any possible uniformity. The establishment by the Council of Europa Nostra in 1963, initially to investigate and promote a sample of 50 projects (Council of Europe, 1974), was again principally intended to achieve a levelling up by example, as was the 1970 attempt to draft outline protection legislation for monuments and sites that could be universally applied. Attempts to stimulate a wider popular constituency of support were typified by European Architectural Heritage Year 1975, by the broader-based work of the Council on 'cities as popular culture' (Mennell, 1976), and by the annual, heavily promoted designation of particular cities as 'European Culture Capitals'.

Compared with the Council of Europe, the European Community has paid little attention to this topic, although it is in its direct interest to do so. Concern for heritage appears marginal and often coincidental. A number of European legal instruments have an impact upon the broad field of urban conservation. Some environmental protection regulations, such as those on motor car exhaust emissions, have an obvious relevance, as do financial subsidy possibilities under the Regional Fund (whose coverage includes almost half of the major European cities) and the European Investment Bank, both of which have been used in heritage conservation projects. The 1991 Treaty of European Union (The 'Single European Act') has a clause conferring unspecified 'new powers' on the Commission in the fields of 'culture' and 'environmental protection'; the relevance of the latter is that so far in practice the term 'environment' has been extended to include the built as well as natural environments. Indeed, it is in 'green' planning that most progress on 'grey' conservation can be expected. The Commission's *Green Book on the Urban Environment* (Commission of the European Community, 1990) does not concern itself, as might have been expected, with features of the natural environment in cities, but with implementing two of the four green plan recommendations that are specifically directed towards the architectural and morphological heritage, namely the provision of more financial resources for the protection and maintenance of historic buildings and areas of 'European importance', and the investigation of the possibility of devising a community-wide system of recognition of such heritage.

But in no sense does any of the above, however commendable in other ways, amount to a specifically European architectural heritage policy, nor is it intended to be such. Its contribution in countries with developed national conservation systems is minimal compared with national efforts. Also relevant to the argument here is the fact that the political messages of place-identity being projected through urban conservation are specifically national, local or regional rather than continental. There is no European policy in the form of sets of specifically European goals or instruments, whether legislative, financial, operational or organizational, for achieving them.

Even more fundamental is the fact that nowhere in the recommendations and resolutions of the international agencies is there any attempt to define a European heritage or to describe what it should encompass. The EU's 'European application' and 'European significance' amount to no more than a selection of the current best national practice as applied to the most spectacularly renowned of the national sites and cities. The avoidance of the specifically European heritage issue in this context is understandable but ultimately unproductive.

Official policies may, however, have a much smaller impact upon the architecture of cities than local practice, whether exercised through commercial or local government implementation agencies. In this respect some attention should be given to a major change, whether in architectural fashion or city development, variously described but resulting in essence in a shift from international modernist styles to the vernacular. The importance of this argument is the relationships of these stylistic changes to political identity. Soane (1994), for example, has described the rise of vernacular architectural and planning styles in Germany in the past few years. He has argued that this reflects changes in political sentiment away from subordination to a largely North American political system and towards a reassertion of what is seen as a more traditional German society, expressed through urban conservation, but also in reconstruction in vernacular styles.

Vernacularism has long been an important element powering the production of heritage, strongly linked to ideas such as 'folk' and 'everyday life'. The significance of its continued rise in importance in urban design and development can be viewed in two contrasting ways. It can be considered (Soane, 1994) to be a reassertion of the local over the international, or to be little more than a new international, widely reproduced, stylistic convention (Whitehand and Larkham, 1992). In either event, it is hard to see the emergence of any specifically European architectural or town planning style: on the contrary, the continuing internationalization of project development and investment is leading, if anything, to a homogeneity in cityscapes which closely follows worldwide fashionable trends.

Tourism and Europe

The second side of the triangle (Figure 5.1), the political implications of tourism, is a central consideration. It refers specifically to the contribution of European tourism to the idea of European political and economic integration. The simple hypothesis is that the experience both of taking holidays in other parts of Europe and of receiving tourists from other parts of Europe increases mutual knowledge, understanding and thus ultimately provides the popular support for the supranational political entity that is so markedly lacking in Europe. The opportunity appears to be inviting and of enormous potential, if only because more Europeans are choosing to visit their continental neighbours than ever before in history. Undoubtedly, the widening experience of foreign countries disseminated through tourism has led to an international exchange of many previously local cultural products, gastronomic specialities and even social behaviour. Similarly the 'demonstration effect' of visitors has long been recognized as a major, if not always welcome, influence upon the economic demands and even social and political ideas in destination regions. Heritage tourism in particular requires an interaction of the individual tourist with local cultures that may be particularly apposite, being flattering to the host culture and financially supportive of it.

There is a widely voiced view that more intra-European tourism will encourage intra-European understanding. The 1980 'Manila Declaration' of the World Tourism Conference linked tourism and world peace, expressing the hope that 'tourism may contribute to a large extent to protecting and developing ... cultural heritage. ... Tourism brings people closer together and creates an awareness of the diversity of ways of life, traditions and aspirations.' The main difficulty with this idea is that it is impossible to demonstrate either negatively or positively. Some indications can, however, be investigated.

It can be argued that tourism tends to both standardize and differentiate. It exploits and thus encourages the propagation of the unique character of places as differentiated products, while also tending to standardize many aspects of the product on offer. So tourism may be a celebration of unique place identities, or an instrument of a homogenization that reduces individuality to an acceptable quaintness or, probably, and paradoxically, both. This dualism may provide a warning or an opportunity for intervention in detail.

Pearce (1977, 1981), among other social psychologists, has experimented with the connection between holiday experience and various measurable attitudes towards foreign countries, peoples and behaviour. The results of such tests, unsurprisingly but encouragingly, demonstrate that those with wider foreign holiday experiences are also more knowledgeable about, and broadly more sympathetic to, other national cultures. This may mean only that those who for one reason or another are internationally orientated tend to travel more and is, in itself, a long way from proving identification with a supranational political entity.

Mutual membership of the EU, or any other international organization, does not appear to influence the direction of tourism flows or, if it does, its effect is minimal compared with other variables. No doubt historians would also add that international conflicts have been as prevalent between countries and peoples that know each other well as between those that do not. In any event no specific cultural or political policy expectations for tourism are implicitly or explicitly formulated within the various agencies of the European Union. Tourism is seen solely as an economic activity producing desirable economic results. It is the concern of economic departments rather than those for cultural affairs; the latter rarely have anything to say about tourism.

There is a superficially appealing reverse argument: that moves towards European integration tend to encourage tourism within Europe, through the removal of bureaucratic formalities and standardization of international transport. However, the sharp growth in tourism in general, specifically long-distance tourism, conceals any such effect among far more significant factors.

The best that can be concluded about such general arguments linking tourism and European integration is that there is no empirical evidence to support cause and effect relationships. This applies to both positive and negative aspects of tourism. There is, however, reasonably convincing empirical evidence for arguments relating to specific tourism situations or places, as Jansen-Verbeke (1990) has demonstrated in Bruges and Costa and van der Borg (1993) have shown in Venice.

There are numerous, well-documented cases (see for example Smith, 1977) where tourism's requirement for a standardized, easily recognizable and mass-reproducible cultural experience has been credited with the trivialization and distortion of local cultures. This can encourage a homogenization in which locality is reduced to a saleable quaintness and can even contribute towards the demise of some cultural characteristics in a number of distinctive European regions. Equally, however, the distinctiveness of local cultures, folklores and languages is a growing tourism resource which Europeans seek out with a daunting seriousness. The floating seminars pioneered by Swan-Hellenic in the Eastern Mediterranean, the campus summer schools at countless universities, the literary and artistic tourist trails, excursions and complete holidays and many similar tourism enterprises, encourage a sympathetic appreciation of the diversity of European cultural heritage, and underpin some concept of a European heritage based on an understanding of its diversity.

These, however, have a significance that is either purely local and specific or, conversely, extremely generalized. They encourage either a sympathetic awareness of the cultural distinctiveness of a particular place or ethnic group or a broad intercultural tolerance based on understanding. Neither of these contributes a specifically European dimension, other than the blandly obvious cultural variety of the continent.

Heritage and tourism —

This third relationship has only an indirect relevance to the argument and has been explored at much greater depth elsewhere (Ashworth and Tunbridge, 1990; Ashworth, 1993b; Dietvorst, 1993). Undoubtedly heritage tourism is a rapidly growing form of tourism and heritage resources are seen as a near-ubiquitous development possibility in places of extremely varied heritage endowment.

The only note of caution that is worth sounding is that although tourist demand for heritage is undoubtedly rising, so also is the supply of heritage places. If all places have a potentially exploitable past and initial investments are low, then inevitably competition between heritage place products will become intense. Tourism is unlikely to be the main justification for the production of heritage. Apart from a select group of sites in especially favoured towns and regions, tourism is likely to be an extra use of heritage which has been developed for other, often political, purposes. Although, as argued earlier, the same heritage resources can be marketed as different products to different markets, success will depend upon the possibility of market segmentation and subsequent segregation.

The probability of conflict between heritage products for tourism and those for local political identity has been argued on the grounds of the essential demand orientation of all heritage production (Ashworth, 1991). Tourists can only be successfully sold their own heritage, to which they can relate, and this will probably be different from that of the local inhabitants. Such a difference becomes serious when tourists have a different cultural and historical experience from that of residents. Even in Europe sharp differences can arise. From the myriad possibilities take, for example, the heritage interpretation of the countries of Central and Eastern Europe currently being used to support a new or rediscovered and essentially fragile national identity; this is very likely to be either irrelevant or offensive to foreign tourists drawn from the very neighbours that are cast in the stereotyped role of national enemy. Conserved German historical architecture or Russian war memorials may have little place in officially promoted Polish or Slovak heritage, however much they relate to potential tourism markets.

Some Strident Objections: Some Modest Suggestions

There are many objections to the argument that heritage should be used for political purposes. These will now be considered together with some suggested policies for modest and marginal change to existing structures rather than drastic reconstruction.

The propaganda argument

This claims that the project involves an unacceptable intervention in the writing and propagation of history, which should be a simple honest account of the past and not a manipulation for political objectives.

The past may be 'just the old things that happened to happen' (Chippendale, 1993, p. 6) but the concern here is not with recording this as history, itself highly selective, but as heritage, a contemporary product. This is an activity in which governments have already assumed large responsibilities, for various ostensible reasons. Major historical resources in most countries are already in official ownership or guardianship, as are many of the most important formal and informal channels of interpretation. Thus selected aspects of the past are being, and will continue to be, interpreted by public agencies for public objectives, whether stated or not, with impacts, whether intended or not, upon place identities and upon the individual's identification with political jurisdictions. It can be done well or badly, consciously or unconsciously, but such deliberate use of aspects of the past is neither new nor confined to Europe. There is only the particular political situation in which Europe finds itself at the end of the twentieth century, with the unique challenge of using the expanding European heritage industry to support the shaping of a new continental political entity.

The impossibility argument

Here the task, although theoretically possible, is seen as being too difficult: in practice it cannot be done because it would be ineffectual, especially given the competition from existing heritages and their present use at the national scale to underpin the nation state. Certainly heritage, as defined above, has a proven track record of outstanding success in formulating and reinforcing place-identities in support of particular state-entities and all that is suggested here is no more than adding to or redirecting a portion of these efforts. Individuals already identify with a whole nesting hierarchy of spatial scales from the local to the international without these necessarily conflicting. The continental scale need not compete with, or seek to replace, the national scale, but should seek to supplement it in the same way as regional and local heritages coexist with that of the nation.

There is a simple and reassuring point that the European case in this respect is not unique: it is only, given the continent's troubled history, more difficult to achieve. The deliberate fostering of place-identities for political purposes is routinely assigned to heritage interpretation in countless nation states and also, significantly, in some federal entities endeavouring to shape a new collective consciousness. Canada, with its inherent diversities and conflicting incipient nationalisms, is a revealing case in point (Ashworth, 1993a).

It is true that the EC (now the EU) has been notably slow to develop the iconic trappings of a popular state. Neither its flag nor its anthem is original, nor are they yet inspiring popular symbols. The EU has no pantheon of heroes, founding fathers or even villains and folk enemies, battles and revolts, such as are the stuff of most national founding mythologies. The Berlaymont or the Place Schumann are hardly sacred symbolic places. In short, European-scale heritage interpretations are poor competition for the strident nationalist interpretation of most European heritage.

The selection argument

It can be argued that the task of selection and of presentation, of which heritage and whose heritage, is too difficult and too sensitive. There is just too much choice from a Europe currently overloaded with heritage and currently busy producing more.

The choice of content of the distinctly European heritage intended to reinforce popular identification with that scale of political entity, needs answers to two main questions. First, which of the many possibilities is to be chosen to provide the unifying themes of such a continental-scale European heritage? The current European Union model favours institutional, bureaucratic, free market, social-capitalist and liberal representative pluralist democratic elements as those they wish to project as essentially European. A review of the long history of attempts at achieving European unity, in its various possible forms, reveals many other models based upon quite different ideological heritages, from medieval Christendom to international Marxism–Leninism. Secondly, what is to be done with 'dissonant heritage', i.e. heritage that does not conform to these prevailing norms and objectives (Tunbridge and Ashworth, forthcoming)? Europe's long history of war, pogrom and persecution between nations, classes, races and religions has left its own legacies, which blatantly contradict any theme of harmonious unity and present a clear challenge to any use of the past to promote integration. Are these unpleasant events to be ignored in a deliberate policy of collective amnesia which contains its own dangers, or somehow re-interpreted within the new European heritage product?

Both of these questions can be seen as part of a wider question – 'Whose Europe is it?' and 'Whose heritage is to be interpreted?' There is also the converse, and probably inevitable question, 'Which Europeans or European ideas are to be written out of the script of such a history by their failure to be incorporated in it?' Is a European heritage to be the heritage of governing groups and dominant ideologies, or is it to include subordinate classes and diverging, even contradictory, ideas? This raises all sorts of obvious but highly tendentious problems.

Towards Policy

There are of course no simple policy responses to these issues, but that in itself is not a sound argument for not posing the questions; they are implicit in all heritage products and will arise regardless of the objective of such heritage. It should also be added that heritage creation is a continuous process that needs constant restructuring and thus constant reassessment. Shifts in population groups leave behind cultural and material relics that no longer reflect relevant or desirable contemporary place symbolisms. Similarly, shifts in dominant ideologies leave memorials of previously prevailing values to haunt and conflict with current interpretations, as can be seen throughout post-communist Europe.

Cultural and tourism policies have been designed to minimize frictions and maximize mutual understanding on the local scale. More broadly, it is possible for heritage to be interpreted and, even more difficult, to be reinterpreted to supplement purely national interpretations with common European themes and even bridge old antagonisms with new reconciliations (Ashworth and Larkham, 1994). Verdun is now interpreted as a symbol of Franco-German reconciliation rather than as an encouragement to continue a hereditary national feud. Among the many cases of 'museums of war and peace' (*Museum International*, 1993) are the Caen memorial (Quetel, 1993), commemorating a common sacrifice of 1944 in a way that few war memorials or battlefield sites attempt explicitly, and Auschwitz (Wikanowicz, 1993), marking a common European atrocity.

Finally, against the daunting task of reformulating the place-identity of a continent by reinterpreting its past, must be balanced the imperatives of its necessity and its urgency. There is no consensus on the nature of the new European entity that will, or should, emerge nor indeed of what a European heritage could be. There is, however, a broad consensus that Europe at the end of the twentieth century is faced with a choice of repeating the nineteenth century as a fragmented and warring set of nations and regions, powered by identities based on exclusive and antagonistic linguistic, ethnic and religious heritages, or moving into the twenty-first century with a new identity based upon a common and distinctive European heritage reflecting some consensus of values.

There are research and policy agendas to reconcile. This chapter is an attempt at least to make clear to those with such powers, the dangers, difficulties and above all opportunities for using these aspects of a European past to shape a European future.

References

Abercrombie, N., Hill, S. and Turner, B. S. (1980) *The Dominant Ideology Thesis*. London: Allen and Unwin.

Ashworth, G. J. (1991) *Heritage Planning*. Groningen: Geopers.

Ashworth, G. J. (1993a) *On Tragedy and Renaissance: The Role of Loyalist and Acadian Heritage Interpretations in Canadian Place Identity*. Groningen: Geopers.

Ashworth, G. J. (1993b) Culture and tourism: conflict or symbiosis in Europe? In W. Pompl and P. Lavery (eds) *Tourism in Europe*. London: Mansell, pp. 13–35.

Ashworth, G. J. and Larkham, P. J. (eds) (1994) *Building a New Heritage: Tourism, Culture and Identity in the New Europe*. London: Routledge.

Ashworth, G. J. and Tunbridge, J. E. (1990) *The Tourist-Historic City*. London: Belhaven.

Bourdieu, P. (1977) *An Outline of a Theory of Knowledge*. Cambridge: Cambridge University Press.

Burtenshaw, D., Bateman, M. and Ashworth, G. J. (1991) *The European City: Western Perspectives*. London: Fulton.

Chippendale, C. (1993) Putting the 'H' in Stonehenge. *History Today*, **43**, 5–8.

College of Europe (1993) Culture and the economy, Culture: building stone for Europe 2002, Bruges. Symposium report.

Commission of the European Community (1990) *Green Book on the Urban Environment* (EUR 12902). Brussels: Commission of the EC.

Costa, P. and van der Borg, J. (1993) *The Management of Tourism in the Cities of Art* (CISET 2). Venice: University of Venice.

Council of Europe (1974) The future of our past. *Ekistics*, **39**, 139–142.

Council of Europe (1979) *Monument Protection in Europe*. Deventer: Kluwer.

Council of Europe (1992) *Handbook of the Council of Europe*. Strasbourg: Council of Europe.

Dietvorst, A. (1993) Planning for tourism and recreation: a market oriented approach. In H. N. Van Lier and P. D. Taylor (eds) *New Challenges in Recreation and Tourism Planning*. Amsterdam: Elsevier, pp. 87–123.

Dobby, A. (1978) *Conservation and Planning*. London: Hutchinson.

Jansen-Verbeke, M. C. (1990) *Toerisme in de Binnenstad van Brugge: Een Planologische Visie*. Nijmeegese Planologische Cahiers, No. 35. Nijmegen: Katholieke Universiteit Nijmegen.

Kain, R. (1981) *Planning for Conservation: An International Perspective*. London: Mansell.

Lumley, R. (ed.) (1988) *The Museum Time Machine: Putting Cultures on Display*. London: Routledge.

Matthew, R., Reud, J. and Lindsay, M. (eds) (1972) *The Conservation of Georgian Edinburgh*. Scottish Civic Trust, Edinburgh: University of Edinburgh Press.

Mennell, S. (1976) *Cultural Policy in Towns*. Strasbourg: Council of Europe.

Museum International (1993) Museums of war and peace. *Museum International*, **93** (1).

Pearce, P. L. (1977) Mental souvenirs: a study of tourists and their city maps. *Australian Journal of Psychology*, **29**, 203–210.

Pearce, P. L. (1981) *The Social Psychology of Tourist Behaviour*. Oxford: Pergamon.

Quetel, C. (1993) The Caen memorial. *Museum International*, **93** (1), 1–11.

Ross, M. (1991) *Planning and the Heritage: Policy and Procedures*. London: Spon.

Smith, V. L. (ed.) (1977) *Hosts and Quests: The Anthropology of Tourism*. Oxford: Basil Blackwell.

Soane, J. (1994) Urban vernacular architectural heritage in Germany. In G. J. Ashworth and P. J. Larkham (eds) *Building a New Heritage: Tourism, Culture and Identity in the New Europe*. London: Routledge, pp. 157–187.

Tunbridge, J. E. and Ashworth, G. J. (forthcoming) *Dissonant Heritage*. London: Belhaven.

Whitehand, J. W. R. and Larkham, P. J. (eds) (1992) *Urban Landscapes: International Perspectives*. London: Routledge.

Wikanowicz, S. (1993) Auschwitz: the strangest museum. *Museum International*, **93** (1), 33–37.

6

Heritage as Planned and Conserved

保守 保查

Peter J. Larkham

The Heritage Concept

All things to all people?

One significant problem underlies any consideration of heritage planning. This is the general lack of any accepted theory, or ethic, of conservation (Worskett, 1982a). The few attempts to promulgate such an ethic have been published in low-visibility sources or have not met with great success among planning practitioners (Briggs, 1975; Faulkner, 1978; Larkham, 1990). Yet, in fields other than the built environment, there are considerable parallels in heritage and conservation problems but far greater advances in conceptualizing. In art, for example, there is a general consensus on the delimitation of fake, restoration and replication; with the intent to deceive being a major consideration, and widespread acceptance that repairs and restorations should be reversible, if not discernible: these arguments are well explored in Jones (1990). In dealing with mechanical devices, however, it appears that constant use means constant replacement of damaged or worn pieces and yet the 'identity' of a vehicle may remain unchanged: this was found to be so in the High Court after the purchaser of the racing Bentley known as 'Old No. 1' challenged its provenance in 1990. Still more unusual is the general acceptance of new vehicles or aircraft, manufactured to original drawings and standards by the original company years after production originally ceased, as being 'original' rather than 'replica'. In this respect, Dron (1991) discusses the example of the 'new' Aston Martin DB4GT Zagato. Historic buildings and townscapes, however, produce higher levels of debate, and issues of fakery, façadism, replication and originality are central to the argument of this chapter.

Some of these ideas have been discussed in Lowenthal's penetrating analysis of the minutiae and ephemera of conservation-related activities (Lowenthal, 1985). He shows clearly that we want old things to *seem* old, with antiquity being valued and validated by decay and the patina of age. There is a need to know the past: a psychological need for a reference-point, although how we 'know' the past varies from personal experience through fallible memory to learned history. Yet history can be simultaneously less and more than the past as it is interpreted selectively by writers and readers. We thus display a marked propensity for changing the past to suit our own changing require-ments. Relics can be adapted, added to, copied and 'interpreted', all of which tend to idealize the past. The 'originality' debate, which is often raised in the context of tourism and its consequences for the built heritage, can thus be seen as largely irrelevant to the concept of heritage planning (Ashworth, 1991; Newby, 1994).

There are three main aspects to 'heritage' which can be identified in the context of planning and conservation. *Preservation* involves the retention, in largely unchanged form, of sites or objects of major cultural significance. Items falling into this category are frequently of national, or perhaps regional, significance. *Conservation* encompasses the idea that some form of restoration should be undertaken to bring old buildings and sites into suitable modern use. *Exploitation* recognizes the value of heritage sites, particularly for tourism and recreation, and encompasses the development of existing sites and new sites. These definitions are explored more fully by Herbert's introduction to this volume. In many respects, it is the theme of exploitation which poses both practical and conceptual problems for conservation. Virtually all forms of tourism involve exploitation, from the more benign signposting or 'blue-plaquing' of heritage attractions (which nevertheless may detract from them: Meinig, 1979) to the extreme of the recreated and re-enacted past, possibly seen at its best in Colonial Williamsburg (USA). Those responsible for the identification and management of heritage attractions, whether quasi-governmental bodies such as English Heritage or Cadw or from the private sector such as Madame Tussaud's at Warwick Castle, are increasingly aware of the potential that tourism has for heritage: tourist income often allows the maintenance of areas or buildings where grant-aid or private funding is absent. This increasing need to attract tourists and their revenues inevitably affects the decisions being made by the agents directly involved: this chapter also argues that those more indirectly involved are increasingly also being affected by decisions to design new buildings in historicist styles, 'enhance' large urban or village centres, and so on. Implicit throughout is an awareness of the increasing tension between tourism and its impact upon heritage and regeneration planning on the one hand, and the nature and scale of the changes to monuments, historic buildings and conserved areas on the other.

Particularly in Western societies, there has been a realization throughout the late twentieth century that 'planning', in the broad sense of the management of the urban and rural landscape, must encompass all three aspects of heritage. Yet the manner in which this is achieved shows great variation from one planning system to another and over time. The major incentive to heritage planning has been economic. Major planning problems have arisen as urban landscapes have aged and the social, economic and cultural conditions under which they were originally created have changed. Adaptation of the townscape to new requirements becomes necessary, but this proves hard to achieve without some wastage of the investment that past societies have made in the shaping of all aspects of urban form. Adaptation is especially problematic where one or another group in society imposes values on places which are hard to quantify in purely economic terms, particularly where these values derive from associations with past events or with reactions to particular visual associations.

This chapter discusses a range of activities falling under the broad heading of 'heritage planning', using examples from the United Kingdom. British legal/administrative conservation systems are discussed, in order to demonstrate some of the problems and successes of the current wave of conservation concern.

Those involved in heritage planning

In order to understand the actual changes occurring on the ground, it is necessary to consider the decision makers involved. These may be divided into two groups: first, those directly involved in changes in that they initiate, design or implement development; secondly, those exercising external, less direct influence, mainly through the statutory system of development control.

Direct agents of change

The initiator of a change and the architect designing it have probably the most direct influence on the townscape. The architect also frequently acts as an intermediary between the local planning authority and the initiator. The initiator is often, but not invariably, the landowner. Specialized contractors and consultants are also important. These agents form a chain, or perhaps more correctly a web, of decision making which begins with the initiator, who makes the initial decision to begin the process of change. Not only is a train of events leading to a change in the physical fabric thus set in motion, but the initiator also exercises a major influence over the choice of other firms and organizations that participate in the later stages of the development process. The reasons underlying the initiation of a change are numerous, but one factor that is often involved is the obsolescence, in one respect or another, of the property (Cowan, 1963). Concern to improve the townscape is rarely a dominant motivating factor.

Two of the most significant characteristics of these direct agents of change are their provenance and type (Whitehand, 1984; Larkham and Freeman, 1988). Decisions made by local agents, especially initiators and architects, tend to result in different types and styles of alteration or addition to the building stock than decisions taken by agents based far from the site of the proposed change. There is a tendency for large national concerns to be based in London, and London-based agents have a large impact. In the case of retail developments, a major feature is the adoption by each chain of its own house style, which is reproduced in many different towns. Whether an initiator is a speculative developer or is building for owner-occupation may well affect the architectural style used. Commercial owner-occupiers may adopt new architectural fashions more rapidly than speculative developers. The latter have typically been more conservative and less likely to adopt new architectural forms.

Indirect agents

The first major group of indirect agents to be involved in the UK development control process is that of the local authority planning officers. They are professionally qualified and are responsible both for large-scale planning and for the detailed control of development. Virtually all proposed changes to the built fabric and material changes of use must receive the permission of the local planning authority. When a formal application for permission is submitted, not only may it be preconditioned by the initiator's prior knowledge of the planning officers' attitudes to certain types of development, but subsequent negotiations between the applicant and the planning officers may be of considerable importance in changing an initially unacceptable application into an acceptable form.

The actual decisions on planning matters are made by the Planning Committee of the local authority, which is composed of elected public representatives, amongst whom aesthetic or technical knowledge or training is rare. These committees discuss the formal recommendation of the chief professional planning officer on each application. It is therefore the professional planners who determine, to a large extent, the nature and detail of the information upon which the committee acts. Nevertheless, the committee makes the final decision. Although frequently accepting the officers' recommendations, committees may act in a variety of ways, suggesting that other pressures have acted upon them (Fleming and Short, 1984; Witt and Fleming, 1984). In addition to debating the principles involved in large projects, some are clearly particularly active in making detailed modifications to applications (Witt and Fleming, 1984, section 5.4).

However, councillors' attitudes to any planning discussion, including that on aesthetic matters, are conditioned not only by the planning officers' recommendations and other lobbying, but also by factors such as ideological and political position, attitude towards the role of the elected representative and perception of the role of planning. Although their position is of paramount importance in the democratic decision-making process, their role as agents of change in the townscape is in practice considerably less influential than that of other agents, including the professional planning officers.

Another indirect agent is the general public. The influence of the public in planning has increased since the mid-1960s, largely as a consequence of a new paradigm in planning (Long, 1975, p. 73). Although individual members of the public rarely respond to invitations to comment on planning applications, local amenity societies, community action groups and other pressure groups do. Because they often possess considerable local knowledge and some professional expertise, they may be able to present the public's viewpoint with force and eloquence. However, the impact of local amenity societies is difficult to assess. They have few sanctions that they could bring to bear on a recalcitrant planning authority, save for the possible stirring up of adverse publicity. Having little leverage to exert, the societies usually rely on persuasion and, increasingly, upon becoming incorporated within the planning system by various consultation processes. Informal contact between societies, councillors and planners is high and there often seems to be a striking similarity between the views of local planners and those of the amenity societies (for example see Barker, 1976). Direct confrontation is often seen as self-defeating in that it may prejudice, to the detriment of future consultations, a close working relationship that has been built up: cooperation is more typical of the dialogue between planners and amenity groups. However much consultation is urged by the Department of the Environment, the roles of amenity societies, residents' associations and similar groups are diverse and vary greatly in their effectiveness.

The significance of the non-involved

Even though 'the public' may be a significant indirect agent of change, the number of individuals directly involved in the amenity movement is small: a recent survey carried out for the Midland Amenity Societies Association gave membership rates ranging from 34.5 per cent in a small wealthy village to 0.02 per cent in a large industrial town (see Larkham, 1992, p. 93). Detailed studies of rates of change in conserved townscapes also imply that, at any given time, the number of non-changers vastly outnumbers those actively involved in making changes to buildings or the townscape (for example see Larkham, 1990, 1992). Yet those who are not actively involved are, nevertheless, indirect or passive 'consumers' of the historic built environment. Their taxes fund the planning system, its handling of development control applications and the physical 'enhancements' of local authorities. Their responses to historic townscapes and buildings are difficult to elicit, but seem to be concerned largely with superficial, external appearance rather than originality or authenticity, as the research reviewed by Hubbard (1993) shows. Moreover,

Table 6.1 Top ten heritage tourism attractions in England (paying visitors only), 1977–1991

1977	1981	1986	1991
Tower of London 3 089 000	Tower of London 2 088 000	Tower of London 2 019 000	Tower of London 1 923 520
St George's, Windsor 989 000	State Apartments, Windsor* 727 000	Roman Baths, Bath 828 492	St Paul's* 1 500 000
Stonehenge 815 000	Roman Baths, Bath 657 000	State Apartments, Windsor 616 000	Roman Baths, Bath 827 214
Roman Baths, Bath 727 000	Stonehenge 546 000	Warwick Castle 580 255	Warwick Castle 682 621
Hampton Court 666 000	Hampton Court 524 000	Beaulieu 500 551	State Apartments, Windsor 627 213
Shakespeare's Birthplace 661 000	St George's, Windsor 500 000	Shakespeare's Birthplace 496 331	Stonehenge 615 377
Beaulieu 582 000	Beaulieu 477 000	Stonehenge 496 138	Shakespeare's Birthplace 516 623
Anne Hathaway's Cottage 522 000	Shakespeare's Birthplace 460 000	Hampton Court 482 000	Blenheim 503 528
Warwick Castle 485 000	Warwick Castle 421 000	Leeds Castle* 433 559	Hampton Court 502 377
Brighton Pavilion 428 000	Salisbury Cathedral* 358 000	Tower Bridge* 419 003	Leeds Castle 497 528

* Newly open, or newly making admission charges.
Source: English Tourist Board (annual) English Heritage Monitor: note that not all tourist destinations responded to this ETB annual survey.

they may often act as active consumers when on holiday: here, the reactions of the heritage providers or managers to actual or perceived demands (see Carr, 1994; Light and Prentice, 1994) are important components of what Urry (1990) has termed the 'tourist gaze'. The importance of the indirect contribution of the public as consumers of commodified heritage is clearly shown in Table 6.1, which gives the top ten tourist attractions in England: significant features are the numbers of paying visitors together with the fact that all sites are heavily 'interpreted' and presented for the tourist trade, with the possible exception of the Stonehenge monument itself. Those unaware of heritage issues in their home areas may become aware when they visit other places as tourists: the relevance of tourism to heritage issues here becomes clear.

Planning and Heritage

Changing ideas

The concept of conservation is now an accepted part of urban planning in most developed countries. This is a reflection of the widespread interest in the past and ways in which it is viewed, used and changed (Lowenthal, 1985). There is a 'conserver society' that creates its own landscapes (Relph, 1982) and which is particularly manifest in the rapid growth of the conservation movement and local amenity societies (Cherry, 1975; Lowe, 1977). This implies that conservation has had, and will continue to have, a significant effect upon urban form, which can clearly be seen in all kinds of urban landscapes (see the examples in Larkham, 1992). The current concern with conservation now appears to be allied with the postmodern reaction in architecture and planning to bland postwar modernism. The latter has been seen by many critics as eroding the unique attributes of places through the imposition of uniform building types and house styles, and the widespread use of materials which are alien to the locale (Relph, 1976, 1987). In the UK at least, interest in conservation is also a reaction against the post-World War II comprehensive clearance and redevelopment (Esher, 1981), whereby large areas of often historical town cores were redeveloped at a scale rarely seen before, except after natural or man-made disaster. The effects of this comprehensive redevelopment have, in fact, been compared directly, and unfavourably, to the devastation caused by war (HRH Prince Charles, 1987).

Conservation is one reaction, particularly common at present, to the problem of ageing urban landscapes. The production and maintenance of the physical fabric of the urban environment absorbs a large amount of the wealth of the developed world. Furthermore, a strong case has been made for the social, cultural and psychological significance of the urban landscape (see Larkham, 1990; Hubbard, 1993). Yet during some periods, for example the 1950s in many Western countries, this wastage received relatively little consideration, as the philosophy of comprehensive clearance was dominant.

During the 1980s, in contrast, it was suggested that interest in conservation in Britain was at its highest for a century (Sutcliffe, 1981) and over a decade later this shows no sign of abating. This change of attitudes has helped to highlight the problem of accommodating the requirements of present societies within the townscape legacy from previous generations. This interest in the past has, indeed, reached such a point that some critics have protested strongly against the concept of conservation in principle (Price, 1981), Britain's 'museum-based culture' (Hewison, 1987; Lumley, 1988) and its accompanying 'conservation-area-architecture' (Rock, 1974).

In general terms, the UK public appears to be inherently conservative and strongly resistant to large-scale change. Particularly since the late 1960s, the British planning system has allowed public involvement through inspection of planning applications and participation in the preparation of structure and local plans. The local voluntary amenity groups, which largely represent the views of the public, have grown rapidly in number since the national Civic Trust was formed in 1957. The number reached a peak in the mid- to late 1970s and declined slightly into the 1980s (information from the Civic Trust: the decline represented a 'weeding' process of inactive societies). These societies claim to represent public opinion, but it is clear that they are directly representative, in terms of numbers of members and also of socio-cultural groups, of only a small proportion of the population. Indeed, many of the criticisms of these societies are that they represent the views of a middle-class, well-educated, self-appointed and vociferous elite, rather than of the public at large (Crosland, 1971; Eversley, 1974). Many critics, not least developers, complain that these amenity societies are wholly negative, anti-development, in their views. 'They have one common denominator . . . the lowest: that no change is always better than change, that their taste is always better than that of any architect or planner in the public service' (Eversley, 1974, p. 14). Price, an architect, noted that an 'élitist delight in the archaic' makes the destruction of an old building exceptionally difficult and attributes this to a varied 'range of prejudice, conceit, ignorance, sloth and feeble thinking' (Price, 1981, p. 40). Indeed, studies of the comments made by amenity societies are few and the impact of these comments is almost impossible to measure. Nevertheless, an examination of the comments made by one society, Wolverhampton Civic Society, shows that the society advised against planning proposals in only 15.4 per cent of cases between January 1970 and June 1985; and in only 18 of 214 cases was the Civic Society's view in significant conflict with the eventual decision of the local planning authority (Larkham, 1985).

But the criticism of the NIMBY (Not In My Back Yard) view is hard to dispel. Published cases where public views, especially of the societies themselves and the Civic Trust, have materially assisted in the delay or withdrawal of development proposals are more common than cases where negotiation has resulted in acceptable amended plans. For example, one developer noted of a site in Ludlow that 'unfortunately, it would appear that due to pressure from the Ludlow Civic Society the opinion of the Planning Officers and certainly that of the councillors was changed and our planning application was refused' (Larkham, 1992, p. 94). It is also evident that much public opinion is selfish, reacting only to immediate threats of development and rarely takes a longer-term or wider spatial view. This is confirmed by detailed examination of individual comments on planning proposals, a sample of which are discussed in Larkham (1990).

Changing legislation

In every country which attempts to conserve parts of its built form through legislative fiat, the detailed form of legislation and the manner of its change over time are crucial. The precise wording of Acts, once passed, may seem academic to the public but, to those deeply involved in the practicalities of conservation, words matter. The UK case is here examined in some detail, since some of the relative minutiae of legislation have recently come under scrutiny. The semantics of words, their dictionary definitions and the meanings imputed to them by legislators, decision makers and others have been discussed at length by planning inspectors of the Department of the Environment when applications are taken to Appeal; by the High Court, the Court of Appeal and, on occasion, by the House of Lords. Although the precise nature of the English legal system detailed here is not replicated everywhere – and it should be noted that there are some variations even within the UK – it is a legal system which has acted as the model for many others. It is instructive to see how an established system has dealt with the debates on conservation and heritage.

The rise of the conservation area

It is generally accepted that the genesis of the conservation area concept in the UK lies in the case of *The Earl of Iveagh* v. *Minister of Housing and Local Government* (Court of Appeal 1964: 1 QB 395). The case involved two adjoining terraced houses in St James's Square, London, owned by the Earl. Building preservation notices had been served on these houses on the grounds that their alteration or demolition would be detrimental to the square. This was challenged by the Earl, the contentious point in this case being whether a building should be listed for its intrinsic architectural or historical interest, or whether it might possess such interest merely because it was a part of a group. The Court of Appeal decided for the Minister, holding that 'a building might be of special architectural or historic interest by reason of its setting as one of a group'. The decision, however, was not unanimous and it was apparent that a more general power was required in the case of 'group value' (Suddards, 1988a, pp. 45–46; Graves and Ross, 1991; Ross, 1991, p. 30). This case led to Duncan Sandys, MP and President of the Civic Trust, drawing up the Civic Amenities Bill on winning first place in the 1966 parliamentary ballot for Private Members' Bills. His Bill received support from Richard Crossman, then Minister of Housing and Local Government, and passed through Parliament with all-party support, although in slightly modified form. Yet there was opposition, principally from the Permanent Secretary of the Ministry, Dame Evelyn Sharp. 'This kind of work [conservation and preservation] was utterly despised by Dame Evelyn. She regarded it as pure sentimentalism, and called it "preservation", a term of abuse' (Crossman, 1975, p. 623).

The new Act was thus largely permissive and a 'declaration of interest'. One of the reasons for its easy and widespread acceptance was probably just that: it provided no new regulatory powers or onerous duties for local or central government. Section 1 of the 1967 Act merely required local authorities, from time to time, 'to determine which parts of their area . . . are areas of special architectural or historical interest, the character or appearance of which it is desirable to preserve or enhance, and shall designate such areas (hereafter referred to as conservation areas)'.

Successive Planning Acts and government guidance suggest that a conservation area is an area:

(a)   of special architectural interest; or
(b)   of special historical interest; or, presumably, both.
      In any event, it must also be an area
(c)   whose character it is desirable to preserve;
(d)   whose character it is desirable to enhance;
(e)   whose appearance it is desirable to preserve; or
(f)   whose appearance it is desirable to enhance; or, again, presumably any
      combination of these. (Mynors, 1984, p. 146)

There were no absolute criteria laid down for designation, save that, to be eligible, an area must be of *special* interest. The effect of designating a conservation area is that 'special attention shall be paid to the desirability of preserving or enhancing its character or appearance' (1971 Town and Country Planning Act, section 277[8]). Although local authorities were enjoined to determine which areas may be suitable for designation, there was no over-riding obligation upon them to make designations. In practice, by 1990 each local authority had made at least one designation, and by 1993 some 8000 areas had been designated. The process of designation is simple. There was no guidance as to what should be included, beyond noting that areas might vary in size between town centres and squares, terraces and smaller groups of buildings; they may centre on listed buildings; and may also feature other groups of buildings, open spaces, trees, historic street patterns and village greens (Ministry of Housing and Local Government, 1969). Designation is made by the local planning authority. Once a local authority has identified an area, the designation takes effect from the date of its formal resolution:

(a) designation is implemented through a notice in the *London Gazette* (or *Edinburgh Gazette* in the case of Scotland) and at least one local newspaper; (b) designation must be registered as a local land charge; and (c) the Secretary of State for the Environment and English Heritage (or the appropriate body in Wales and Scotland) must be informed. It is thus a simple, local and potentially rapid procedure, and one from which there is no appeal. Northern Ireland, however, has a more centralized procedure administered through the Department of the Environment (Northern Ireland) rather than individual local authorities (Hendry, 1993).

The 1974 Town and Country Amenities Act replaced the clumsy and limited control of demolitions within conservation areas. This was another Private Member's Bill, passed between the two general elections of that year, albeit with government support (Ross, 1991, p. 126). It significantly enlarged the scope of control within conservation areas by bringing the demolition of unlisted buildings in a conservation area within the remit of listed building consent requirements; although the prospect of applying for listed building consent relating to an unlisted building was a problem for subsequent years.

More recently, the 1990 Town and Country Planning Act and 1990 Planning (Listed Buildings and Conservation Areas) Act have 'tidied up' the current planning legislation, though there are no substantive changes in the thrust of conservation area legislation; indeed, much of the wording of earlier Acts is preserved.

Responsibility for conservation policy was moved in 1992 to the newly created Department of National Heritage (DNH). The DNH now has responsibility for general oversight of the conservation area – and listed building – systems, although their application in practice through appeals and so on still rests with the DoE and the Secretary of State for the Environment (Department of National Heritage, 1992). How this uneasy division of responsibilities will work in practice is yet to be resolved and the lengthy gestation period of the Planning Policy Guidance Note on conservation and listed buildings, caused in part by this interdepartmental problem, is perhaps a bad omen.

The listed buildings system

The listing of buildings of national architectural or historic interest began as a reaction to wartime bomb damage and the system was then formalized in the 1944 and 1947 Town and Country Planning Acts (Harvey, 1993). The principles of listing have remained unchanged, although there have been changes in practice as the country has been covered by the initial listing and resurvey campaigns (Robertson *et al.*, 1993).

Strict guidelines exist on how buildings are selected for listing. Although local authorities – and indeed members of the public – may put forward buildings for selection, the actual decision is made by the relevant Secretary of State on the advice of English Heritage, Scottish Heritage or Cadw, whose inspectors will visit likely buildings and make recommendations. The current criteria for listing were originally drawn up by the Historic Buildings Council at the outset of the national resurvey in the 1980s. In 1987 the criteria were amended to permit the inclusion of a small number of post-1939 buildings. These criteria form a set of general principles and suggest that listing should include all buildings built before 1700 which survive in anything like their original condition. As selection has moved towards the present there is rapidly increasing selectivity, with only a few outstanding buildings built after 1939 being listed.

All listed buildings must possess 'special' interest. Although this is not legally defined, guidelines suggest that, in listing buildings, particular attention is paid to special value within certain building types, either for architectural or planning reasons, or as illustrating aspects of social or economic history; to technological innovations, to association with historic characters or events, or their group value, especially as models of town planning (squares, terraces or model villages). Listed buildings are divided into three grades. There is no provision for these in the statutes, but the grades have acquired a particular importance for grant purposes and for their treatment in assessing listed building consent applications. Thus this system has been given a quasi-legal status. In all, the total of listed buildings, in all grades, is now approximately half a million in England alone.

Problems of these systems

This examination of legislative development has emphasized terminology, much of which has caused problems and much remains undefined in statute or guidance (Millichap, 1989a). Both conservation areas and listed buildings must be of 'special' interest. Although conservation areas should be of 'architectural or historical' interest, the Secretary of State has decided, in the case of wartime prefabricated buildings at Bletchley Park used for the breaking of German codes, that historic interest alone will not secure listing (Lock, 1993; Morton, 1993). 'Character or appearance' is mentioned, but these could be quite different criteria; and, although local authorities are encouraged to carry out character assessments to support designation decisions, policy development and development-control decisions, only a small proportion of areas have such statements (Suddards and Morton, 1991). Indeed, Morton's research suggests that only some 10 per cent of areas possess such statements (Morton, 1994) (see also Jones and Larkham, 1993). The final dichotomy is 'preserve or enhance', both of which have been stressed in guidance, yet there is increasing unease at the nature and scale of current 'enhancement' works which seem neither to preserve nor enhance the historic character or appearance of these areas (Booth, 1993). There are national criteria for listing that are applied by expert advisers whose conclusions, however, may often not match the perceptions of the general public (Hubbard, 1993); and the merits of this process of identification and protection must be questioned.

The significance of the concern with legislative language is highlighted by recent court cases dealing with conservation issues. As the planning system is quasi-judicial in its operation, any court decisions act as precedents and shape future decision making by local authorities. In the late 1980s, several influential decisions attempted to clarify these procedures and terms and had a significant impact upon the interpretation of the law relating to conservation areas and listed buildings. The statutory duty of local authorities (or other 'decision makers') to pay 'special attention' to conservation areas (section 277(8) of the 1971 Act as amended by the 1974 Act; now section 72 of the 1990 Act) had not previously been defined, and Suddards (1988a, p. 51) felt that

> many local planning authorities might say that a conservation area policy is not required because it would in any event pay special attention (i.e. attention over and beyond that which it would normally pay to any other area) to the sort of area which would be designated as a conservation area.

In the case of *Steinberg and Sykes* v. *Secretary of State for the Environment and Another* (1989 JPL 259), two residents in a conservation area were aggrieved at a grant of planning permission at Appeal for a two-storey house in Camden. Steinberg and Sykes challenged the Secretary of State's decision in the High Court on the ground that the inspector had failed to take into account the statutory requirement to 'pay special attention'. Lionel Read, QC agreed that this obligation had not been fulfilled, stating that nowhere in the inspector's decision letter did he explicitly mention the obligation to pay special attention to the desirability of preserving or enhancing the character of the conservation area.

The Appeal decision was therefore quashed (Millichap, 1989b; Stubbs and Lavers, 1991). The implications of this decision were significant for decision making in conservation area development control and it was seized upon by conservationists, with the Civic Trust (1989, p. 1) stating that

> it is not enough to say that a particular development will do no harm. The positive tests required by Section 277(8) [of the then 1971 Act] must be applied. Of course, opinions will vary as to whether a particular development will preserve or enhance the local scene but the Steinberg case will serve to enable the proper issues to be addressed in the future.

The apparent importance of *Steinberg* is the interpretation of the phrase that 'the concept of avoiding harm is essentially negative. The underlying purpose of Section 277(8) seems to me to be essentially positive' (Lionel Read, QC, speaking in the *Steinberg* case). In other words, a proposed development should not merely cause no harm, it must positively enhance the area. A series of cases have tested this proposition (Stubbs and Lavers, 1991). Most importantly, in the case of *South Western Regional Health Authority* v. *Secretary of State for the Environment* (1989), Sir Graham Eyre noted that section 277(8) contained no exclusive test that could be applied by decision makers to determine the outcome of every application within a conservation area. Harm may mean that the character or appearance will not be preserved or enhanced, but this is not necessarily so. It may be that a proposal would preserve or enhance some aspects of an area, but harm others (in fact, many applications, if strictly examined, would fall into this category). The decision maker then has to balance preservation and enhancement against potential harm: it should not be supposed that all harm must be avoided.

In the case of *Unex Dumpton Ltd* v. *Secretary of State for the Environment and Forest Heath District Council* (Ferguson, 1990), the inspector had arguably considered whether the proposed development would preserve or enhance the conservation area, but not (in the post-*Steinberg* way of thinking) whether they would harm the area's character or appearance, let alone whether this harm would be demonstrable. During this case, Roy Vandermeer, QC gave the following useful determinations.

1. As a general rule Inspectors cannot avoid the need to consider whether development proposals cause harm to interests of acknowledged importance and they should grant permission if they do not.
2. Inspectors considering proposals in a conservation area have, by Section 277 of the [1971] Act, a special duty imposed on them to pay special attention to the desirability of the proposals enhancing or preserving the special character of the conservation area and it must be apparent from the decision that this duty has been discharged otherwise an error of law will have occurred.
3. If Inspectors find that the proposed development will not preserve or enhance the conservation area it is very likely that he [*sic*] will conclude that harm would be caused to the conservation area.
4. What falls to be considered is the appearance of the conservation area, not simply each individual component within it. Accordingly, it is possible that a proposal to replace one building with another in a conservation area will not harm the conservation area.

Millichap (1989a) examined a number of post-*Steinberg* appeal decisions, noting the problems of identifying 'demonstrable harm' and the tendency to treat 'preservation' and 'enhancement' as alternatives, although many decision letters refer to preservation *and* enhancement rather than preservation *or* enhancement, as does the legislation. He concludes that applicants and decision makers should beware of the ability to promote the interpretation of the section that favours their aims, suggesting that further official guidance is necessary.

In the case of the *Bath Society* v. *Secretary of State for the Environment and Another* (*Journal of Planning and Environment Law Bulletin*, 1991), the Court of Appeal held that the failure of an inspector hearing a planning appeal relating to a conservation area to consider recommendations for the appeal site contained in the local plan constituted a failure to pay 'special attention' and resulted in a flawed decision. Lord Justice Glidewell, in the Court of Appeal, thus set out the proper approach in considering an application for planning permission within a conservation area.

1. The decision-maker had two statutory duties to perform, imposed by Section 277(8) as well as Section 29(1) of the Act.
2. In a conservation area the requirement under Section 277(8) to pay 'special attention' should be the first consideration for the decision-maker. It was to be regarded as having considerable importance and weight.
3. If, therefore, the decision-maker decided that the development would enhance or preserve the character or appearance of the area, that had to be a major point in favour of allowing the development.
4. There would, nevertheless, be some cases in which a development could simultaneously enhance the character of an area but cause some detriment. That detrimental effect was a material consideration.
5. If the decision-maker decided that the proposed development would neither preserve nor enhance the character of the area, it was almost inevitable that the development would have some detrimental effect on it. Then, the development should only be permitted if the decision-maker concluded that it carried advantages outweighing the failure to satisfy the Section 277(8) test and such detriment as might inevitably follow.

Shortly after the *Bath Society* case, the Court of Appeal also ruled on the case of *South Lakeland District Council* v. *Secretary of State for the Environment and Carlisle Diocesan Parsonages Board*. This case dealt with the relationship between section 72(1) and 'neutral' development which did not harm the character or appearance of a conservation area. In doing no harm, it was argued that such neutral development acted to 'preserve' character or appearance. In accepting this argument, the court overruled the narrow interpretation of preservation adopted by the High Court in the *Steinberg* case in 1989 (Stanley, 1991, p. 1014).

The case has now been heard in the House of Lords. The judgment of Lord Bridge of Harwich, in dismissing the appeal by South Lakeland District Council, agreed with the Appeal Court's interpretation of section 277(8) and, therefore, its reinterpretation of the *Steinberg* judgment.

> It not only gives effect to the ordinary meaning of the statutory language; it also avoids imputing to the legislature a rigidity of planning policy for which it is difficult to see any rational justification. . . . where a particular development will not have any adverse effect on the character or appearance of the [conservation] area and is otherwise unobjectionable on planning grounds, one may ask rhetorically what possible planning reason there can be for refusing to allow it. (House of Lords, 1992)

This virtual reversal of *Steinberg* principles again has significant repercussions on how development control decisions affecting conservation are – or should be – made.

In the case of *R.* v. *Canterbury City Council ex parte Halford*, a decision by Canterbury City Council to extend the designated Barham conservation area was quashed by the court. This raised the question of the definition of conservation area boundaries and established that, in the absence of a right of appeal against conservation area designation, a judicial review may be sought by an interested party. A key issue in this case was the concept of the 'setting' of the conservation area. The High Court accepted that conservation areas should not be enlarged (and thus, arguably, originally defined) merely to include 'buffer zones'. It would appear, from this case, that land devoid of intrusive historical or architectural interest may be included within a conservation area so long as it comprises a relatively small proportion of the total area's extent: it seems unjustified to expand a conservation area specifically to include such land (Jarman, 1992; Millichap, 1992).

It should be noted that the Barham conservation area extension was quashed not on these grounds, but on the narrow ground that tree preservation had not been considered; this technicality has now been overcome and the designation made. Nevertheless, the airing of these issues in open court is significant.

A recent case (*Wansdyke DC* v. *Secretary of State*) suggests that a development which clearly harms a conservation area may be sanctioned if, in so doing, other significant conservation interests would be promoted. A proposed sports development for a rugby club in the Bathampton conservation area was found, on appeal, to be damaging to the area. However, allowing this proposal would mean the likely development of a park-and-ride area and superstore on a site vacated by the rugby club to the direct benefit of a nearby conservation area: Bath. Since Bath is generally accepted as an 'internationally important' area, the inspector ruled that the benefits of decreasing vehicular congestion through providing the park-and-ride facility, and attracting shoppers away from the city centre to the new superstore, would outweigh the accepted damage to Bathampton.

This is a clear case of an exception being made to the general policies on conservation and development, following that of the *Bath Society* case: even if a given proposal is not in accordance with the legislative criteria, there may be other planning arguments in its favour leading to acceptance (Millichap, 1993). The implications for heritage planning are significant: here, for the first time, it is explicitly recognized that conservation is subordinate to other goals, and that demonstrable harm to conservation interests can be acceptable.

The saga of Peter (now Lord) Palumbo's attempts to develop his site at No. 1 Poultry was finally decided on 28 February 1991 in the House of Lords (Watson, 1991). Five Law Lords decided that the appeal decision by the former Secretary of State, Nicholas Ridley, was correct in granting permission for James Stirling's new building on the corner site occupied by a group of eight listed Victorian buildings. However, they did not endorse Ridley's views that the new building was a 'possible masterpiece', being of such quality that it would contribute 'more both to the immediate environment and to the architectural heritage than the retention of the existing buildings'. Instead, Lord Ackner stated that 'in allowing this appeal, your lordships are in no way either expressly or implicitly concurring with the views of the Secretary of State' (quoted in Bar-Hillel, 1991, p. 22). Furthermore, the House of Lords regards this ruling as an exception, rather than forming a precedent. Yet, although dealing explicitly with listed buildings, this case has implications for development in conservation areas. SAVE Britain's Heritage, which fought the case against Palumbo, based its arguments on the fact that the relevant circular makes no mention that the possible quality of a proposed replacement building could be a material consideration. SAVE's legal adviser said of the original Appeal decision that

> everyone will be trying to get through this loophole . . . unless the decision is challenged, future listed building inquiries will be bogged down in arguments about taste and aesthetics of new buildings instead of presuming, as the circular says, in favour of old ones. (David Cooper, quoted in Bar-Hillel, 1991, p. 22)

It is difficult to argue, as the Law Lords did, that this case will not set a precedent. The validity of Circular 8/87 (DoE, 1987) and its presumption in favour of retaining listed buildings remains official policy, and Lord Bridge was correct in alluding to the 'special circumstances' of this particular site. Nevertheless, although each planning application should be treated on its own merits, the law operates on the basis of precedent and case law, and the government accepts that 'the Courts are the ultimate arbiters' (DoE, 1991, para. 19). Future Appeal decisions and court cases regarding development in conservation areas must be expected to raise the case of No. 1 Poultry.

Conclusions from UK conservation legislation and case law

In 1984, Mynors stated that 'the law as it now stands is somewhat complex – it is no wonder that there are several inconsistencies in the drafting of the later amending legislation!' (Mynors, 1984, p. 145). Since then, there has been a specific conservation areas and listed buildings Act, bringing together and tidying up the many changes and developments in conservation legislation. Yet confusions remain in abundance. This examination of legislative development and legal quibbles suggests many. Must all development 'enhance' a designated conservation area? Or is development which does no demonstrable harm thus acting to 'preserve' it? How is an area's 'character' or 'appearance' defined?

The policies and procedures laid down by statute are interpreted by official guidance, usually in the form of circulars. These interpretations may change from time to time, as the political complexion of government changes, or even as influential individuals within the system change (as with the evident differences of opinion held by three Secretaries of State for the Environment during the No. 1 Poultry case). Yet both the statutes and the guidance are interpreted by users and, as a last resort, by the courts. The latter evidently place great reliance upon precedent.

The implications for conservation and heritage planning are plain. There are many areas of uncertainty contained in the statutes, circulars and even in successive court decisions. These uncertainties often revolve around varying interpretations of specific words, as the above cases demonstrate. Various practices are hardly made explicit, as with the provisions for extending or de-designating conservation areas and the lack of guidance on what precisely may constitute a conservation area. In one case, which gained wide publicity, it was accepted that a group of listed buildings could be replaced with a new building, designed by a prominent architect, at least in part on the grounds of the possible quality of the replacement.

Many of these problems stem from the basis of subjectivity implicit in conservation, and in the concept of amenity in planning in general. Some of the terms used are hardly amenable to casting in terms of 'objective', quantifiable standards. They will, therefore, continue to lend themselves to a variety of interpretations. Mynors's statement of 1984 remains true in spirit despite the 1990 Acts.

Listed Buildings and Conservation Areas: Current Concerns

Despite the successes of conservation in the past few years, along with the rise of a variety of research-based and practice-based ideas for wider urban management, a growing concern has been evident in a wide literature over the concept of conservation areas.

Designation

Conservation areas in Scotland have been examined by Campbell (1986), who showed the *ad lib* methodology with which they were designated and suggested that future designations should be restricted and that efforts should concentrate on effective management and enhancement. The Department of the Environment's consultation paper containing proposals to integrate the designation process with the local plan-making process (DoE, 1989) was widely criticized (for example by Williams, 1990), and the proposal was later abandoned. In a commentary on the important *Steinberg* case, Ferguson (1990, p. 9) noted that

> where an unworthy conservation area is designated, any development will nonetheless be required to preserve or enhance the character or appearance of that area. This is particularly unfortunate given that, as yet, there is no appeal on the merits against designation of a conservation area, nor is it necessarily the subject of prior consultation.

Motivations for designation such as 'snob zoning' to prevent change and development, political motivation and designation to enhance development control powers all devalue the process and deviate from the original Act (Stansfield, 1991). Reade's critique of the system, based on a study of Upper

Bangor, sharply criticized the system of designation and management (Reade, 1991, 1992a, 1992b).

> Is an area so defined because it is *already* seen as rather special, and is thus valued and cared for and thought to merit protection against insensitive development? Or is it, by contrast an *unappreciated* area, whose potential architectural or historic interest is to be *made* manifest to all? For clearly these are two different cases. Neither the legislation itself, nor the advice note which accompanies it distinguishes between them. (Reade, 1992a, p. 25)

Then, however designated, areas must be managed. Resources must be deployed and policies developed; it must be understood that the character of conservation areas does change through time:

> Most conservation areas do not stand still. . . . Consequently they require managing to make best use of the opportunities that will arise, and there is a need for the appraisal statement prepared for the justification of the designation of the conservation area to go much further than simply a statement acknowledging the special architectural and historic interest of the area. It clearly needs to set out the local planning authority's policies and objectives in protecting the area, and should also, where applicable, address issues such as how the Council will undertake enhancement work when resources permit. Such a document would not only convey the Council's policies and intentions, but help to persuade developers and applicants that their proposals need to comply with the Council's management plan for the conservation area. (Ward, 1992, p. 234)

Debasing the coinage versus maintaining standards

Taking the idea of the conservation-worthiness of designated areas further, Morton (1991; Suddards and Morton, 1991) examined the question of whether continued designations devalue the concept and found that the process of designation is not rigorous, is not democratic and, in some cases, the reasons for designation are not well understood. His views have subsequently become widely accepted. Others have suggested that since the criteria for designation are only loosely governed by statute, the system is open to abuse and is being abused; *inter alia*, it has been suggested that a description of the essential character or appearance of the area should be an essential part of the designation (Graves and Ross, 1991). Hamshere (1991) has stressed the shortcomings of conservation areas, and the differing aims of designating authorities. He argued that 'a comprehensive evaluation of conservation areas, in terms of their social as well as economic impact, is long overdue' (Hamshere, 1991, p. 248).

The character and quality of areas

Robinson (1991) has dealt with the current concerns of continual erosion of character through unsympathetic attention to detail and inadequate maintenance, accusing some local authorities of 'incompetence and lack of concern'.

Many others have agreed with this, in particular suggesting that historic areas are losing individual character through inadequate attention to detail (Coupe, 1991; Davies, 1991; Suddards and Morton, 1991). Indeed, a series of reports on individual town centres published by the Georgian Group documents the nature and scale of this type of problem even within historic town centres such as Stratford-upon-Avon and Cirencester, widely regarded for their qualities of architecture, design and historic associations (see, for example, Georgian Group, 1992). The English Historic Towns Forum similarly suggests, in a recent and widely publicized report, that the scale of inappropriate changes is such that legislative change – and greater use of Article 4 Directions reducing permitted development rights – is required to curb them and to retain the character of conservation areas (English Historic Towns Forum, 1992).

In short, as speakers at an RIBA conference at Dartington in 1991 argued, the concept of conservation is widely felt to have become devalued. It is noteworthy how the current expressions of concern, which have quite suddenly come to the fore in the period 1990–93, closely parallel those of Worskett (1975) and Reynolds (1975), both articles published during European Architectural Heritage Year.

The similar problems of listed buildings

All four of the key conservation studies, of Bath, Chester, Chichester and York, sponsored by the Ministry of Housing and Local Government and published in 1968, found that the listing of buildings in their area was unsatisfactory and recommended alternative criteria (Smith, 1969). Since then a campaign of relisting has been completed, the criteria have been amended and increasing numbers of postwar buildings are being listed through thematic rather than geographical surveys (Robertson *et al.*, 1993). Yet numerous local cases show that listing does not preclude neglect (sometimes deliberate) or demolition. Even now, some types of buildings remain under-represented, with vernacular building types particularly at risk: for example, Scottish vernacular is discussed in Horne (1993). A recent paper prepared by an officer of Dudley Metropolitan Borough Council criticizes the reliance on national, rather than local, significance:

> Sandwell's experience indicates that judging national or regional importance is all too subjective, in that the assessment of merit is dependent on the surveyor's knowledge and perceptions, and that there can be no real comparison between vastly different types of buildings and structures. The local planning authority has even suggested that historic prejudices emerge, with a 'clear bias' against structures associated with trade unionism, religious non-conformity and other movements which challenged the *status quo*. (*Planning*, 1992, reporting on a paper prepared by Peter Boland)

Further, there are strong opposing views in that some people think that listing has gone too far, while conservationists believe that it has not gone far enough (Suddards, 1988b). One recent radical proposal suggested five grades of listing, to offset the tendency of the present system to treat buildings in isolation, thus precluding considerations of urban design and the impact of change on wider urban areas (Noakes, 1991). So far, however, official reaction to the growing concerns of the listing system has been to initiate and hasten the national resurvey.

Examples of UK Conservation Planning

Conservation areas and the cathedral city of Worcester

The historic cathedral city of Worcester can be used to exemplify the concerns set out so far (Vilagrasa and Larkham, 1992). Here, immediately following World War II, the opportunity was taken to prepare a major redevelopment plan (Minoprio and Spencely, 1946). This had many similarities with many of the contemporary 'master plans' for postwar rebuilding of historic cities, whether the aims were to replace bomb-damaged areas or to clear slums and semi-derelict industrial areas. A superimposition of the 1946 plan on the 1930s Ordnance Survey map of the city centre shows that new road alignments were planned; the majority of the remaining medieval alignments were to be widened, new buildings constructed and the entire river frontage cleared of its slums and industry. The riverfront area was to be redeveloped for substantial public buildings and open space. Few of the older street-blocks and buildings would remain unscathed. In common with many such redevelopment proposals, including those for the cities that suffered significant wartime bomb damage, there is little evident concern in the plans for the retention of any older fabric. This 'master plan' was not implemented to any great extent but was influential in shaping subsequent plans that were, more or less, adhered to. Few of the proposed new roads were built, although the City Walls ring road was built in part during the 1980s and some public buildings were constructed in the cleared waterfront area; nevertheless, the implementations were very different in form from those envisaged in 1946.

Some of these differences become evident in local planning documents of 1954 and 1963, with the latter in particular proposing a zoning of acceptable land uses in the central area. Following closely upon the designation of the historic core as a conservation area, a 'continuous retail frontage' policy was adopted in 1971. This aimed to preserve the continuous retail frontage within certain key streets of the centre, by excluding some uses that alter the character of such areas by occupying retail premises but which do not use any retail display within the shopfront. These are often known as 'dead frontages': such uses include estate agencies, financial services and betting shops. This was unusually early for such a policy to be devised and examinations of planning appeals show dead frontages becoming an important issue only in the early to mid-1980s. This policy was extended to other streets in 1985. In addition, some of the central streets were pedestrianized during the mid-1980s.

By the mid-1980s, therefore, Worcester had undergone a considerable amount of redevelopment, although the majority of this had occurred in a piecemeal fashion. Most medieval street alignments and a considerable number of plots remained, although the majority of these plots were substantially altered. By 1987 the city had 911 listed buildings; the Cathedral attracted some 300 000 tourists and the central area had 1 372 400 square feet of gross retail floorspace in 610 retail units. In 1989 the total annual retail spend estimated for the population living within 30 minutes of Worcester was £802.4 million and this is expected to rise to £984 million by the year 2000 (information from the Department of Technical Services, Worcester City Council). There are, therefore, considerable implications for continued pressure for retail change in this regional centre.

Conscious conservation planning came relatively late to Worcester. Although 1971 marked an early conservation area designation, it clearly showed a move away from the influence of the 1946 plan. Yet, between designation and the mid-1980s, applications for changes of building use, alterations to shopfronts, and significant alterations to listed buildings showed significant increases and, although the amount of new construction dropped dramatically, the number of individual plots amalgamated and otherwise changed in new developments was substantial (Vilagrasa and Larkham, 1992, Figures 5, 7–9). In terms of major morphological constituents of streets, plots and buildings, therefore, Worcester avoided the most significant damage proposed in 1946 but, despite the 1971 designation, smaller-scale changes to the area's character and appearance have continued apace. It is instructive to note that there has been a clear trend for new buildings to be proposed in modernist styles, only to become altered to Georgian styles during the process of development control negotiation; but the majority of these occurred before conservation area designation. Since then, refurbishment of original buildings is the preferred option of the planners, and only when an irreversibly ruinous condition is clearly demonstrated is the replacement of an existing building permitted, usually with one which perpetuates or reproduces some of the details of the original façade. Façadism, replication and pastiche designs have become commonplace in the core of Worcester (*ibid.*, pp. 20–22). Both this approach and the earlier push for Georgian styling show that arguments of originality have been convincingly lost, while a superficial historicism retains some, at least, of the external characteristics of the area. It could clearly be argued that the legal requirements to pay special attention to the character or appearance of the area have been met.

'Enhancements' to conservation areas

It will be recalled that the legislation exhorts us to preserve *or enhance*. Many of the early post-1967 enhancement schemes tended to enhance through removal of 'clutter', especially by the placing of power and telephone wires underground. Ian Nairn (1955) and Gordon Cullen (1961) were early advocates of 'tidiness' – not specifically for conservation reasons, but generally in terms of 'good urban design'. Many proposals to rationalize the proliferation of street signs, obtrusive in many historic areas, in the interests of conservation or good townscape design have been unsuccessful owing to the statutory obligation for signs to be of specified dimensions, colours and locations. Recent helpful suggestions are given in Davis (1993). Yet a trenchant criticism of more recent 'enhancement' schemes is that they merely add clutter to historic townscapes, particularly by the use of unsuitable street paving materials and street furniture. The proliferation of catalogues of 'heritage' castings for lighting, seating, litter bins and bollards, and the indiscriminate use of these items throughout the country, has been condemned (Booth, 1993):

> Throughout Britain there seems to be a feeling that 'nineteenth-century' cast iron goes with all periods of townscape. The message that this is a quality environment is expressed by having the lettering picked out in gold. . . . At first this approach was individual, but its repetition throughout our historic towns serves more to destroy individuality than enhance it. (Newby, 1994, p. 221)

The issue of the significant change to character caused by the virtual removal of vehicular traffic has, however, rarely been addressed; improvements to pedestrian environments and, particularly, tourist experiences thus brought about have outweighed considerations of pure character and appearance.

A recent questionnaire of local authority conservation practice suggested that of 289 responding authorities in Britain, just over 1000 pedestrianization schemes were reported as 'enhancements', with a further 300 street furniture schemes. Landscaping, building development, façade refurbishment and other schemes together totalled only some 650 schemes (Jones and Larkham, 1993, Figure 6.1). This highlights the perceived importance (to planners at least) of a traffic-free environment in conserved areas ever since the first such scheme in Norwich in the late 1960s. This is usually restricted to town centres, although the problems of through traffic, on-street parking and incorporation of traffic-calming measures are important in residential and village areas. Indeed, traffic flows and related issues such as car parking are central to both the continued functioning, and the character and appearance, of the majority of conservation areas.

Where the Highway Authority is investing in 'improvements', these usually relate only to safety, parking and traffic flow issues, often at the expense of visual character. This limitation has been highly damaging to the historic character and appearance of conservation areas. To avoid this, most district planning authorities consider that a good working relationship between themselves and the Highway Authority is essential. Yet many districts report little or no contact with the Highway Authority, and many, such as Stratford-upon-Avon, complain of poor workmanship, the use of inferior materials and poor results even within nationally significant conservation areas. Likewise, the reinstatement of surfaces, especially of special finish and expensive material, by statutory undertakers has long been a particular problem. The recent privatization of many statutory undertakers and the rise of other major undertakers, such as cable television companies, is also reportedly leading to problems.

Yet traffic improvements can be secured without compromising area character. Traffic management schemes for College Green and Queen's Square in Bristol have been achieved with integral conservation elements through close liaison between departments, which enabled conflicting aims of aesthetic improvement and efficient traffic movement to be reconciled. Norwich likewise has good interdisciplinary cooperation, with teams composed of engineers, landscape architects and conservation officers even able to adjust schemes on site to suit the exact peculiarities of a street (Jones and Larkham, 1993, pp. 97–98; Davies, 1993, p. 24).

The example of façadism

Even within designated conservation areas, and even affecting listed buildings, a relatively recent trend in development has tended to devalue historic structures. This is the practice of 'façadism': developing a wholly new structure to modern design and standards behind the retained front wall of an older building (Saunders, 1986; Barrett and Larkham, 1994). This has been particularly marked in central urban areas and affects buildings particularly of the Victorian period.

It is argued that the visual impact on the townscape is minimized by preservation of the existing façade. The number of these conversions already existing is surprisingly large and many cannot be identified as such from the street. This is not an entirely modern phenomenon, as examples of refronting are known from the Georgian period onwards. In Solihull High Street, a conservation area designated in 1968, there has been very little pressure to build completely new buildings, but seven planning applications were made proposing the retention of façades. All these examples of façadism were approved by the Planning Committee. In only one case was there a problem: the application in 1973 in which the developer, a London-based property company, wished to build a replica of the existing façade while the local planning officers wished the original façade to be retained. Because of this conflict, the developer withdrew from the project (Larkham, 1986). Yet in central Birmingham there have been significant conflicts over this tactic, leading to appeals to the Secretary of State against local refusals of schemes. These appeals have been upheld, leading to significant numbers of façadist schemes being developed contrary to local policy and wishes (Barrett, 1993; Barrett and Larkham, 1994).

During the 1980s, Birmingham attempted to develop its conservation strategy for the city centre, to initiate a stronger negotiating position concerning the form of redevelopment, and to demand the greater retention of historic structures. In 1986 the authority had stated its position of wanting refurbishment as the preferred option, seeing façadism as the last resort, with a desire to retain more interiors (Birmingham City Council, 1986). Negotiation on a scheme for 75–77 Colmore Row, carried out in 1986, obtained substantially more retention of rooms, stairs and interior features than the previous façadist schemes in Birmingham – an important success for the City's planners. However, following this, an application was submitted for a large redevelopment at 55–73 Colmore Row by Barclays Bank. The scheme involved the demolition of all but the façades of the Victorian Italianate palazzo-styled buildings owned by the bank along Colmore Row, Church Street and part of Barwick Street. The authority wanted greater retention of the building, along the line of the earlier scheme at 75–77 Colmore Row. However, the application was not determined and was taken to Appeal following a breakdown in negotiations between the developer and the authority. The scheme was granted on Appeal, with the inspector indicating that the scheme satisfied conservation objectives, concluding that the façades alone were of real importance in satisfying conservation aims, and that the proposed buildings provided an economic reuse of the site. The decision to allow this façadism was based on the presumption in favour of development at the national legislative level and the relatively low emphasis even then placed on Victorian architecture in the national context. This illustrated the differences in opinion concerning the worth of Victorian architecture between the local planners and the DoE. The authority did manage to secure the retention of the Banking Hall, but failed to win the desired greater retention of internal features (Barrett and Larkham, 1994).

There are many criticisms of façadism. One philosophical objection is that it may be seen as having little regard for the historic totality of the building, leading to the loss of important interior features, or the townscape, which can lead to the loss of the townscape 'grain' via plot amalgamation (Saunders, 1986). Façadism thus gives a misrepresented view of the townscape: indeed, it 'makes a complete nonsense of the concept of conservation. It is ridiculous to have a street made up of historic front walls' (R. Bearman of the Stratford Society, quoted in Beard, 1982). Current guidance on conservation areas by English Heritage and the recent draft Planning Policy Guidance Note on conservation areas and listed buildings both contain an implicit presumption against façadism, based on concern for the stability of structures during such operations and an apparent philosophical antipathy towards the practice, which is becoming increasingly widely held among conservation planners (English Heritage, 1993; DoE and DNH, 1993). Yet an authoritative commentary on these documents strongly suggests that this presumption is without legal basis: structural problems can be overcome through planning conditions and obligations, while

> the second basis for the implicit 'presumption against façadism' is really a 'philosophical antipathy' to the practice. In terms of pure architectural/ conservation theory a view of this kind can, of course, be justified in an academic context. However, the planning system (even when dealing with conservation

interests) is concerned with rather more than just architectural theory and academic fashions . . . if such a purist view of this sort would involve action which has no foundation in law then it is clear that the planning system cannot condone an approach which would involve *ultra vires* action. (Linklaters & Paines, 1993, pp. 6–7)

Are Conservation, Planning and Heritage Irreconcilable?

It has been shown that the concept of 'heritage' contains within it some contradictory concepts. Particularly within UK legal usage, there has long been a conception that conservation and preservation are two different and mutually irreconcilable entities. This is shown by the repeated usage, for conservation areas, of the words 'preserve or enhance'. The 'or' is a deliberate legal usage, persisting through several Acts and campaigns to amend the wording to 'preserve and enhance'; for example at the London Conservation Areas Conference in 1992 (see also Linklaters & Paines, 1993, pp. 20–21). The exploitation element of 'heritage' also tends to contradict both preservation and conservation; in particular, the trends towards 'museumification' or 'Disneyfication' have been of particular concern to many critics (*Heritage Outlook*, 1982; Worskett, 1982b; Lumley, 1988). In many cases involving relatively recent developments, particularly in the postmodern period, there are concerns that the original features which led to value being attached to areas or buildings have been lost. Originality and verisimilitude have lost; pastiche and replication have won. Indeed, it is clear that many of these cases of pastiche and replication are explicitly part of that 'double-coding' which characterizes postmodernism in architecture, according to Charles Jencks (1992), its most vociferous champion.

It is also clear that there have been many successes in planning for the heritage. This is particularly so for identifiable city centre tourist destinations, where (a) heritage tourism capitalizes on the already existing resources of the historic city; (b) tourist use of the existing infrastructure and services of the city will incur only marginal costs; and (c) a relatively small investment will create employment in urban areas with few alternatives (Ashworth and Tunbridge, 1990). This has been shown to be true in Canterbury, although this tourist-dependent city economy has policies dating to 1983 and there is an absence of a long-term and identifiable tourism strategy for the 1990s (Page, 1992).

Yet although increasing wealth and leisure time have led to increasing tourism, which has acted as a spur to heritage planning, the relationship between planning, heritage and tourism is one of paradox (Ryan, 1990, Chapter 7; Urry, 1990, Chapter 6). Crowds conflict with area character and appearance, and with building integrity: some National Trust properties are forced to issue timed tickets as building structures cannot cope with the weight of so many visitors, while the wear of feet erodes floors in many historic structures. But crowds also bring prosperity to fund refurbishment.

It is the extremes of tourism – sudden numbers or sudden wealth – which can do most harm. Tourism also conflicts with culture, resulting often in revalued or sanitized history, as purveyed in many 'heritage parks' and city centres (for example, Hewison, 1987; Newby, 1994).

But the response of conservation planning to such trends and pressures is problematic. In the UK, with a market economy and well-developed planning system, much 'heritage' is provided by bodies such as museum trusts and governmental organizations (see Table 6.1, for example; few of the attractions listed are owned by private heritage operators), over whom individual local planning authorities have relatively little control. More control can be exerted over property developers and designers through the conservation system described above, and its invaluable adjunct, the standard development control system. In this forum, debates over originality and related theoretical or philosophical issues carry little weight and, as has been shown, there is a clear tendency for the historical townscape to become increasingly a recreation, pastiche or façade.

However, it can be seen from this discussion of UK conservation planning that the legislative approach to conservation is wholly separate to that for all other planning activity, and this is a potential cause of problems. Aspects of this theme are discussed in Jewkes (1993, pp. 417–422) and Linklaters & Paines (1993, especially pp. 4–5). This separation is most clearly shown in the 1990 revision of the Planning Acts, which produced a Town and County Planning Act and a separate Planning (Listed Buildings and Conservation Areas) Act, and by the creation in 1992 of a new Department of National Heritage, although its heritage functions cannot be wholly divorced from the planning functions retained by the Department of the Environment. The legal encouragement to designate areas and buildings, their (undefined) special interest and the enhancement of areas in particular is one system. The day-to-day development control planning system is a separate system; yet they overlap where areas are designated as conservation areas. Here, 'special attention' must be paid to the examination of development proposals. It is also evident that, although many local planning authorities employ highly trained conservation officers, not only are they most frequently used to give advice to development-control sections, but their status and career paths are uncertain and conservation budgets are among the earliest cutbacks in times of recession (Jones and Larkham, 1993).

From the confusions which have been demonstrated in this chapter – between legal and lay interpretations, the actions on the ground resulting from the interaction of a conservation system with the remainder of the planning system and the all-embracing problem of a lack of coherent conservation philosophy – the UK should not be viewed as a model of conservation planning. Nevertheless, conservation of sorts has been contained within our legal system since the 1882 Ancient Monuments Act and, despite some key losses of buildings and areas, significant parts of our built heritage retain a recognizable historic ambience. Because of the intellectual and emotional confusions surrounding conservation, heritage and tourism, perhaps this is the success of our system. Regardless of the 'originality' debate, heritage tourism remains a popular activity (see Table 6.1); and most towns have retained significant amounts of their heritage identity to satisfy the majority of residents and visitors alike.

Acknowledgements

The ideas in this chapter have developed in particular from a number of recent collaborative ventures, and I should like to acknowledge the influence of Professor Greg Ashworth, Professor Joan Vilagrasa, Dr Andrew Jones and Heather Barrett. Work on this chapter was supported by the Faculty of the Built Environment, University of Central England.

References

Ashworth, G. J. (1991) *Heritage Planning*. Groningen: Geo Pers.
Ashworth, G. J. and Tunbridge, J. E. (1990) *The Tourist-Historic City*, London: Belhaven.
Bar-Hillel, M. (1991) Conservationists' nightmare or developers' dream? *Chartered Surveyor Weekly*, 14 March, p. 22.
Barker, A. (1976) *The Local Amenity Movement*. London: Civic Trust.
Barrett, H. (1993) Investigating townscape change and management in urban conservation areas. *Town Planning Review*, 64, 435–456.
Barrett, H. and Larkham, P. J. (1994) *Disguising Development: Façadism in City Centres*. Research Paper No. 11. Birmingham: Faculty of the Built Environment, University of Central England.
Beard, P. (1982) All the world's a stage . . . *Sunday Times*, 28 March, p. 14.
Birmingham City Council (1986) *Conservation in the Environment: A Strategy for Birmingham*. Draft report. Birmingham: Development Department, Birmingham City Council.
Booth, E. (1993) Enhancement in conservation areas. *The Planner*, 79, 22–23.
Briggs, A. (1975) The philosophy of conservation. *Journal of the Royal Society of Arts*, 123, 685–695.
Campbell, K. (1986) *Scotland's Conservation Areas: Retrospect and Prospect*. Research Paper No. 6. Edinburgh: Department of Town and Country Planning, Heriot-Watt University/Edinburgh College of Art.
Carr, E. A. J. (1994) Tourism and heritage: the pressures and challenges of the 1990s. In G. J. Ashworth and P. J. Larkham (eds) *Building a New Heritage: Tourism, Culture and Identity in the New Europe*. London: Routledge, pp. 5–68.
Charles, HRH Prince (1987) Speech given at the Mansion House, London, 1 December.
Cherry, G. E. (1975) The conservation movement. *The Planner*, 61, 3–5.
Civic Trust (1989) Conservation areas: the important 'Steinberg' test. *Heritage Outlook*, 9, 1.
Coupe, M. (1991) The character and appearance of conservation areas. *Conservation Bulletin*, 14, v–vi.

Cowan, P. (1963) Studies in the growth, change and ageing of buildings. *Transactions of the Bartlett Society*, 1, 55–84.

Crosland, A. (1971) *A Social Democratic Britain*. Fabian Tract No. 404. London: Fabian Society.

Crossman, R. H. S. (1975) *The Diaries of a Cabinet Minister*. Vol. 1: *Minister of Housing, 1964–66*. London: Hamish Hamilton and Jonathan Cape.

Cullen, G. (1961) *Townscape*. London: Architectural Press.

Davies, P. (1991) 'Improvements' in conservation areas. *Conservation Bulletin*, 13, 6.

Davis, C. J. (1993) *Traffic Measures in Historic Towns: An Introduction to Good Practice*. London and Bath: Civic Trust and English Historic Towns Forum.

Department of National Heritage (1992) Circular 1/92: *Responsibility for Conservation Policy and Casework* (also published as Department of the Environment Circular 20/92). London: HMSO.

Department of the Environment (1987) Circular 8/87: *Historic Buildings and Conservation Areas – Policy and Practice*. London: HMSO.

Department of the Environment (1989) *Listed Buildings and Conservation Areas*. Consultation paper. London: DoE.

Department of the Environment (1991) *Planning Policy Guidance: General Policy and Principles*. Consultation paper on draft revision of PPG 1. London: DoE.

Department of the Environment and Department of the National Heritage (1993) Draft Planning Policy Guidance Note 15: *Historic Buildings and Conservation Areas*. London: DoE and DNH.

Dron, T. (1991) Risen ghosts. *Thoroughbred & Classic Cars*, September, 26–31.

English Heritage (1993) *Conservation Area Practice*. London: English Heritage.

English Historic Towns Forum (1992) *Townscape in Trouble*. Bath: EHTF.

Esher, L. (1981) *A Broken Wave: The Rebuilding of England 1940–1980*. London: Allen Lane.

Eversley, D. (1974) Conservation for the minority. *Built Environment*, 3, 14–15.

Faulkner, P. A. (1978) Definition and evaluation of the historic heritage; Is preservation possible? Preservation within a philosophy (Bossom Lectures). *Journal of the Royal Society of Arts*, 126, 452–80.

Ferguson, C. M. (1990) Steinberg reconsidered. *Journal of Planning and Environment Law*, January, 8–10.

Fleming, S. C. and Short, J. R. (1984) Committee rules OK? An examination of planning committee action on officer recommendations. *Environment and Planning A*, 16, 965–973.

Georgian Group (1992) *Stratford-upon-Avon*. London: Georgian Group.

Graves, P. and Ross, S. (1991) Conservation areas: a presumption to conserve. *Estates Gazette*, 9137, 108–110.

Hamshere, J. D. (1991) Regeneration catalysts or exclusion zones? *Town and Country Planning*, 60, 247–248.

Harvey, J. H. (1993) The origin of listed buildings. *Transactions of the Ancient Monuments Society*, 37, 1–20.

Hendry, J. (1993) Conservation areas in Northern Ireland: an alternative approach. *Town Planning Review*, 64, 415–435.

Heritage Outlook (1982) Letters following publication of Worskett (1982b). *Heritage Outlook*, 2, 80–81.

Hewison, R. (1987) *The Heritage Industry: Britain in a Climate of Decline*. London: Methuen.

Horne, M. (1993) The listing process in Scotland and the statutory protection of vernacular building types. *Town Planning Review*, 64, 375–393.

114   *Peter J. Larkham*

House of Lords (1992) Judgment in the South Lakeland Case. London: HMSO.
Hubbard, P. (1993) The value of conservation: a critical review of behavioural research. *Town Planning Review*, 64, 359–373.
Jarman, D. (1992) Drawing the line on conservation areas. *Planning*, 965, 16–17.
Jencks, C. A. (1992) *The Language of Post-Modern Architecture*. London: Academy Editions.
Jewkes, P. (1993) Protecting the historic built environment. *Journal of Planning and Environment Law*, May, 417–422.
Jones, A. N. and Larkham, P. J. (1993) *The Character of Conservation Areas*. London: Royal Town Planning Institute.
Jones, M. (ed.) (1990) *Fake? The Art of Deception*. London: British Museum Publications.
Journal of Planning and Environment Law Bulletin (1991) Conservation areas – the duty under Section 277(8) of the Town and Country Planning Act 1971. *Journal of Planning and Environment Law Bulletin*, March, 3–4.
Larkham, P. J. (1985) *Voluntary Amenity Societies and Conservation Planning*. Working Paper No. 30. Birmingham: Department of Geography, University of Birmingham.
Larkham, P. J. (1986) Conservation, planning and morphology in West Midlands conservation areas, 1968–1984. Unpublished PhD thesis. Birmingham: Department of Geography, University of Birmingham.
Larkham, P. J. (1990) Conservation and the management of historical townscapes. In T. R. Slater (ed.) *The Built Form of Western Cities*. Leicester: Leicester University Press, pp. 349–369.
Larkham, P. J. (1992) Conservation and the changing urban landscape. *Progress in Planning*, 37, 83–181.
Larkham, P. J. and Freeman, M. (1988) Twentieth-century British commercial architecture. *Journal of Cultural Geography*, 9, 1–16.
Light, D. and Prentice, R. (1994) Who consumes the heritage product? Implications for European heritage tourism. In G. J. Ashworth and P. J. Larkham (eds) *Building a New Heritage: Tourism, Culture and Identity in the New Europe*. London: Routledge, pp. 90–116.
Linklaters & Paines (1993) *Revisions to Policy on Listed Buildings and Conservation Areas: Response to Consultation Draft PPG 15*. London: Linklaters (unpublished).
Lock, D. (1993) Bletchley site makes history. Letter to the Editor, *Planning*, 1012, 2.
Long, A. R. (1975) Participation and the community. *Progress in Planning*, 5, 61–134.
Lowe, P. D. (1977) Amenity groups and equity: a review of local environmental pressure groups in Britain. *Environment and Planning A*, 9, 35–58.
Lowenthal, D. (1985) *The Past Is a Foreign Country*. Cambridge: Cambridge University Press.
Lumley, R. (ed.) (1988) *The Museum Time Machine: Putting Cultures on Display*. London: Routledge.
Meinig, D. W. (1979) The beholding eye. In D. W. Meinig (ed.) *The Interpretation of Ordinary Landscapes*. New York: Oxford University Press, pp. 33–48.
Millichap, D. (1989a) Conservation areas and Steinberg – the Inspectorate's response. *Journal of Planning and Environment Law*, July, 499–504.
Millichap, D. (1989b) Conservation areas – Steinberg and after. *Journal of Planning and Environment Law*, April, 233–240.
Millichap, D. (1992) Neglected area of conservation law. *Planning*, 965, 17.
Millichap, D. (1993) Exceptions to the rule. *Planning*, 1002, 17.

Ministry of Housing and Local Government (1969) Development Control Policy Note 7: *Preservation of Historic Buildings and Areas*. London: HMSO.

Minoprio, A. and Spencely, H. (1946) *Worcester Plan: An Outline Development Plan for the City of Worcester*. Worcester: City Council.

Morton, D. (1993) Making sense of history. *Planning*, 1010, 6–7.

Morton, D. (1994) The designation debate. In P. J. Larkham (ed.) *Conservation Areas: Issues and Management*. Conference Proceedings Series, Faculty of the Built Environment, University of Central England, 7–16.

Morton, D. M. (1991) Conservation areas: has saturation point been reached? *The Planner*, 77, 5–8.

Mynors, C. (1984) Conservation areas: protecting the familiar and cherished local scene. *Journal of Planning and Environment Law*. March and April, 144–157; 235–247.

Nairn, I. (1955) *Outrage*. London: Architectural Press.

Newby, P. T. (1994) The significance of tourism for heritage conservation. In G. J. Ashworth and P. J. Larkham (eds) *Building a New Heritage: Tourism, Culture and Identity in the New Europe*. London: Routledge, pp. 206–228.

Noakes, T. (1991) Listing and the urban context. *Urban Design Quarterly*, September.

Page, S. (1992) Managing tourism in a small historic city. *Town and Country Planning*, July/August, 208–211.

Planning (1992) Campaign for local view on listing gains ground. *Planning*, 992 (30 October), 4.

Price, C. (1981) The built environment: the case against conservation. *The Environmentalist*, 1, 39–41.

Reade, E. (1991) The little world of Upper Bangor. Part 1: How many conservation areas are slums? *Town and Country Planning*, 60, 340–343.

Reade, E. (1992a) The little world of Upper Bangor. Part 2: Professionally prestigious projects or routine public administration? *Town and Country Planning*, 61, 25–27.

Reade, E. (1992b) The little world of Upper Bangor. Part 3: What is planning for anyway? *Town and Country Planning*, 61, 44–47.

Relph, E. (1976) *Place and Placelessness*. London: Pion.

Relph, E. (1982) The landscapes of the consumer society. In B. Sadler and A. Carlson (eds) *Environmental Aesthetics: Essays in Interpretation*. Western Geographical Series No. 20. Victoria: Department of Geography, University of Victoria, pp. 47–65.

Relph, E. (1987) *The Modern Urban Landscape*. London: Croom Helm.

Reynolds, J. P. (1975) Heritage Year in Britain: the aims and objectives of conservation. *Town Planning Review*, 46, 355–364.

Robertson, M. *et al.* (1993) Listed buildings: the national resurvey of England. *Transactions of the Ancient Monuments Society*, 37, 21–94.

Robinson, J. M. (1991) Civic offence. *Architects' Journal*, 10 July, 24–27.

Rock, D. (1974) Conservation: a confusion of ideas. *Built Environment*, 3, 363–366.

Ross, M. (1991) *Planning and the Heritage*. London: Spon.

Ryan, C. (1990) *Recreational Tourism*. London: Routledge.

Saunders, M. (1986) Façadism. *Transactions of the Ancient Monuments Society*, 36, 227–240.

Smith, D. (1969) The Civic Amenities Act. *Town Planning Review*, 40, 149–162.

Stanley, N. (1991) The Bath Society case – a Pandora's box? *Journal of Planning and Environment Law*, November, 1014–1015.

Stansfield, K. (1991) Imitation or imagination? *Public Service and Local Government*, July/August, 20–21.

Stubbs, M. and Lavers, A. (1991) Steinberg and after: decision-making and development control in conservation areas. *Journal of Planning and Environment Law*, January, 9–14.

Suddards, R. W. (1988a) *Listed Buildings*, 2nd edn. London: Sweet and Maxwell.

Suddards, R. W. (1988b) Listed buildings: have we listed too far? *Journal of Planning and Environment Law*, August, 523–528.

Suddards, R. W. and Morton, D. M. (1991) The character of conservation areas. *Journal of Planning and Environment Law*, November, 1011–1013.

Sutcliffe, A. R. (1981) Why planning history? *Built Environment*, 7, 65–67.

Urry, J. (1990) *The Tourist Gaze: Leisure and Travel in Contemporary Societies*. London: Sage.

Vilagrasa, J. and Larkham, P. J. (1992) *Redeveloping and Historic City Centre: Worcester, 1947–1990*. Occasional Publication No. 37. Birmingham: School of Geography, University of Birmingham.

Ward, R. (1992) Letter to the Editor. *Journal of Planning and Environment Law*, March, 234.

Watson, I. (1991) Demolition upheld in No. 1 Poultry decision. *Chartered Surveyor Weekly*, 28 March, 73.

Whitehand, J. W. R. (1984) *Rebuilding Town Centres: Developers, Architects and Styles*. Occasional Publication No. 19. Birmingham: Department of Geography, University of Birmingham.

Williams, M. (1990) Conservation areas: preparing the ground for reform. *Estates Gazette*, **9002**, 57–60.

Witt, S. J. C. and Fleming, S. C. (1984) *Planning Councillors in an Area of Growth: Little Power But All the Blame?* Geographical Paper No. 85. Reading: Department of Geography, University of Reading.

Worskett, R. (1975) Great Britain: progress in conservation. *Architectural Review*, 157, 9–18.

Worskett, R. (1982a) New buildings in historic areas 1: conservation: the missing ethic. *Monumentum*, **25**, 155–161.

Worskett, R. (1982b) I'm worried about Walt. *Heritage Outlook*, **2**, 34–35.

7

Heritage as Informal Education

Duncan Light

Historic buildings and monuments have long been recognized as having educational and inspirational value and have been popular destinations from the earliest days of tourism. While some were intent on formal study of the past, many people sought a more informal understanding and appreciation of what they saw. But heritage sites do not readily explain themselves and need to be made intelligible to their visitors. Alongside the growth of tourist consumption arose an activity dedicated to making heritage places understandable and meaningful; this activity subsequently became known as heritage interpretation.

By the second half of the twentieth century, heritage interpretation had become a formal, professional and widespread activity. Popular interest in the past attained unprecedented levels, particularly during the so-called 'heritage boom' of the 1980s. Increasingly, visitors to heritage sites sought to learn about and understand the past and, moreover, were prepared to use their leisure time for this purpose. Heritage interpretation underwent a similar boom and is now a central component of modern heritage tourism.

This chapter considers the twin themes of heritage interpretation and informal education, in the context of the modern 'heritage industry'. The two themes are closely linked and may indeed be considered as different sides of the same coin: heritage interpretation employs a range of presentational techniques as a means of facilitating informal education during leisure time. In this discussion 'informal education' refers to that self-motivated, voluntary, exploratory, non-coercive learning and understanding which can take place during a visit to a heritage site. Such informal education may be distinguished from more formal, school-based education in a number of ways (Lewis, 1980; Hammitt, 1984; Screven, 1986). First, there is no compulsion on the visitor to learn, or even try to learn, during their visit. Learning, which is entirely voluntary, depends on the motives of the visitor, who is free to decide how to use his/her time. Secondly, informal education takes place during leisure time and within a leisure environment. It is very different from formal education, which is structured, curriculum based and takes place in a classroom. Thirdly, in a formal school environment the main means of communication is the teacher. In the informal learning context of a heritage site the teacher is replaced by various forms of interpretive media. Overall, the role of interpretation at a heritage site is to provide visitors with an opportunity to learn. It clearly cannot compel such learning.

While the focus of this chapter is on heritage sites, considerable reference is made to research studies based on museums. This is justified on the grounds that many museums, particularly those recently established, are increasingly orienting themselves towards leisure and tourism. Together with more 'traditional' types of heritage site, they now form central components of the modern heritage tourism industry. Moreover, there is considerable overlap between principles and practices of heritage interpretation and those of museum presentation. Museums are increasingly concerned with issues of communication and informal education for people who are visiting during leisure time and are using heritage interpretation to cope with this demand.

The Origins of Heritage Interpretation

Early educational interest in historic sites

Travellers have always sought information about the places they visit, and the educational roles of historic sites have long been recognized. Travel to historic sites became an established part of the informal education of the English landed classes (Dent, 1975). From the sixteenth century onwards the association between historic buildings, travel and education was well established in the form of the 'Grand Tour' – 'a tour of certain cities and places in western Europe undertaken primarily, but not exclusively, for education and pleasure' (Towner, 1985, p. 301). This Grand Tour became an integral part of the education of the English aristocracy. It embraced many of the historic buildings and monuments of Europe, culminating in Italy, where these early tourists spent their time studying the legacy of classical civilization. The relationship between visiting historic places and informal education was clearly apparent at this time but such travel was the preserve of an elite. In the eighteenth century the Grand Tour was undertaken by only 0.2 to 0.3 per cent of the English population (Towner, 1985).

The influx of 'Grand Tourists' generated services, one of which was the provision of guided tours for travellers seeking to understand the places they visited. Many British expatriates offered their services as guides to English visitors. By the mid-eighteenth century, Rome had been systematized into a six-day tour of the city and its antiquities (Feifer, 1985), and guiding offered a regular source of employment at some places for over four centuries (Towner, 1985). By this time, the beginnings of what is now termed heritage interpretation were evident. The essential elements are a resource, either natural or human-made; a visitor seeking to learn; and the intervention, either directly or indirectly, of an interpreter.

When the Napoleonic wars curtailed travel in Europe, would-be British tourists turned their attention to their own country. Around the same time, the Romantic revival generated interest, especially among writers, poets and artists, in wild and remote places, and in ruins from previous eras. Wales, Scotland and some of the more inaccessible parts of England rapidly became popular among travellers (Zaring, 1977). The Romantic 'travellers' had a desire to understand and appreciate what they encountered, but their preference for solitude meant that they eschewed guided tours. Instead, guidebooks and topographical descriptions rose to popularity as travellers recorded their observations for the benefit of those following them. The popularity of these books should not be underestimated: a guidebook to Raglan Castle, South Wales published in 1792 had run to its eleventh edition by 1829 (Kenyon, 1988).

Interest in visiting and learning about the past grew in the nineteenth century, particularly among the expanding middle class with its increasing access to leisure. The acute sense of dislocation felt by many people following urbanization and industrialization (Lowenthal, 1985) stimulated interest in historic places, which offered stability and comfort in an uncertain age. In this context historic places were increasingly preserved to allow people to visit them. An early example in Britain was the taking of ancient monuments into public guardianship after 1882. Once established, such monuments were opened for public access. Interpretation of such sites used both guidebooks and guided tours, although the former became known for their scholarly and inaccessible style.

Early museums and exhibitions

The nineteenth century was an important period for the establishment of museums. Early museums were designed to be imposing places, frequently resembling cathedrals, in which the visitor felt awe and reverence (Lewis, 1980; Horne, 1984; Urry, 1990). Their concern was scholarship and curatorship, not presentation; the display of objects, not the communication of ideas (Lewis, 1980). Their collections were expected to speak for themselves and there was little attempt to make them understandable to visitors – indeed Lewis questioned whether museums of this period were ever intended to educate the populace.

In the mid-nineteenth century international exhibitions rose to prominence in London. These exhibitions were places of display and spectacle, where themes of commerce, industry and empire were presented to a mass audience. Greenhalgh (1989) observed that the organizers of such events usually intended formal educational missions for them. However, they were frequently appropriated for popular entertainment, something the organizers had not intended and were far from happy about. In France, a similar practice of *Expositions Universelles* was established from 1855 onwards. Again the aim was mass education, but unlike in Britain where education and entertainment were seen as dichotomous, in France they were regarded as naturally complementary. The *Exposition* of 1878 emphasized display media as a means of educating; it featured elaborate reconstructions of other places and working displays. The 1900 Paris *Exposition* included a reconstruction of the medieval city with hundreds of people in authentic costume (Greenhalgh, 1989). These *Expositions*, with their elements of informal education, entertainment, fun and enjoyment, and the use of unusual and stimulating media, are clear harbingers of modern heritage interpretation.

One Scandinavian visitor, Artur Hazelius, to the London Great Exhibition of 1851 and the Paris *Exposition* of 1878 was particularly inspired by the techniques of display and presentation encountered there (Aldridge, 1989). Hazelius, aware that traditional folk life in Sweden was under threat from industrialization, planned to preserve traditional buildings and ways of life (Trinder, 1976). The result was Skansen Open Air Museum (the first of its kind in the world) in Stockholm, which opened in 1891 and can also be regarded as an antecedent of modern heritage interpretation (Phillips, 1989). The site had traditional rural buildings, guides dressed in historic costume, and performing musicians and dancers (Bennett, 1988). The open-air museum concept proved extremely popular and rapidly spread to the rest of Europe, and later to America. There it merged with a practice of nature interpretation and conservation which the American National Park Service had been using since the 1920s. These two sources – the open-air museum with its concern for the built environment in Europe, and the established practice of interpreting the natural environment in America – can be identified as the origins of modern heritage interpretation (Aldridge, 1989; Phillips, 1989).

The popularization of heritage interpretation

Until the latter half of the twentieth century, interpretation was an uncoordinated and unprofessionalized activity, which lacked a coherent philosophical basis. It was not until 1957 that a formal philosophy of heritage interpretation was expounded by Freeman Tilden, in a book entitled *Interpreting Our Heritage*. Tilden is frequently considered the 'father' of interpretation, although it is clear that he was not so much inventing a new activity as systematizing and formalizing, with considerable eloquence, a set of ideas and practices already in existence in both America and Europe.

Tilden defined interpretation as 'an educational activity which aims to reveal meanings and relationships through the use of original objects, by first-hand experience, and by illustrative media, rather than simply to communicate factual information' (1977, p. 8). In recognition of the importance of heritage places for leisure and tourism, interpretation was a means of explaining the history and significance of an historic site to the people who visited it, and of allowing them to achieve a better understanding.

Although Tilden emphasized that education was at the heart of interpretation, he was clearly thinking of informal education. He recognized that visitors to heritage sites were engaged in leisure activity – 'The man on holiday does not wish to be lectured' (1977, p. 111) – and that interaction with interpretation was voluntary (Sharpe, 1982). Tilden stressed that the aim of interpretation was not instruction (formal education between teacher and pupil) but provocation, and the revelation of the larger truth lying behind any simple statement of fact. Furthermore, interpretation was an activity that should 'capitalize on mere curiosity for the enrichment of the human mind and spirit' (1977, p. 8). Tilden offered a set of principles of good interpretation, of which probably the most important is the need for interpretation to be relevant and accessible to the people who use it.

Tilden identified interpretation as an altruistic activity – a public service (Sharpe, 1982) – but also acknowledged that it had secondary roles. One product of good interpretation was the enhanced protection of the resource: 'through interpretation, understanding; through understanding, appreciation; through appreciation, protection' (Tilden, 1977, p. 38).

The early development of heritage interpretation in Britain

Following the publication of Tilden's book, heritage interpretation was widely promoted and adopted. The basic elements of the activity – a resource, a visitor and an interpreter acting as a broker between the two (Uzzell, 1985) – were largely unchanged. What distinguished heritage interpretation in the postwar years from earlier interpretation was the existence of a formal philosophy of 'informal education', and the greatly increased level of the activity. The rapid development of interpretation must be viewed in the context of the rapid expansion of leisure, tourism and travel in the postwar years. Unlike the Grand Tour, visiting heritage places now became a more general, though still socially selective, form of tourism, at a time of increased leisure time and personal mobility. Interpretation was a service to cater for the growing numbers of people who wished to visit, understand and appreciate their past. Largely designed for visual consumption, interpretation's role was to complement what Urry (1990, 1992) has termed the 'tourist gaze'.

In Britain, the early development of interpretation was at sites in the natural environment but interpretation soon departed from Tilden's ideal of altruistic, informal education (Light, 1991a). In the postwar decades, the scale of rural recreation was perceived as a threat to the countryside and some British interpreters viewed interpretation as a solution to many conservation problems (Stansfield, 1983). This position was based on Tilden's claim that interpretation could lead to the protection of the resource. Interpretation was to manage visitors in the rural environment (Prince, 1982a, 1983; Uzzell, 1989). The two forms were 'soft' management, which utilized interpretation to explain to visitors the problems and pressures facing the countryside; and 'hard' management, which attempted to attract visitors to specific interpretive facilities in the countryside. The former strategy aimed at gaining sympathy for conservation, the latter at relieving visitor pressure on more sensitive rural areas. The two most widely employed media were the visitor centre and the nature trail.

Education was still central to interpretation of the countryside, and as Prince (1982a) noted, effective education was central to the use of interpretation as a conservation tool. However, the nature of this education had departed from Tilden's original ideals of altruistic, informal education. For example, the Countryside Commission (Aldridge, 1975) argued that its ultimate aim was to communicate and *explain* a conservation message (Phillips, 1989). The emphasis on 'explaining' suggests that Tilden's ideals of revelation and provocation had been lost; hence, Goodey (1979, 1982) argued that interpretation in Britain had emerged in a more formal and rigid way than was originally intended.

Interpretation of built heritage took longer to become established, but the European Architectural Heritage Year in 1975 did much to promote interpretation of the built environment (Stansfield, 1983). Urban interpretation largely mirrored its rural counterpart, with the emphasis on projecting a conservation message. At a time when postwar modernization and reconstruction was radically altering the character of the built environment (Hewison, 1987), this need seemed all the more urgent. The two main media of countryside interpretation were adapted to urban contexts as heritage centres and town trails (Light, 1991a).

European Architectural Heritage Year also acted as a stimulus to heritage education, the urban equivalent of environmental education. Both environmental and heritage education are distinct from interpretation in that they are more formal and school-based (Hammitt, 1984) and, as Aldridge (1989) noted, they only shared general objectives. However, the growth of formal heritage education was a further stimulus to the provision of interpretive facilities at built environment sites, although it was not until the 1980s that interpretation of the built environment became a widespread activity. At around this time, museums also began to define themselves as educational institutions with visitor learning as a central part of their mission (Lewis, 1980; Shettel, 1989). Techniques and practices of interpretation were increasingly adopted in museums (Stansfield, 1983), while heritage interpretation also used some aspects of the museum display philosophy.

Interpretation and the Contemporary Heritage Industry

The heritage boom, and its influence on interpretation

The 1980s witnessed the rapid emergence of the 'heritage industry' (Hewison, 1987), largely the response of the leisure industry to public demand. Visits to heritage attractions rose substantially, from 52 million to 68 million between 1977 and 1991 (ETB, 1978; BTA/ETB, 1992). Consequently, there was a rapid increase in the number and range of heritage attractions open to the public. Between 1977 and 1991 the number of historic buildings increased from 1208 to 1932, a rise of 60 per cent (ETB, 1977; BTA/ETB, 1992), while the number of museums has almost doubled since 1971 (Merriman, 1991).

Two types of heritage attraction in particular – heritage centres and modern museums – rose to prominence in the 1980s. Heritage centres marked a departure from the traditional concept of a museum, being described by Hewison (1989) as museums without collections. The emphasis in such centres was on presentation and interpretation of a place, person or event. The growth of independent museums in the 1980s was largely led by the private sector and was, like heritage centres, oriented towards the tourist industry. Consequently, they avoided the intimidating image traditionally associated with museums and aimed instead at dynamic, visually appealing and user-friendly presentations (Capstick, 1985; Urry, 1990).

These developments had significant implications for heritage interpretation. First, there was an explosive growth in interpretation of built heritage. Not only are there more heritage attractions, but more of them employ heritage interpretation. Moreover, this interpretation is being encountered (or consumed) by more people than ever before, who are more familiar with, and expect, interpretation when they visit heritage sites. Without doubt, interpretation is now a central corollary of the tourist gaze, and the desire to gaze upon history (Urry, 1990).

Secondly, a greater range of types of heritage are currently being interpreted and overall there is greater plurality and anti-elitism in the interpretive messages available to visitors to heritage sites. Whereas much early interpretation of the built environment was concerned with elite heritage – such as castles and stately homes – more recently there has been a boom in the presentation and interpretation of more vernacular and everyday subjects (Urry, 1990). The new generation of what Urry (1990) terms 'post-modern' museums focuses on an increasingly diverse and specialist range of subjects, especially industrial history (Hewison, 1987).

Thirdly, the heritage boom has acted to rejuvenate the informal educational role of interpretation (Light, 1991a). Unlike many sites in the countryside, most built heritage sites are not endangered by excessive visitor numbers (with obvious exceptions such as Stonehenge) – indeed many recent heritage centres and open-air museums have been designed and built specifically to accommodate large numbers of people. As a result interpretation at heritage sites no longer has visitor management and the need to communicate a conservation message as a primary concern; instead it is closer to Tilden's original ideal of altruistic education.

Indeed, in recent years learning, leisure and tourism have become more interlinked (Roggenbuck *et al.*, 1990; Urry, 1990; Martin and Mason, 1993). There is certainly a growing interest in education among both producers and consumers within the contemporary heritage industry. Many heritage attractions are being established with some degree of education as their *raison d'être*. For example, the Jorvik Viking Centre is managed by York Archaeological Trust, an educational charity which has 'as its prime objective the education of the public in archaeology' (Addyman and Gaynor, 1984, pp. 9–10). Similarly, the Ironbridge Gorge Museum was established as an educational trust (West, 1988), and Wigan Pier Heritage Centre started with three full-time teachers and a range of educational facilities for schools (Lewis, 1988).

Public sector agencies have similarly been charged with educating the public. English Heritage has among its statutory duties to 'promote the public's enjoyment of, and advance their knowledge of, ancient monuments and historic buildings' (Historic Buildings and Monuments Commission, 1984). In Wales, Cadw (Welsh Historic Monuments) similarly aims to 'maintain and present to the public for their appreciation, education and enjoyment the monuments in the care of the Secretary of State' (Cadw, 1992). In this context the formal educational market for heritage attractions is buoyant – Cooper and Latham (1988) estimated that 12 million school visits are made to heritage attractions each year.

Informal education as a motive for visiting heritage sites

A degree of learning also appears to be increasingly important to the consumers of heritage sites (Light and Prentice, 1994). Underpinning the growth of the heritage 'industry' in the 1980s has been a huge increase in popular interest in the past. While for many people heritage sites may simply represent a pleasant day out, many others may seek a better understanding of what they encounter. A range of research findings suggests that informal learning is both a motive for, and a requirement of, visiting heritage sites. Two types of research project are reviewed here: studies of the motives of visitors to heritage sites; and studies of how heritage sites (particularly museums) are perceived by their visitors and non-visitors.

Studies of the motives of visitors to heritage sites indicate that learning is an important component of such motives. From a review of literature over the period 1968–86, Thomas (1989) concluded that a significant proportion of visitors to heritage sites actively pursued heritage information or education. Summarizing a series of studies undertaken at ancient monuments in Wales in the mid-1980s, Thomas suggested that two broad reasons for visiting were

Table 7.1 Requirements of visitors to ancient monuments in Wales

To relax	20%
To be entertained	14%
To be informed	45%
To be educated	17%
Uncertain	4%

Sources: Thomas (1989); Herbert (1989).

apparent: a specific interest in castles and historic places, and a more general interest and sightseeing motive (see also Light and Prentice, 1994). Thomas (1989, p. 90) claimed that 'for a significant minority of visitors the pursuit of heritage information and education are primary motivating factors'.

Another part of the same study investigated requirements and expectations from visiting heritage sites (see Table 7.1). A large majority of visitors (62 per cent) indicated some degree of education as a requirement from their visit. However, the distinction between formal and informal education could hardly be clearer: relatively few visitors sought to be educated, but a majority sought to be informed. Herbert (1989, p. 198) commented: 'whereas a small majority seek to be "taught" about a site in any formal sense, there is a large group which is interested in acquiring some knowledge.'

Studies of the ways in which heritage sites are perceived by their visitors and non-visitors also suggest that education is seen as an important part of their roles. Prentice (1993) noted that large proportions of visitors at heritage sites, especially professionals and managerial workers, perceived their function to be either educational or informational. Prentice also established that a large majority of visitors favoured the provision of information at historic properties, which shows that visitors wanted to understand how people in the past had lived.

Research on perceptions of museums has produced similar results. Hood (1983) established that people who visited museums frequently were those seeking the opportunity to learn, the challenge of new experiences and worthwhile use of their leisure time. Among occasional and non-visitors, learning was not a requirement of their leisure time. Similarly, non-visitors to a museum in Hull (largely manual workers) considered museums to be boring and uninviting. A large majority regarded them as educational, suggesting that they found this association unattractive as they did not regard education as a legitimate use of their leisure time (Prince, 1985). In a study of public attitudes to museums, Merriman (1989, 1991) noted that frequent visitors to museums were almost unanimous (93 per cent) in the view that it was 'definitely' important to know about the past, while only 49 per cent of non-visitors said likewise. Frequent visitors were also likely to agree strongly (53 per cent) with the statement that museums were places where they learned a lot, but only 21 per cent of non-visitors said the same.

The evidence assembled here supports the claim that a desire for informal learning and understanding is a genuine reason for visiting heritage sites and museums (particularly among the middle classes). There have been several attempts to place this desire in an explanatory theoretical framework (Merriman, 1991).

A socio-psychological understanding of leisure (Driver and Tocher, 1979; Iso-Ahola, 1980, 1983; Prince, 1983; Dunn Ross and Iso-Ahola, 1991) has suggested that motives for leisure activities are goal driven and linked to the expected benefits or rewards to be gained from the activity. An individual will undertake those activities which, when successfully completed, produce a sense of competence, satisfaction and fulfilment. Activities which have previously been successful and fulfilling are more likely to be repeated, so prior experience and socialization are important influences. More specifically, a basic motivator for leisure activity is to seek new information and experiences (another is the desire to escape, or leave something behind).

For some visitors (especially those from the middle classes) a heritage site offers the rewards necessary to make it a worthwhile use of leisure time. For many visitors to heritage sites, some degree of understanding, appreciation and informal education will always be important components of the visit. Heritage sites, particularly their interpretive media, offer the challenge of encountering and successfully manipulating new information, and the reward of competence and understanding of the significance of the site and its history (Prince, 1983). The degree of informal learning sought from the visit will vary among individuals depending on, among other things, the prior level of interest and knowledge of the subject (Griggs and Alt, 1982); the motive for visiting (Alt and Griggs, 1984); and on the composition of the visitor group (McManus, 1987, 1988).

Merriman (1989, 1991) added a further perspective to this model. By drawing on the social theory of Bourdieu (1984), Merriman suggests that visiting heritage sites and museums is a way of demonstrating and affirming social status and position. People will seek to identify with some activities and groups, and to distinguish themselves from others (Walsh, 1992). One way of doing this is by the accumulation of 'cultural capital' appropriate to the image or lifestyle with which they wish to identify. Museums and heritage sites have high cultural associations and visiting them is linked with being 'cultured'. Thus, Merriman suggests, visiting museums and heritage sites is a way of acquiring cultural capital. In order to understand and appreciate a form of cultural production (such as a museum or heritage site) it is necessary to have experienced the socialization which provides the necessary 'cultural competence' (Walsh, 1992). Those who were not socialized in this way (who tend to be manual workers) will not possess this competence and so will exclude themselves from visiting (Merriman, 1991). However, leisure time and heritage visits may also be used for social advancement. With the growth of the middle classes in recent decades (Thrift, 1989), those wishing to demonstrate upward social mobility visit museums and heritage sites to improve their cultural capital (Merriman, 1991).

More specifically, heritage interpretation and informal education may be important elements of the process by which some individuals accumulate cultural capital at museums and heritage sites. For some, simply entering the site may be sufficient, but for others it may also be necessary to demonstrate assurance in understanding and appreciating the resource. To do this means paying at least some attention to interpretive facilities, and since most interpretation still relies on the written word, this involves reading and understanding. This is an important reason why heritage sites have a disproportionate appeal to the middle classes, for whom the written word is traditionally an important part of their culture (Prince, 1983), and who are able to extract information from text (Walsh, 1992). However, the expansion of secondary education has given more people the intellectual ability to make use of interpretation, while the general trend towards improving presentations at museums and heritage sites has made interpretation more accessible to visitors (Merriman, 1991).

Given these arguments, it might be expected that many visitors to heritage sites would see interpretive facilities as an important part of the visit. The evidence unequivocally supports this claim: recent research at heritage sites (Herbert, 1989; Light, 1991b; Prentice, 1993) has indicated that, in a variety of ways, interpretation is important to many of the people who visit these attractions. For example, a large majority of visitors notice interpretive media; generally upwards of 50 per cent examine them carefully and read what they look at; a large majority consider that interpretive displays have helped them to enjoy their visit; and visitors are almost unanimous in agreeing that interpretation has increased their understanding of the site. Clearly, those who want some degree of informal education from their visit are appropriating the interpretive facilities they encounter.

The evidence lends considerable empirical support to the claim that informal education is both an important motive of, and a requirement from, visiting heritage sites. Further, theoretical studies provide a fuller understanding of these motives. Interpretation provides a service which is required by many visitors to heritage sites, and many might be expected to have learnt something from their visit. However, although the desire for some degree of informal learning or understanding may be apparent, this does not necessarily mean that people do learn from their encounters with interpretation; in fact the educational effectiveness of interpretation has received very little attention, and is poorly understood. Some of the key issues relating to its effectiveness are addressed in the following section.

The Educational Impact of Heritage Interpretation

Changing conceptions of the learner

Much early provision of interpretation was based on a poor understanding of the people who used it. Many providers lost sight of the extent to which learning was self-motivated, informal, and undertaken during leisure time. While intended to have an educational role, many interpretive and museum presentations were designed with little consideration of the people who would use them. A frequent assumption of the designers of interpretation and exhibitions was that visitors would share their values, interests and understanding of the subject (Lewis, 1980; Hooper-Greenhill, 1988). This assumption was untenable, but the result was that many presentations made little attempt to communicate to an uninformed audience and were unintelligible to the non-specialist. In a powerful critique directed at museums, but which is equally applicable to much heritage interpretation, Lewis (1980) argued that modern museums were notable for their communicative incompetence. While they were catering effectively for informed visitors with specialist interests, they were far less effective for the public as a whole.

Similarly, both Prince (1982a) and Alt and Griggs (1984) contended that much interpretation and museum design adopted a model inappropriate to an informal educational environment. This model, known as behaviourism, emphasized stimulus–response relationships, and viewed learning as the response to a particular stimulus. Applied to interpretation, this model resulted in an emphasis on the interpretive medium – the stimulus – as the key factor in influencing learning (Prince, 1982a). Underpinning much exhibition design was the assumption that 'by organizing exhibition material in a certain way, a drive to learn will be set in operation and the visitor will learn in the way the exhibition designers intended' (Alt and Griggs, 1984, p. 386). Even if visitors did not visit a museum with an intent to learn, this model assumed that the nature of the displays would make them want to do so. A tenet of this approach was the setting of clear behavioural (learning) objectives, which visitors were expected to attain after encountering interpretive media (Screven, 1976; Shettel, 1989). If visitors failed to achieve these objectives, the fault was identified as being with the interpretation (Alt, 1977; Alt and Griggs, 1984).

Clearly, this model ascribes an essentially passive role to visitors, denies their free will, and sees them as unthinking responders to stimuli. Moreover, it assumes that visitors are a homogeneous group, whereas their reasons for visiting and their expectations differ. In particular, there is no recognition that visitors may visit a museum or heritage site with no intent to learn (Alt, 1977). Such a model was obviously inappropriate to heritage sites where learning is voluntary and informal. However, a consequence of this view of the learner was that much interpretation in Britain may not have been as educationally effective as its sponsors had intended, not necessarily because of bad design, but because too much was expected from visitors (Alt and Griggs, 1984).

More recently, there has been a reappraisal of the nature of visitors to heritage sites. The model of the visitor as a responder to stimuli has largely been replaced by a more dynamic model derived from cognitive psychology.

This emphasizes that learning is influenced by a number of visitor characteristics such as motivations and expectations; prior interest and experience; prior knowledge; and the importance of perception, with an emphasis on active exploration of an environment – rather than passive response (Alt, 1977; Hammitt, 1981, 1984; Prince, 1982a, 1982b; Alt and Griggs, 1984; Miles *et al.*, 1988). Such a model is more appropriate to voluntary learning in a leisure environment where people may have come for a variety of reasons.

A changing understanding of the visitor has led to attempts to redefine what interpretation can realistically be expected to achieve. Hammitt (1984) defined interpretation's role as that of 'familiarizing' users with a resource's facilities, opportunities and management policies; this familiarization is clearly a form of informal education. Lewis (1980) identified the strengths of regarding museums as free and non-coercive learning environments, and highlighted the potential of museums as 'facilitative' of learning for those who wish to learn. This principle applies equally to interpretation.

Visitors to heritage sites and museums are also now regarded as a differentiated group (Prentice, 1993). Miles (1986) identified three segments of museums visitor – a small, highly motivated group of people who will learn in any circumstances; a small group who will not be interested in any sort of educational experience; and a large intermediate segment with varying willingness to learn from their visit and who can be motivated to do so to some degree (see also Herbert, 1989). This schema is expanded in Table 7.2 to include the motives, requirements and likely interaction with interpretation of these three groups. Interpretation's role is to cater mainly for the third group (although it will obviously also be used by the first group) by providing opportunities for informal learning and understanding for visitors who require it. Interpretive media and messages need to be designed so as to facilitate effective communication for such an audience.

There is also greater recognition of the need for the providers of interpretation to know and understand their audience (Screven, 1986; Hooper-Greenhill, 1988; Ames, 1989; Stevens, 1989). Only when, for example, the extent of visitors' interest in a site, their requirements for understanding it better, and their level of background knowledge have been investigated, can the interpretation be designed to be appropriate to its users. This entails market research, which has an increasingly important role in the heritage tourism industry.

Education – or entertainment?

A further recent development within heritage interpretation is a much greater emphasis on the entertainment value of interpretive facilities (Light, 1991a) as a means of providing visitors with fun and enjoyment as part of an encounter with interpretation. In itself, this is not a recent development, as Sharpe (1982) observed: while entertainment was not an objective of interpretation, good

Table 7.2 Different segments of visitors to museums and heritage sites

Segment	Motives for visiting	Requirements from visit	Implications for interpretation
1. Highly motivated to learn (perhaps 5% of visitors)	To learn about and understand the history of the site	Detailed learning and understanding	Extensive attention and probably extensive learning
2. Can be motivated to learn	Various – but probably with some element of interest and curiosity in history and the past	Some degree of intellectual stimulation, informal learning and understanding. For some an element of entertainment and fun may also be important	At least some attention to interpretation and at least some learning, more so among more motivated individuals. Less motivated people can perhaps be motivated to pay more attention by well-designed interpretation
3. Not at all motivated to learn	Somewhere to take children; somewhere to pass a wet afternoon; somewhere to kill time	Few specific requirements or expectations	Little if any attention to interpretation; little or no learning

Source: Adapted from Miles (1986).

interpretation should be entertaining, in order to maintain the interest of an audience. However, the new generation of private sector heritage sites faces the need to be commercially successful and profitable in a competitive market. To this end, they place a very high priority on the entertainment value of interpretation not only to ensure the enjoyment and satisfaction of visitors but to maintain commercial viability.

This emphasis has produced radical changes in the interpretive media used at heritage sites, and many sites are adopting dynamic, exciting, multi-media presentations. Lumley (1988) identified two distinct trends. The first is the move towards creating ostensibly authentic heritage places, as exemplified by the new generation of open-air museums. The second trend is the antithesis of the first, and involves the use of elaborate, state of the art technology to create a novel historic 'experience'. Such sites – of which Jorvik Viking Centre is the leading example – frequently use 'postmodern' display media such as sound, smell and heat to create this experience (Walsh, 1992).

Critics of the heritage industry argue that at many heritage sites and museums the influence of the market has meant that an educational role has been subordinated to entertainment and the satisfaction of visitor expectations (Lumley, 1988; Walsh, 1992). Underpinning this stance is the assumption that entertainment is not compatible with informal education. Ames (1988, 1989) suggested that where the two are combined, entertainment will usually prevail. Similarly, Binks (1986) commented that there is a danger of losing sight of educational objectives which are not always easily defined and measured. Indeed, many museums may not even try to educate their audiences and are preoccupied with other concerns, such as making money (Fleming, 1986). West argues that this is the case at the Blists Hill open-air museum, where the educative function is 'almost entirely subordinated to the opportunism of commodity exchange' (1988, p. 57).

The new emphasis on sophisticated, entertaining interpretive media has generated further concern. Increasingly at heritage sites, the interpretation is dominating the resource being interpreted, in contrast with earlier practice, which treated interpretation as secondary. As Stevens (1989, p. 103) noted, 'the media is becoming the message'. The implications for the educational role of interpretation have been questioned. Screven (1986) and Ames (1988, 1989) argued that interpretive media may so overwhelm the message that for visitors the main memory is of the interpretive 'experience' and little more. Museums may consequently be stimulating and entertaining visitors but educating very few. Similarly, Walsh (1992) suggested that the emphasis on 'media as spectacle' may drown out any educational message. In a critique of Jorvik Viking Centre, Schadla-Hall (1984) recognized its success as entertainment but doubted that the centre actually educated or informed its visitors.

Underpinning these critiques are the assumptions that the legitimate role of interpretation is education; that this role has been subsumed beneath an emphasis on entertainment, or drowned by overpowering display techniques; and that education and entertainment are incompatible. While there is evident validity in some of these critiques, the situation is not so straightforward. At the root of these concerns is a long-standing ambivalence in Britain towards entertainment, and a belief that pleasure and learning are dichotomous and incompatible (Greenhalgh, 1989). But as Walsh (1992) noted, the two are not mutually exclusive; it is not possible to define where education stops and entertainment – or fun – takes over. Vergo (1989) suggested that even the most overtly entertainment-oriented presentations will have, in the broadest sense, some educational value, even if it is only the widening of horizons and experiences. Instead of being dichotomous it is more likely that education and entertainment can be closely linked: there has long been recognition that the educational impact of a presentation can be enhanced if it is entertaining and stimulating (Fleming, 1986; Screven, 1986; Ames, 1989). So, rather than speaking of education *or* entertainment, it may be helpful to talk of the two being intertwined, perhaps as Urry's notion of *'edu-tainment'* (1991, p. 51), a combination of popular education and commercial entertainment which characterizes modern heritage sites. Sweeping statements about entertainment having eclipsed education are unhelpful, and rarely supported by empirical evidence.

Other concern has focused on the content of interpretive messages presented at heritage sites, and their educational value. Various authors (Wright, 1985; Hewison, 1987; Jenkins, 1992; Walsh, 1992) have accused the heritage industry of presenting a superficial, unchallenging and ultimately false version of the past. Heritage sites, aiming to ensure the satisfaction of their visitors and maintain their market share, are concerned to give their customers what they want; they are certainly disinclined to challenge or disturb them. Hewison (1987) has argued that nostalgia has been central to the rise of the heritage industry, and that an underlying motive for visiting heritage sites is escapism. Since visitors want a version of the past which conforms to their expectations, this is what the heritage industry sells them (Brigden, 1982; Kavanagh, 1983). The pressure of the market is to provide cheap thrills, rather than authoritative interpretation: as a result truth is the casualty (Cossons, 1989). Many heritage sites are presenting a safe, sanitized, easily consumable and uncontentious past, with a strong element of entertainment. Hence Hewison's bold assertion that 'heritage is bogus history', and that 'many of its products are fantasies of a world that never was' (1987, pp. 144, 10).

Again this debate calls into question the educational value of much heritage interpretation. Critics suggest that in presenting an incomplete or inaccurate representation of history, heritage sites are not effectively catering for public interest in the past. According to Fowler (1989), far from being educative, much interpretation makes little contribution to a deeper popular under-standing of history, but instead simply reinforces existing perceptions and stereotypes. Others make the same point with reference to specific attractions: Hewison (1987) argues that the main purpose of Wigan Pier heritage centre is to create an emotional – rather than an informative – experience, while Walsh (1992) questions whether visitors to the Imperial War Museum actually learn anything about the horrors of war. But other writers are less pessimistic. Lowenthal contended that it is better to have a misguided understanding of history than none at all; better 'a lighthearted dalliance with the past than a wholesale rejection of it' (1981, p. 232).

Once again, while there is validity in this critique, the issue suffers from oversimplification, since ultimately very little is known of how and what visitors learn at heritage sites. While many heritage sites clearly do present a bland and uncontentious account of their past there are problems in arguing that visitors are gullible and unquestioning about the representation of history they encounter, and are unable to discriminate between accurate and meretricious interpretation (Urry, 1990). Some argue that the public can recognize shallow and sanitized interpretation of the past, and that coming years will see a reaction against such presentations (Hewison, 1991; Fowler, 1992).

Overall, it is clear that issues concerning the educational role of heritage interpretation are hotly debated. Equally clear is 'that the educational impact of interpretation is poorly understood, a surprising situation given that its primary aim is educational. The need is for research into the educational impact of heritage interpretation (Rumble, 1989; Prentice, 1993). Relatively little is known of the ways in which visitors interact with interpretive media;

the circumstances which can assist or hinder the encounter, whether in fact they actually learn anything, and the circumstances that affect this learning. The final section attempts to address some of these issues.

An empirical study of visitors' learning at heritage sites

This section reports an empirical study undertaken by the author (Light, 1991b) of the educational effectiveness of interpretation at four ancient monuments – Caerphilly Castle, Raglan Castle, Tintern Abbey, and Tretower Court and Castle – in South Wales. These sites featured varying combinations of three media – exhibitions, outdoor panels and stereo-audio tours – commonly used to interpret monuments. A majority of visitors at the four sites encountered the interpretive media; large majorities declared an interest in them; and nearly all paid at least some attention to them (Light, 1991b).

Any investigation of informal learning in a leisure environment poses considerable methodological problems (Light, 1988), and it is perhaps for this reason that so little investigation of learning has been undertaken. Some discussion of the methodology of this study is therefore necessary.

To assess visitors' learning from interpretation, recognition tests in the form of multiple-choice questions were employed. Miles *et al.* (1988) considered these to be the best type of test for assessing learning performance. Visitors were asked six site-specific questions and given a choice of four responses, one of which was the correct answer. The location of the correct answer was varied for different questions. To control for guessing, respondents were asked to state 'don't know' rather than guess. Although some authors (Prentice and Prentice, 1989; Prentice, 1991) have advocated the use of statistical corrections to control for guessing, these were not employed in this study, since they were designed for a formal, classroom environment, and are inappropriate for an evaluation of informal, leisure-based learning. At each site, the six test questions were carefully chosen to give coverage of all of the site's interpretive media and themes.

Any attempt to investigate visitor learning from interpretation must make some assessment of prior knowledge, so that any increases in this knowledge can be attributed to the site's interpretation. One commonly adopted technique is the use of 'before' and 'after' tests, where one sample of visitors is interviewed before visiting the site to produce a baseline of prior knowledge against which the responses of visitors leaving the site can be compared. Such an approach is problematic, not least in that it fails to consider how much new information is learnt by each individual (Prince, 1982a). For this study, an alternative approach was adopted. When visitors answered a test question correctly, they were asked if they knew that information before their visit. This allows each respondent to establish their own baseline of prior knowledge, and subsequent increases on that baseline can be assessed (Prince, 1982a).

A final issue concerns objectives or criteria of success for an evaluation of

Table 7.3   Responses to the statement: 'You have not learnt anything from your visit here'

	All sites	Caerphilly	Raglan	Tintern	Tretower
Agree	7%	12%	4%	5%	7%
No opinion	1%	1%	–	1%	2%
Disagree	92%	87%	96%	94%	91%
N =	1197	324	355	369	149

the educational effectiveness of interpretation. The need for clear objectives is recognized since, as Putney and Wager (1973, p. 43) noted, 'you cannot say how well you are doing until you have specified what you are trying to accomplish'. While some authors (Screven, 1976) have advocated clear objectives that specify exactly what a visitor is expected to learn, others have rejected this notion as inappropriate to an informal learning environment (Alt and Griggs, 1984). However, an investigation of learning needs to be undertaken with reference to some form of yardstick, although, as Griggs (1984) notes, this need not be too precise. For this study, two objectives suitable to an informal learning environment were formulated:

1.   For interpretation to be judged at least marginally successful, a majority of visitors who had paid some attention to interpretation should learn something new from their visit.
2.   Learning should be greater among visitors who define themselves as showing greater interest and attention to interpretation: i.e. those who declared that they were 'very interested' in the interpretive media, and who had read (or listened to) *all* the information they encountered. Hereafter this group is known as 'highly motivated' individuals.

An initial indication of the educational impact of interpretation can be gained from visitors' own assessment of how much they had learned (see Table 7.3). This table clearly indicates that at all sites, very large majorities of visitors considered that they had learnt something from their visit. At this level, whether or not visitors had actually learnt anything is irrelevant; what is more important is that they think they have learnt something; learning can therefore be identified as a perceived benefit of their visit (Prentice, 1993). The figures are very similar across sites, suggesting that different interpretive media do not influence the perception of having learnt something new.

We can now focus on the first of the two evaluation objectives. Responses to the six test questions asked at each site are presented in Table 7.4. The responses are confined to those respondents who had seen or used the interpretive media. At all sites, large majorities of visitors were able to answer at least one question correctly, with the average response being considerably higher. Few people answered none of the questions correctly. However, these figures are rather misleading in that they fail to consider questions answered correctly where the answer was known before the visit, and those answered

Table 7.4 Number of test questions answered correctly by visitors

No. of correct answers	Caerphilly	Raglan	Tintern	Tretower
0	13%	4%	4%	1%
1	16%	14%	9%	3%
2	20%	19%	17%	7%
3	23%	24%	26%	13%
4	18%	22%	25%	27%
5	9%	13%	15%	33%
6	2%	5%	4%	16%
Mean	2.5	3.0	3.2	4.3
N =	314	352	366	108

Rounding errors mean that percentages may not add up to exactly 100.

correctly without prior knowledge (which represents learning from the interpretation). It is necessary to distinguish between questions answered correctly with and without prior knowledge. These figures are presented in Tables 7.5a and 7.5b.

Table 7.5a shows that at Caerphilly, Raglan and Tretower a majority of visitors had little prior knowledge of the site. Most answered none of the test questions correctly on the basis of previous knowledge, although a few *were* able to give correct answers to at least one question on the basis of prior knowledge. The responses differ between the sites, and prior knowledge was greatest at Tintern, where two-thirds of visitors answered at least one question correctly on the basis of previous knowledge. Here, some of the interpretive material is duplicating the background knowledge of some visitors. Overall these findings confirm that, while many people visit historic sites from an existing interest, few have specific and detailed prior knowledge. Almost all visitors have the potential to learn new information if they are inclined to do so.

Table 7.5b presents the most important findings for the providers of interpretation: the amount of new learning which takes place from an encounter with interpretation. The results are initially encouraging. At all sites, upwards of 75 per cent of visitors were able to answer at least one question correctly without prior knowledge, and this indicates new learning from the interpretation. Clearly, with respect to the first of the learning objectives, interpretation is at least a marginal success, since a majority of people who use interpretation are able to answer at least one question correctly. In fact the average number of questions answered correctly without prior knowledge is more than one at all sites.

Responses to the test questions support the claims discussed earlier (see Table 7.2) that, with respect to learning, three segments of visitors can be identified (Miles, 1986; Herbert, 1989). A small group of visitors (average 7 per cent across the four sites) answered all six questions correctly; these are those individuals who are highly inclined to learn from their visit. Similarly,

Table 7.5a Number of test questions answered correctly by visitors with prior knowledge

No. of correct answers	Caerphilly	Raglan	Tintern	Tretower
0	56%	73%	34%	85%
1	24%	16%	35%	10%
2	13%	8%	16%	4%
3	5%	3%	8%	–
4 or more	2%	1%	7%	1%
Mean	0.7	0.4	1.2	0.2
N =	314	352	366	108

Table 7.5b Number of test questions answered correctly by visitors without prior knowledge (new learning)

No. of correct answers	Caerphilly	Raglan	Tintern	Tretower
0	22%	12%	16%	1%
1	22%	17%	21%	3%
2	26%	21%	26%	11%
3	20%	21%	24%	17%
4	8%	18%	10%	27%
5	2%	9%	3%	29%
6	–	3%	–	13%
Mean	1.8	2.6	2.0	4.0
N =	314	352	366	108

a small group were unable to answer any test question, or gained no new knowledge (average 13 per cent across the four sites). These are likely to be those visitors who are completely disinclined to learn (although their numbers are probably underestimated since such people are unlikely to even look at interpretive media, and this group is not included in the table). The third group is that for whom informal learning is important to some degree (which makes up 80 per cent or more of visitors), and who gain varying amounts of new knowledge.

New learning varies significantly among the sites: Table 7.5b indicates that at Tretower 99 per cent of visitors learnt something new, and 69 per cent were able to answer four or more questions correctly. Making comparisons between sites is difficult because the nature of the test questions was site specific. However, Tretower, with only audio interpretation (a stereo-audio tour), was different from the other sites which featured visual, text-based media. The stereo-audio tour is closely associated with personal, home-based entertainment and has been found to generate more interest and attention among visitors than visual media (Light, 1991b). On the evidence of this study, audio interpretation seems to be considerably more effective in educational terms than written media.

For a further insight into how visitors learn from interpretation, the

Table 7.6 Visitors' learning from an interpretive exhibition at Caerphilly Castle

Extent of reading those displays looked at	Number of displays looked at		
	All	Most	Some
Completely	93%	85%	*
Partly	76%	66%	64%
Hardly	*	*	*

Figures are percentage of visitors who learnt something new from their visit.
* = Number of observations less than 20.
N = 283.

Table 7.7 Visitors' learning from outdoor interpretive panels at Tintern Abbey

Extent of reading those panels looked at	Number of panels looked at		
	All	Most	Some
Completely	80%	79%	78%
Partly	*	76%	52%

Figures are percentage of visitors who learnt something new from their visit.
* = Number of observations less than 20.
N = 346.

relationship between learning and attention to interpretive media was invest-igated. Visitors' attention was expressed as a table: one axis represented the extent to which visitors had looked at interpretive media, while the other represents the extent to which they read what they looked at. The extent of visitors' learning can then be identified for each cell of the table. This procedure was adopted for all four study sites: for the sake of brevity the results from just two sites – Caerphilly and Tintern – are presented here. Table 7.6 shows the relationship between learning and attention for an exhibi-tion at Caerphilly; Table 7.7 presents the same data for Tintern. The relation-ship is clear. At Caerphilly, of those who read completely *all* the exhibition displays, 93 per cent learnt something new, while only 64 per cent of those who looked only partly at some displays did likewise. Similarly at Tintern, 80 per cent of people who read all the panels completely learnt something new, while of those who read only some of the panels partly the figure was 52 per cent.

The extent of a visitor's attention is clearly an important influence on the extent of their learning: greater attention to interpretive media unsurprisingly increases the likelihood of learning something new. Light (1991b) has argued that visitors' attention is the product of an interaction between characteristics of the interpretive medium itself and the users of that medium. Similarly, Alt (1977) suggested that the effectiveness of interpretation is an equation between the visitor and interpretive medium. Various properties of the interpretive medium may influence how visitors attend to it, including the quantity of information presented, readability of text, and the use of aural rather than

Table 7.8 Learning among visitors with different degrees of motivation*

	Caerphilly		Raglan		Tintern		Tretower	
	(a)	(b)	(a)	(b)	(a)	(b)	(a)	(b)
	88.8%	76.9%	96.1%	85.6%	80.0%	88.5%	98.7%	100%
	2.18	1.60	3.14	2.33	2.13	2.13	4.03	4.04
N =	45	257	101	249	30	277	76	28

(a) = 'Highly motivated' sample of visitors.
(b) = Remainder of visitors.
* Top figure is the percentage of people who learnt something new from their visit. Bottom figure is the average number of questions visitors answered correctly without knowing the answer before their visit (new learning).

written presentations. Visitors' motives for visiting were also an important influence on their attention, and people who visited because of a declared interest in historic sites showed more interest and attention to interpretive media. An important finding for this discussion is that the prior motives and interests of visitors are important influences on their attention, and presumably their requirements for learning and understanding about the place they are visiting. Visitors with greater requirements for informal learning will pay more attention to interpretive media.

The second performance criterion for this study stated that visitors who could be described as 'highly motivated', and who had paid extensive interest and attention to the interpretation, should demonstrate greater learning than the rest of the visitors. Such visitors are likely to be those for whom learning and understanding are important parts of their visit to a heritage site, and correspond to the first visitor segment identified in Table 7.2. Table 7.8 presents the extent of new learning for both this 'highly motivated' sample and the remainder of visitors at the four study sites.

The findings of Table 7.8 lend partial support to the suggestion that 'highly motivated' individuals display greater learning. At both Caerphilly and Raglan those visitors who had read completely all interpretive material learnt more than other visitors – a greater proportion learnt something new, and answered a higher average number of questions correctly without prior knowledge. However, this pattern is not replicated at Tintern and Tretower. Since the extent of visitors' motivation is controlled for at a self-defined maximum level, it appears that attributes of the interpretive media, rather than of the visitors, may explain why this 'highly motivated' sample does not learn more than the remainder of visitors. At Tintern, the lack of greater learning on the part of the 'highly motivated' sample may mean that the interpretation was replicating their background knowledge, so they were less well able to acquire new knowledge. Alternatively, it may reflect a failure on the part of the interpretation to communicate effectively; perhaps, despite having read all the interpretive material available, the 'highly motivated' sample of visitors was no better able to comprehend and understand parts of it than the remainder of visitors.

At Tretower, the lack of difference between the two samples may reflect the exceptional properties of the stereo-audio tour, which seems to be equally effective for all visitors, regardless of the extent of their involvement with interpretation. The higher average number of questions answered correctly without prior knowledge, when compared with other sites, lends support to this idea. The novelty value, dynamic aural presentation, and entertainment associations of the stereo-audio tour may contribute to its greater educational success, and greater popularity among visitors.

In summary, this section has demonstrated that interpretation is successful in communicating to visitors (at least in the short term), and that a majority of visitors learn informally at least something new from their visit. The inter-relationships of the various elements which influence the extent and effective-ness of informal education at heritage sites are summarized in the model presented in Figure 7.1.

Concluding Comments

Heritage interpretation is a central component of modern heritage tourism. Central to its success has been the increasing interest and curiosity about history and the past among the public, an interest which extends to their choice of leisure activities, and generates visits to heritage sites. An examina-tion of motives for visiting heritage sites confirms that a desire for some degree of informal understanding and learning is a significant component; moreover, many heritage sites and museums are perceived as having educational proper-ties by both their visitors and non-visitors. The discussion noted that individual leisure needs, which include the desire for understanding and competent manipulation of knowledge, and social needs, in particular the desire to accumulate cultural capital, are important motives for visiting museums and heritage sites. Interpretation plays an important role in catering for these motives. As a consequence, it has boomed in parallel with the emergence of the heritage 'industry'. It is now an activity which receives considerable finance; employs an increasing number of people; and embraces an increasing number of museums which have oriented themselves towards the leisure industry. To Goodey (1990), interpretation is almost synonymous with the heritage industry itself. Since the desire for activities involving learning is arguably likely to grow in coming years, the future for heritage interpretation seems assured.

At the heart of interpretation is informal education. Interpretation is designed to communicate the significance of heritage places, in a manner appropriate to visitors engaged in leisure activities during their leisure time. However, there is evidence that much interpretation has not been designed with effective communication in mind; still less has it adopted Tilden's ideals of revelation and provocation. It may simply be that Tilden's vision of inter-pretation was too demanding to put into practice, but more probably inter-preters were ill equipped or unaware of how to face the challenge. Many

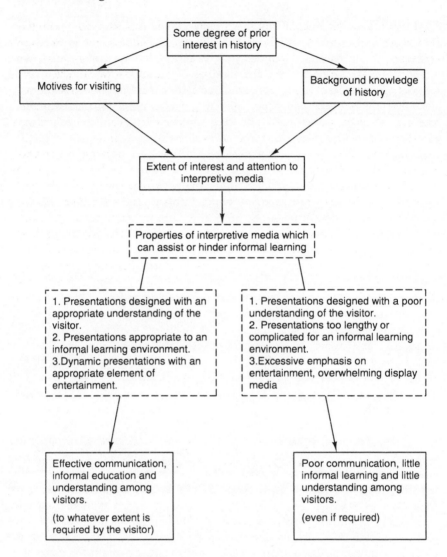

Figure 7.1 Factors influencing informal education at heritage sites.

interpreters failed to appreciate who their visitors were, and misunderstood the nature of informal, voluntary, leisure-based learning, so that, as practised, interpretation frequently became a more formal and rigid didactic activity. Much interpretation was designed with only cursory regard for the expectations and background knowledge of its intended users. More recently, as the need to 'stay close' to visitors has been recognized, there has been greater concern with effective communication and how to achieve it. That this is often allied with entertainment is a cause for concern among some purists.

The educational effectiveness of interpretation is in essence a poorly under-stood issue. Some critics have argued that the educational role of interpretation has been hijacked by entertainment, or swamped by an overemphasis on display media: they question whether interpretation does educate its users, and whether the providers of interpretation attach any importance to such concerns. Others accept interpretation's educational impact, but question whether inter-pretation does little more than peddle stereotypical, clichéd and unchallenging representations of the past. Yet empirical support for such assertions is rarely available. Very little is known of the educational impact of heritage interpreta-tion. The results reported here indicate that many visitors do learn something new from their visit, and that this was influenced by their attention and motives. If interpretation is effective in its informal educational role then further research is needed into how such learning is influenced by entertaining interpretation; how display media can enhance or overwhelm an educational message; and whether consumers of interpretation are accepting or critical of how the past is represented. It is fair to say that many aspects of heritage tourism are poorly understood, none more so than the educational impact of interpretation. This issue represents a significant research challenge for the 1990s.

References

Addyman, P. and Gaynor, A. (1984) The Jorvik Viking Centre: an experiment in archaeological site interpretation. *International Journal of Museum Management and Curatorship*, **3**, 7-18.

Aldridge, D. (1975) *Guide to Countryside Interpretation Part One: Principles of Countryside Interpretation and Interpretive Planning*. Edinburgh: HMSO.

Aldridge, D. (1989) How the ship of interpretation was blown off course in the tempest: some philosophical thoughts. In D. L. Uzzell (ed.) *Heritage Interpretation*, Vol. I. London: Belhaven, pp. 64-87.

Alt, M. B. (1977) Evaluating didactic exhibits: a critical look at Shettel's work. *Curator*, **20**, 241-258.

Alt, M. B. and Griggs, S. A. (1984) Psychology and the museum visitor. In J. M. A. Thompson, D. A. Bassett, D. G. Davies, A. J. Duggan, G. D. Lewis and D. R. Prince (eds) *The Manual of Curatorship: A Guide to Museum Practice*. London: Butterworth, pp. 368-393.

Ames, P. J. (1988) Meshing mission and market. *Museums Journal*, **88**, 33-36.

Ames, P. J. (1989) Marketing in museums: means or master of the mission. *Curator*, **32**, 5-15.

Bennett, T. (1988) Museums and 'the people'. In R. Lumley (ed.) *The Museum Time Machine: Putting Cultures on Display*, London: Routledge, pp. 63-85.

Binks, G. (1986) Interpretation of ancient monuments – some current issues. In M. Hughes and L. Rowley (eds) *The Management and Presentation of Field Monuments*. Oxford: Oxford University Department for External Studies, pp. 39-45.

Bourdieu, P. (1984) *Distinction: A Social Critique of the Judgement of Taste*. London: Routledge and Kegan Paul.

Brigden, R. (1982) Where will it all end? *Museums Journal*, **81**, 199-203.

BTA/ETB (British Tourist Authority and English Tourist Board) (1992) *English Heritage Monitor 1992*. London: English Tourist Board.

Cadw: Welsh Historic Monuments (1992) *Cadw: Welsh Historic Monuments Executive Agency Annual Report and Accounts 1991/2.* Cardiff: Cadw: Welsh Historic Monuments.

Capstick, B. (1985) Museums and tourism. *International Journal of Museum Management and Curatorship*, 4, 365–372.

Cooper, C. P. and Latham, J. (1988) The pattern of educational visits in England. *Leisure Studies*, 7, 255–266.

Cossons, N. (1989) Plural funding and the heritage. In D. L. Uzzell (ed.) *Heritage Interpretation*, Vol. II. London: Belhaven, pp. 16–22.

Dent, K. (1975) Travel as education: the English landed classes in the eighteenth century. *Educational Studies*, 1 (3), 171–180.

Driver, B. L. and Tocher, S. R. (1979) Towards a behavioural interpretation of recreational engagements with implications for planning. In C. S. van Doren, G. B. Priddle and J. E. Lewis (eds) *Land and Leisure: Concepts and Methods in Outdoor Recreation*, 2nd edn. London: Methuen, pp. 86–104.

Dunn Ross, E. L. and Iso-Ahola, S. E. (1991) Sightseeing tourists' motivation and satisfaction. *Annals of Tourism Research*, 18, 226–237.

ETB (English Tourist Board) (1977) *English Heritage Monitor 1977.* London: English Tourist Board.

ETB (English Tourist Board) (1978) *Sightseeing in 1977.* London: English Tourist Board.

Feifer, M. (1985) *Going Places: The Ways of the Tourist from Imperial Rome to the Present Day.* London: Macmillan.

Fleming, D. (1986) From shepherds' smocks to EEC. *Museums Journal*, 85, 179–186.

Fowler, P. (1989) Heritage: a post-modernist perspective. In D. L. Uzzell (ed.) *Heritage Interpretation*, Vol. I. London: Belhaven, pp. 57–63.

Fowler, P. (1992) *The Past in Contemporary Society: Then, Now.* London: Routledge.

Goodey, B. (1979) The interpretation boom. *Area*, 11, 285–288.

Goodey, B. (1982) Values in place: interpretations and implications from Bedford. In J. R. Gold and J. Burgess (eds) *Valued Landscapes.* London: Allen and Unwin, 10–34.

Goodey, B. (1990) Interpreting with change. *Interpretation Journal*, 45, 5–6.

Greenhalgh, P. (1989) Education, entertainment and politics: lessons from the Great International Exhibitions. In P. Vergo (ed.) *The New Museology.* London: Reaktion, pp. 74–98.

Griggs, S. A. (1984) Evaluating exhibitions. In J. M. A. Thompson, D. A. Bassett, D. G. Davies, A. J. Duggan, G. D. Lewis and D. R. Prince (eds) *The Manual of Curatorship: A Guide to Museum Practice.* London: Butterworth, pp. 412–422.

Griggs, S. A. and Alt, M. B. (1982) Visitors to the British Museum (Natural History) in 1980 and 1981. *Museums Journal*, 82, 149–155.

Hammitt, W. E. (1981) A theoretical foundation for Tilden's interpretive principals. *Journal of Environmental Education*, 12, 13–16.

Hammitt, W. E. (1984) Cognitive processes involved in environmental interpretation. *Journal of Environmental Education*, 15, 11–15.

Herbert, D. T. (1989) Does interpretation help?. In D. T. Herbert, R. C. Prentice and C. J. Thomas (eds) *Heritage Sites: Strategies for Marketing and Development.* Aldershot: Avebury, pp. 191–230.

Hewison, R. (1987) *The Heritage Industry: Britain in a Climate of Decline.* London: Methuen.

Hewison, R. (1989) Heritage: an interpretation. In D. L. Uzzell (ed.) *Heritage Interpretation*, Vol. I. London: Belhaven, pp. 15–23.

Hewison, R. (1991) The heritage industry revisited. *Museums Journal*, **91**, 23–26.

Historic Buildings and Monuments Commission (1984) *Introducing . . . The Historic Buildings and Monuments Commission for England.* London: Historic Buildings and Monuments Commission (unnumbered).

Hood, M. G. (1983) Staying away: why people choose not to visit museums. *Museum News*, **61** (4), 50–57.

Hooper-Greenhill, E. (1988) Counting visitors or visitors who count. In R. Lumley (ed.) *The Museum Time Machine: Putting Cultures on Display*. London: Routledge, pp. 213–232.

Horne, D. (1984) *The Great Museum: The Re-Presentation of History*. London: Pluto.

Iso-Ahola, S. E. (1980) *The Social Psychology of Leisure and Recreation*. Dubuque, Iowa: William Brown.

Iso-Ahola, S. E. (1983) Towards a social psychology of recreational travel. *Leisure Studies*, **2**, 45–56.

Jenkins, J. G. (1992) *Getting Yesterday Right: Interpreting the Heritage of Wales*. Cardiff: University of Wales Press.

Kavanagh, G. (1983) History and the museum: the nostalgia business. *Museums Journal*, **83**, 139–141.

Kenyon, J. R. (1988) *Raglan Castle*. Cardiff: Cadw: Welsh Historic Monuments.

Lewis, B. N. (1980) The museum as an educational facility. *Museums Journal*, **80**, 151–155.

Lewis, P. (1988) Wigan Pier strikes back. In J. Iddon (ed.) *The Dodo Strikes Back* (Proceedings of a one-day conference held at St Mary's College, Strawberry Hill, April), pp. 10–14.

Light, D. (1988) Problems encountered with evaluating the educational effectiveness of interpretation. *Swansea Geographer*, **25**, 79–87.

Light, D. (1991a) The development of heritage interpretation in Britain. *Swansea Geographer*, **28**, 1–13.

Light, D. (1991b) *Heritage places in Wales and their interpretation: a study in applied recreational geography*. Unpublished PhD thesis, University of Wales.

Light, D. and Prentice, R. C. (1994) Who consumes the heritage product? Implications for European heritage tourism. In G. J. Ashworth and P. Larkham (eds) *Building a New Heritage: Tourism, Culture and Identity in the New Europe*. London: Routledge, pp. 90–116.

Lowenthal, D. (1981) Conclusion: dilemmas of preservation. In D. Lowenthal and M. Binney (eds) *Our Past before Us: Why Do We Save It?* London: Temple Smith, 213–237.

Lowenthal, D. (1985) *The Past Is a Foreign Country*. Cambridge: Cambridge University Press.

Lumley, R. (1988) Introduction. In R. Lumley (ed.) *The Museum Time Machine: Putting Cultures on Display*. London: Routledge, pp. 1–23.

McManus, P. M. (1987) It's the company you keep . . . The social determination of learning-related behaviour in a science museum. *International Journal of Museum Management and Curatorship*, **6**, 263–270.

McManus, P. M. (1988) Good companions: more on the social determination of learning related behaviour in a science museum. *International Journal of Museum Management and Curatorship*, **7**, 37–44.

Martin, B. and Mason, S. (1993) The future of attractions: meeting the needs of the new consumers. *Tourism Management*, **14**, 34–40.

Merriman, N. (1989) Museum visiting as a cultural phenomenon. In P. Vergo (ed.) *The New Museology*. London: Reaktion, pp. 149–171.

Merriman, N. (1991) *Beyond the Glass Case: The Past, the Heritage and the Public in Britain*. Leicester: Leicester University Press.

Miles, R. S. (1986) Museum audiences. *International Journal of Museum Management and Curatorship*, 5, 73–80.

Miles, R. S., Alt, M. B., Gosling, D. C., Lewis, B. N. and Tout, A. F. (1988) *The Design of Educational Exhibits*, 2nd edn. London: Unwin Hyman.

Phillips, A. (1989) Interpreting the countryside and the natural environment. In D. L. Uzzell (ed.) *Heritage Interpretation*, Vol. I. London: Belhaven, pp. 121–131.

Prentice, M. M. and Prentice, R. C. (1989) The heritage market of historic sites as educational resources. In D. T. Herbert, R. C. Prentice and C. J. Thomas (eds) *Heritage Sites: Strategies for Marketing and Development*. Aldershot: Avebury, pp. 143–190.

Prentice, R. (1991) Measuring the educational effectiveness of on-site interpretation designed for tourists: an assessment of student recall from geographical field visits to Kidwelly Castle, Dyfed. *Area*, 23, 297–308.

Prentice, R. (1993) *Tourism and Heritage Attractions*. London: Routledge.

Prince, D. R. (1982a) *Evaluating Interpretation: A Discussion*. Centre for Environmental Interpretation Occasional Paper No. 1. Manchester: Centre for Environmental Interpretation.

Prince, D. R. (1982b) *Countryside Interpretation: A Cognitive Evaluation*. Centre for Environmental Interpretation Occasional Paper No. 3. Manchester: Centre for Environmental Interpretation.

Prince, D. R. (1983) Behavioural consistency and visitor attraction. *International Journal of Museum Management and Curatorship*, 2, 235–247.

Prince, D. R. (1985) The museum as dreamland. *International Journal of Museum Management and Curatorship*, 4, 243–250.

Putney, A. D. and Wager, J. A. (1973) Objectives and evaluation in interpretive planning. *Journal of Environmental Education*, 5, 43–44.

Roggenbuck, J. W., Loomis, R. J. and Dagostino, J. (1990) The learning benefits of leisure. *Journal of Leisure Research*, 22, 112–124.

Rumble, P. (1989) Interpreting the built and natural environment. In D. L. Uzzell (ed.) *Heritage Interpretation*, Vol. I. London: Belhaven, pp. 24–32.

Schadla-Hall, R. T. (1984) Slightly looted: a review of the Jorvik Viking Centre. *Museums Journal*, 84, 62–64.

Screven, C. G. (1976) Exhibit evaluation – a goal-orientated approach. *Curator*, 19, 271–290.

Screven, C. G. (1986) Exhibitions and information centers: some principles and approaches. *Curator*, 29, 109–137.

Sharpe, G. W. (1982) An overview of interpretation. In G. W. Sharpe (ed.) *Interpreting the Environment*. New York: John Wiley, pp. 3–26.

Shettel, H. (1989) Evaluation in museums: a short history of a short history. In D. L. Uzzell (ed.) *Heritage Interpretation*, Vol. II. London: Belhaven, pp. 129–137.

Stansfield, G. (1983) Heritage and interpretation. *Museums Journal*, 83, 47–51.

Stevens, T. (1989) The visitor – who cares? Interpretation and consumer relations. In D. L. Uzzell (ed.) *Heritage Interpretation*, Vol. II. London: Belhaven, pp. 103–107.

Thomas, C. J. (1989) The roles of historic sites and reasons for visiting. In D. T. Herbert, R. C. Prentice and C. J. Thomas (eds) *Heritage Sites: Strategies for Marketing and Development*. Aldershot: Avebury, pp. 62–93.

Thrift, N. (1989) Images of social change. In C. Hamnett, L. McDowell and P. Sarre (eds) *The Changing Social Structure*. London: Sage, pp. 12–42.

Tilden, F. (1977) *Interpreting Our Heritage*, 3rd edn. Chapel Hill: University of North Carolina Press. (First published 1957.)

Towner, J. (1985) The Grand Tour: a key phase in the history of tourism. *Annals of Tourism Research*, 12, 297–333.

Trinder, B. (1976) Industrial conservation and industrial history: reflections on the Ironbridge Gorge Museum. *History Workshop*, 2, 171–176.

Urry, J. (1990) *The Tourist Gaze: Leisure and Travel in Contemporary Societies*. London: Sage.

Urry, J. (1991) The sociology of tourism. In C. Cooper (ed.) *Progress in Tourism, Recreation and Hospitality Management*, Vol. III. London: Belhaven, pp. 48–57.

Urry, J. (1992) The tourist gaze and the environment. *Theory, Culture and Society*, 9, 1–26.

Uzzell, D. L. (1985) Management issues in the provision of countryside interpretation. *Leisure Studies*, 4, 159–174.

Uzzell, D. (1989) Introduction: the visitor experience. In D. L. Uzzell (ed.) *Heritage Interpretation*, Vol. II. London: Belhaven, pp. 1–15.

Vergo, P. (1989) The reticent object. In P. Vergo (ed.) *The New Museology*. London: Reaktion, pp. 41–59.

Walsh, K. (1992) *The Representation of the Past: Museums and Heritage in the Post-modern World*. London: Routledge.

West, B. (1988) The making of the English working past: a critical review of the Ironbridge Gorge Museum. In R. Lumley (ed.) *The Museum Time Machine: Putting Cultures on Display*. London: Routledge, pp. 36–62.

Wright, P. (1985) *On Living in an Old Country*. London: Verso.

Zaring, J. (1977) The Romantic face of Wales. *Annals of the Association of American Geographers*, 67, 397–418.

8

Heritage as Formal Education

Richard C. Prentice

The National Curriculum in England and Wales has brought renewed interest in the potential of educational markets by the managers of built heritage attractions. Similarly, the early 1990s have seen an upsurge in schools' interest in both the environment and built heritage, partly in line with the demands of the new 6–14-year-old curriculum guidelines. However, this interest extends beyond the remit of the National Curriculum and, as Historic Scotland's Education Officer recently commented:

> There is a big focus on the environment and heritage just now and schools are spending much more time looking at their local area. I don't have to try and 'sell' something that people are not interested in – there is a great willingness and interest on the part of teachers.[1]

To meet this demand, curriculum-specific literature is being produced by the several state agencies and national trusts which manage many of the formal built heritage attractions of Britain. Innovations, however, go beyond the provision of literature. Indeed, Historic Scotland has made teaching support material available on the NERIS CD-ROM database, to which many schools subscribe.

The main purpose of this chapter is to raise, by the means of two case studies, the issue of the *effectiveness* of educational visits to built heritage attractions. One case study is of schools; the other is of a university. The message of these case studies is that there is a substantially unmet need for the evaluation of the effectiveness of field visits as a market for heritage attractions.

Educationalists' Interests in Field Visits

In Britain it would be wrong to equate the beginnings of educationalists' interest in heritage solely with the demands of more recent curriculum guidelines. This interest has an antecedent in, for example, the fieldwork emphases in geography of the 1970s and 1980s (e.g. Countryside Commission for Scotland, 1982; Central Regional Council and Countryside Commission for Scotland, 1984), the widespread adoption of *topic work* (thematic or project work) in primary schools (Tann, 1988), and the 'living history' movement (children dressing up in period costumes and role playing) of the 1980s (Fairclough and Redsell, 1985). Indeed, for the mid-1980s it was estimated that educational visits by schools in England annually totalled over 12 million, equivalent to 5 per cent of all recorded sightseeing visits to attractions (Cooper and Latham, 1988a). Expressed another way, it was estimated that on average each pupil at school in England made 1.6 educational visits per annum, although this average concealed sizeable regional variations; in the North-West of England fewer visits were made, and in the South-West and in East Anglia far more than average. The major sector of this educational market for visits was found generally throughout England to be pupils of primary age, with the exception of theatres, which were dominated by secondary schools.

Indicators of the volume of visits made nationally tell us little about the reasons *why* such visits are made. Such reasons are to be found in educational theories and practices. Both the contemporary teaching of history and geography, in particular, emphasize field visits and other activities as essential to learning. Some insight into contemporary educational debate is needed if the market for educational visits is to be understood.

In the traditional teaching of history, the concepts of time and change, cause and effect, were rarely well developed. Contemporary teaching of history, in contrast, emphasizes these concepts: 'History is concerned with the causes and effects of change over time; with the ways in which, and the reasons why, societies in the past were different from ours, and what caused them to change' (Cooper, 1992, p. 6). Potentially, visits can help in teaching children to develop concepts of time (before, after; sooner, later; now, then) and in enabling them to understand sequences of events (Hill and Morris, 1991). A sense of chronological sequence has featured prominently in debates about primary curricula in history over the past decade (DES, 1985a, 1985b). However, sequencing illustrates only one type of historical change, that in which unambiguous differences are apparent. As Pluckrose has commented, 'Leaps through time may illustrate change by contrast: they do not illustrate its nature' (1991, p. 17). Historical change is often slow and imperceptible: 'Historical change is a paradox. There is alteration and yet there is similarity and sameness' (ibid.). Visits to attractions need to avoid presenting contrast alone, otherwise pupils and students will fail to grasp the full nature of historical change.

Activities can also contribute to an understanding of change and stability, similarities and differences and growth and decay. They help to make children aware of their own origins in the past, and of the background to the present. Equally, the objective of empathy with the points of view of past people (DES, 1985a) is potentially aided by activity-based learning, so long as it is remembered that children on visits are seeing and handling only relics of the past, not the past itself, and that these relics represent evidence on which an understanding can be based (Pluckrose, 1991). Historical empathy is the ability to enter into some informed appreciation of the predicaments or views of people in the past, and requires an awareness of anachronism. Simply dressing up, for example, does not in itself overcome such anachronism. Failing the achievement of these objectives, as a minimum, visits may be used to stimulate the curiosity of children; itself an important objective.

In terms of developing a critical ability, visits can be seen as a means of prompting, or as a background to, historians' procedures. They enable discussion, the examination of assumptions, the challenging of interpretations, and the setting forth of a case based upon evidence. This learning objective emphasizes the development of the ability to ask questions, and to answer them from historical sources (the so-called *first record*), and from a range of intellectual skills and experience gained from being a historian (the so-called *second record*) (Nichol, 1984). Visits may be seen as prompting questions of the kind, 'What was it like to be . . .?'

Visits are only part of a repertoire of means to achieve these objectives; others include talking, listening, writing, reading, painting, drawing, modelling, singing, role-playing and dancing. This repertoire links closely with that advocated for contemporary arts education in the development of expression, creativity and critical ability. We would be foolish to ignore another similarity between the teaching of history and that of arts: the arts may at the same time be perceived as cultural self-education, as identity, as continuity with the past, as repossessing or reviving a culture, or as innovating a new culture (Turner and Stronach, 1993). Likewise, educational visits to heritage attractions for the teaching of history fulfil many purposes.

The teaching of geography at both school and university level has a long tradition of field study. Geography has been defined as an observational science – 'all geography begins with somebody, somewhere, making observations' – and

> In broad terms, progression in geography means advancing from the simple to the complex, from the known and directly observable towards the unknown and less-observable, from the concrete towards the abstract, from the small-scale towards the large-scale, from the particular towards the general. (Bailey, 1989, p. 187)

Field study is part of this inherent observational process. Because of this emphasis on observation, the teaching of geography may conceal the value system which produces the observations. In terms of heritage, geographers can counter this bias in their teaching of a sense of place. Wiegand (1992) has developed Relph's (1976) arguments about experiencing places as an outsider and as an insider, and the variation shown in the Relph–Wiegand typology serves to remind us of the multi-faceted nature of the experience of place. Seven types of experience of place are defined, using different dimensions of belonging: recognizing that here you belong; recognizing values but not necessarily sharing them; recognizing the distinctiveness of the attributes of one place compared to another; imagining a place from indirect observation; knowing a place through the location of a specific activity only; knowing a place as a collection of attributes rather than as fused with personal meaning; and being alienated from a place. Field visits have the potential to increase the experience of place, from the latter towards the former types of experience listed from this typology: in effect, potentially to change the student's experience from that of an outsider (the last three types of experience) to that of an insider (the first three types). For more distant places, *locality packs* (Geographical Association, 1992) of photographs, aerial images, maps, written material and artefacts can be used to provide an indirect experience of place. Such packs are not confined to distant places, and form the basis of a common type of educational pack at attractions.

The National Curriculum now specifies the Programmes of Study and the standards of attainment to be reached, for both history and geography, for most schoolchildren aged 6 to 14 years in England and Wales, although the structures originally introduced have been modified to make them less prescriptive (Dearing, 1993). This curriculum derives from Parliamentary Orders made under the Education Reform Act 1988. The Attainment Targets and their constituent Statements of Attainment at ten levels now specify the knowledge, skills and understanding which pupils of different abilities and maturities are expected to have by the end of each of four Key Stages as they progress through school. In effect, the Statements of Attainment mean that the curriculum is perceived as assessment-led by teachers (Naish, 1992; Dearing, 1993). The Programmes of Study specify the matters, skills and processes which are required to be taught to pupils. Content is important in the National Curriculum, for pupils are unable to satisfy the Statements of Attainment without demonstrating a knowledge and understanding of the historical or geographical (or other disciplinary) content of the programme studied. Early monitoring results suggest that the curriculum has led to a more structured approach to classroom teaching, with clearer specification of content and process (Naish, 1992), but it has also been criticized as being overcrowded, over-prescriptive and not necessarily relevant to less academic pupils (Dearing, 1993).

What does the curriculum imply for the manner in which heritage attractions are to be developed? The National Curriculum represents an opportunity for the managers of heritage attractions to develop appropriate teaching materials and services to encourage visits; it also represents a body of knowledge and skills, which will increasingly be brought to attractions by their visitors either as schoolchildren, or subsequently as adults. This longer-term implication is beyond the scope of this chapter, but is an important aspect of future planning and assessment of effectiveness for heritage managers. The immediate opportunity is that of responding effectively to demands for educational products and services. When the National Curriculum was introduced, both history and geography were mandatory subjects at Key Stages 1 to 4, but with the slimming down of the curriculum, these subjects are now compulsory only at Stages 1 to 3 (Dearing, 1993). Even with these adjustments, the curriculum still retains much of potential interest to heritage attraction managers.

The concepts of sequence and causation, as noted earlier, are important to the contemporary teaching of history and are important processes in the Attainment Targets set for the subject (DES, 1991a). For example, at Level 2, pupils are expected to be able to place familiar objects in chronological order, to suggest reasons why people in the past acted as they did, and to identify differences between past and present times. By Level 8, pupils are expected to be able to explain the relative importance of several linked causes, and to show an understanding of the diversity of people's ideas, attitudes and circumstances in complex historical situations. The importance of interpretation in history is also measured through an Attainment Target. At Level 2, pupils are expected to show an awareness that different stories about the past can give different versions of what happened. By Level 8 they are expected to be able to show how attitudes and circumstances can influence an individual's interpretation of historical events or developments.

In developing the National Curriculum for history, local history was seen as a twofold resource. First, it was a means of providing local examples to illustrate more general history; secondly, it was a means of developing observation and perceptions of the interconnections of different aspects of history (National Curriculum History Working Group, 1990). Explicitly, the use of the term 'heritage' was avoided in the design of the curriculum, 'because it has various meanings and is in danger of becoming unhelpfully vague' (ibid., p. 10). The managers of heritage attractions may usefully bear this distinction in mind when developing their educational products and services.

By comparison, the Attainment Targets specified for geography are both more specific and more content orientated. The geography curriculum has been perceived by many geography teachers as being characterized particularly by 'content overload' (Naish, 1992). Attainment Targets relating to environmental geography and the knowledge and understanding of places offer most linkages to heritage resources, although these are somewhat tenuous in comparison with those already discussed for history. For example, at Level 2 for environmental geography, pupils are expected to identify how people obtain materials from the environment, to describe ways in which people have changed the environment, and to suggest how they could improve the quality of their own environment (DES, 1991b). By Level 8, pupils are expected to understand why some environmental systems are fragile. Concerning place, at Level 2 pupils are expected to be able to describe similarities and differences between their local area and another locality; by Level 8, they are expected to understand the identification of geographical patterns, relationships and processes in their home region as well as international differences, linkages, trade and decision making. Some relationship to the generalization away from immediate observation noted above as a teaching technique may be seen here. But for heritage attractions, the curriculum effectively limits the main market for educational visits to younger children.

Attractions as the Suppliers of Educational Services

For attractions where entrance fees were charged, school visits have been considered essential in contributing towards fixed costs mainly out of season, and at other 'quiet' periods (Cooper and Latham, 1988b). Not only are school visits important because of their volume and educational benefit; they also contribute more widely to the conservation and presentation of heritage.

The National Curriculum has stimulated the development of products and services for educational visits by the managers of some heritage attractions. Although this is far from a universal trend, progress has been made since the 1980s, when educational objectives were of surprisingly varied importance to the major agencies (Prentice and Prentice, 1989), the National Trust for Scotland being a notable exception (Ritchie, 1982). The National Curriculum has become an essential reference-point for much of the recent educational documentation produced for teachers by heritage attraction managers in England and Wales.

The (English) National Trust has recently promoted its sites to teachers explicitly for skills-based learning for history and geography under the National Curriculum (National Trust, 1991a). The Trust is seeking to expand its educational provision beyond the 8–12-year-old age range, to cover all four Key Stages, to support GCSE, A-level and further education courses. Both national topic-based and regional site-based literature have been produced by the Trust to link with the National Curriculum. National topic-based publications include *Cross-currents: A Coastal Studies Handbook for Teachers* and *Rural Landscapes: A Resource Book for Teachers* (National Trust, 1990, 1992). Regional site-based publications include *Working with the National Trust. Educational Resources in Buckinghamshire* (National Trust and Buckinghamshire LEA, 1991), *Fountains Abbey: A Resource Book for Teachers* and *Directory for Schools Visits. The National Trust East Anglia* (National Trust, 1991b, 1991c). A common feature of these publications is their explicit reference to the National Curriculum. For example, Wicken Fen in Cambridgeshire is promoted as both a combined fenland history and geography study unit and an environmental studies unit. In the combined history and geography unit, reference is made to Key Stages 1 and 2 for history, and Key Stages 1 to 3 for geography. Other organizations too have direct relevance for the National Curriculum; for example, the World Wildlife Fund published *Learn to Travel*, on responsible travel and tourism, as a guide for teachers of 7–12-year-olds (Mason, 1992).

Other teaching guides, not directly addressing the National Curriculum, are also becoming increasingly common. English Heritage has produced a series of teachers' guides in its 'Education on Site' series. These include *Learning from Objects* (Durbin *et al.*, 1990), *Maths and the Historic Environment* (Copeland, 1991) and *Using Listed Buildings* (Keith, 1991). Indicative of the role of sponsorship in many recent developments, and designed to increase public and schools' awareness of environmental issues in the Yorkshire Dales, a tea company has recently sponsored a spotting booklet, *Discovering the Moors and Dales with Yorkshire Tea and the National Trust* (Taylor's Tea and Coffee, 1992).

With developments of this kind, the managers of heritage attractions need to pay more attention to their effectiveness.

Case Studies and the Analysis of Effectiveness

Effectiveness can be studied in two ways. First, in terms of the extent to which visits are made by one part of the educational sector. This is a traditional 'output' measure of effect, sometimes called a surrogate measure of effectiveness. It tells us nothing about the outcomes, which at best can only be somewhat cautiously inferred (more visits, better outcomes). Secondly, the issue of learning outcomes is addressed by reference to another part of the educational sector; this provides a more direct measure of outcomes.

The issues concerning outputs and outcomes as indicators of effectiveness are raised by the following two case studies. These have been chosen to illustrate both the differences inherent in considering outputs and outcomes and the diversity faced by attractions managers seeking to develop business from the educational sector. The first case study focuses on school visits to attractions in south-west Wales in the early 1990s. The second reviews educational visits made by geography undergraduates to a built heritage monument (a Norman castle) in south-west Wales. Both case studies raise issues rather than draw definitive conclusions and show the need for further research.

Case Study 1: School Visits to Heritage Attractions

The first case study indicates the extent and determinants of visits to attractions and, by so doing, explores demand for visits to attractions, including heritage attractions. The case study relates to subjects generating demands for site visits. Systematic information on the distances travelled and the volume of school visits by subject has generally been lacking (see, however, Cooper and Latham, 1988a). The two counties of Dyfed and West Glamorgan are richly endowed with built heritage attractions and allow a detailed investigation of the nature and determinants of demand.

The material upon which the study was based was collected by a postal questionnaire in late 1992. Two hundred questionnaires were mailed to a random selection of primary and secondary schools in Dyfed and West Glamorgan. Return postage was enclosed, with a letter inviting support for the survey. After prompting, 89 usable replies were received, a response rate of 44 per cent, which is a rate almost the same as that reported by Cooper and Latham (1988a); of schools that replied, 77 per cent (69 schools) were primary schools and 23 per cent (20 schools) were secondary. This difference is to be expected, as there are far fewer secondary schools than primary schools in the area. Similarly, the average size (median) of the more numerous primary schools in the achieved sample was much smaller than for their secondary equivalents: 170 full-time pupils compared to 912. However, the range in school size was also quite substantial for primary schools: a quarter had fewer than 64 pupils and a quarter more than 232; this reflects rural–urban differences. There is no reason to suppose that the achieved sample is unrepresentative of the population of schools from which it was drawn.

Cooper and Latham (1988a) reported that the most popular destinations for school visits in England were historic buildings, museums, galleries and theatres, the latter particularly for secondary schools. For the south-west Wales schools in the academic year 1991/92 the countryside headed the list of destinations surveyed, followed by museums, theatres, castles and technology centres (Table 8.1). Differences between the earlier findings for English schools and those in south-west Wales may result from different patterns of visiting or from varying survey methods. For south-west Wales secondary schools, towns and factories were also popular destinations, as were heritage attractions.

The merits and demerits of small rural primary schools are recurrent features of educational debate and protest in Wales. The present analysis touches on this debate. Pupils in the smaller (mainly rural) primary schools would seem, when compared to their larger (mainly urban) counterparts, to partake equally in field visits. If the smaller primary schools are defined as those with under the average (median) number of pupils, with the exceptions of visits to museums and technology centres, for which smaller schools were less likely to have made visits (differences significant statistically using a two-sample chi-square test at respectively 0.06 and 0.07),[2] primary school size was not associated with the propensity to have visited attractions for field study. This would suggest that in general the smaller primary schools in the area are just as able as their larger counterparts to provide field study across the full range of destination types visited in the study of any subject.

By contrast, the differences between subjects in terms of field destinations

Table 8.1a Proportions of Dyfed and West Glamorgan schools making visits to attractions in the academic year 1991/92: all schools*

	1	2	3	4	5	6
Castles	71.9	19.1	51.7 (0.034)	2.2	2.2	22.5
Abbeys	25.8	4.5	15.7	3.4	3.4	11.2
Museums	82.0	25.8 (0.007)	53.9	6.7	20.2	31.5 (0.038)
Galleries	27.0	3.4	6.7	4.5	2.2	20.2
Theatres	77.5	3.4	6.7	44.9 (0.001)	3.4	37.1 (0.002)
Technology centres	62.9	4.5	1.1	0.0	46.1	16.9
Factories	36.0 (0.023)	14.6	4.5	2.2	14.6	13.5
Offices	10.1	2.2	1.1	3.4	0.0	4.5
Countryside	91.0	57.3 (0.001)	24.7	9.0	32.6	38.2 (0.001)
Towns	52.8 (0.001)	36.0 (0.001)	19.1	5.6	7.9	12.4

* Students/pupils studying:
1 = Any subject   2 = Geography   3 = History
4 = Literature   5 = Science   6 = Thematic projects.
Where appropriate ($p < 0.05$), the significance levels of two sample chi-square coefficients (corrected for continuity) are shown in parentheses, indicating differences between primary and secondary schools, as shown in Table 8.1b.
Source: Sample survey of schools, 1992.

are quite substantial among the sample of south-west Wales schools (see Table 8.1). Differences have only been recorded in the table by age range of pupils (primary/secondary) where these are unlikely to have occurred by chance from sampling error in the survey; had the achieved sample been larger, other weaker differences might have been identified. As it is, those differences found reveal different priorities in applied work across the schools' curricula. For geography students, the countryside is by far the most popular field destination, followed by visits to towns. However, there is substantial variation by the age range of pupils. Compared to their younger counterparts, secondary pupils are much more likely to be taken to the countryside, or to towns for geographical field visits, and much less likely to be taken to museums. Museums and castles are the most frequent destinations for historical visits, castles particularly so for secondary pupils. For literary visits, theatres are the most frequent destinations, especially for those studying at secondary level, a finding replicating that of Cooper and Latham (1988a). Technology centres and the countryside are the most popular destinations for science visits, irrespective of the age of pupils. For thematic or topic work, the

Table 8.1b Proportions of Dyfed and West Glamorgan schools making visits to attractions in the academic year 1991/92: differentiated by primary and secondary schools (%)*

	1	2	3	4	5	6
Castles	–	–	44.9 *75.0*	–	–	–
Abbeys	–	–	–	–	–	–
Museums	–	33.3 *0.0*	–	–	–	37.7 *10.0*
Galleries	–	–	–	–	–	–
Theatres	–	–	–	33.3 *85.0*	–	46.4 *5.0*
Technology centres	–	–	–	–	–	–
Factories	29.0 *60.0*	–	–	–	–	–
Offices	–	–	–	–	–	–
Countryside	–	46.4 *95.0*	–	–	–	47.8 *5.0*
Towns	40.6 *95.0*	20.3 *90.0*	–	–	–	–

* Numbers 1–6, as Table 8.1a. Figures in roman refer to primary schools; figures in italic refer to secondary schools. Where there is no statistically valid difference, no figures are entered into the table. *Source*: Sample survey of schools, 1992.

countryside, theatres and museums are popular destinations, but only for primary pupils. The countryside and towns were equally popular for urban and rural schools, suggesting that the immediate vicinity of the schools does not constrain fieldwork.

Cooper and Latham (1988a) reported that, in England, the average distance travelled from school to site was 40 miles, or for primary pupils, 33 miles. They reported a maximum distance of 87 miles for primary pupils (Cooper and Latham, 1988b) and an overall maximum of 100 miles. The south-west Wales survey looked at distance travelled in a slightly different manner, headteachers being asked how far they thought it reasonable for their pupils to travel to a site from school for a day's study visit. The generalized demand curve, as defined by their responses, is shown in Figure 8.1. The localized nature of trip-making found for England was also evident in south-west Wales. Fewer than a quarter of headteachers thought that a distance of over 50 miles was reasonable; indeed, a quarter thought that 25 miles was a reasonable limit. In terms of reasonable travel distances, there was little difference between the views of the headteachers of the primary and secondary schools (Figure 8.1); this was unlike results reported by Cooper and Latham (1988a).

The range of destination types used in fieldwork is also of interest, and the

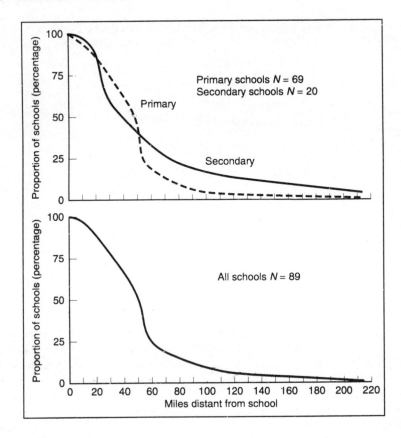

Figure 8.1   Generalized maximum demand curves for school visits from Dyfed and West Glamorgan.
Source: Sample survey of schools, 1992.

ten types can be used to produce an indicator of destination range. However, it needs to be acknowledged that not all types of possible field destination are included among the ten listed in Table 8.1. The indicator should only be used as a guide to the varying ranges of destination types visited, rather than as a definitive statement. With the ten types, the indicator derived ranges from zero (no destination of any of the ten types visited by a school) to ten (at least one visit made to each destination type by a school). On average (median), the schools surveyed had a range of five types of destination visited (Table 8.2); however, 36 per cent had made visits to at least one of seven types of destination. Variation by subject was again apparent. Literature pupils were the most likely to have visited none of the destination types surveyed, and geography and history pupils the most likely to have visited at least one of the attraction types. Compared to the individual subjects studied, pupils on thematic projects showed the greatest diversity in the range of attractions visited.

Table 8.2 Range of visits by subject by schools in Dyfed and West Glamorgan (%)*

Index	1	2	3	4	5	6
0	0.0	32.6	32.6	51.7	39.3	44.9
1	2.2	14.6	12.4	28.1	22.5	11.2
2	4.5	28.1	21.3	11.2	18.0	7.9
3	9.0	11.2	16.9	4.5	11.2	5.6
4	20.2	4.5	9.0	4.5	5.6	11.2
5	18.0	7.9	4.5	0.0	2.2	7.9
6	10.1	0.0	2.2	0.0	1.1	2.2
7	21.3	0.0	1.1	0.0	0.0	5.6
8	13.5	1.1	0.0	0.0	0.0	3.4
9	1.1	0.0	0.0	0.0	0.0	0.0
10	0.0	0.0	0.0	0.0	0.0	0.0

* Students/pupils studying:
1 = Any subject   2 = Geography   3 = History
4 = Literature   5 = Science   6 = Thematic projects.
Source: Sample survey of schools, 1992.

The range of field visits appeared to be strongly age-related. Secondary schools generally showed the greatest range of attractions visited. However, as the secondary schools were generally larger than their primary equivalents, this greater range may also be related to size. Fourteen of the 20 secondary schools had visited six or more attraction types in the survey year, compared to 39 per cent of primary schools (a difference statistically significant at 0.03). A similar pattern was repeated for geography visits, with 18 of the 20 secondary schools making visits to at least two of the attraction types, compared to 52 per cent of primary schools (a difference valid at 0.01).[3] Literary visits showed a similar difference; whereas 85 per cent of the 20 secondary schools had made at least one literary visit, only 38 per cent of primary schools had done likewise (a difference also valid at 0.01).[4] A similar direction of difference was apparent for history visits, with 75 per cent of secondary schools having visited at least two attraction types, compared to 49 per cent of primary schools, and for science visits, 80 per cent of secondary schools having visited at least one attraction type compared to 55 per cent of primary schools (differences significant respectively at 0.07 and 0.08). By contrast, thematic visits are predominantly a primary school activity, for whereas 62 per cent of primary schools had visited at least one attraction type for thematic study, only 30 per cent of secondary schools surveyed had done likewise (a difference statistically valid at 0.02). Taken as a whole, these findings show that the secondary school visits market in south-west Wales is unambiguously more differentiated by subject studied than that for younger pupils.

In view of the controversy and debate the National Curriculum has caused in England and Wales, its impact upon school visits is of particular interest.

Table 8.3 Role of the National Curriculum in Dyfed and West Glamorgan schools in helping to justify field visits (%)

	Geography	History	Literature	Science
More visits	42.9	45.3	12.3	26.8
Same number	56.0	53.5	83.6	67.1
Fewer visits	1.2	1.2	4.1	6.1

Source: Sample survey of schools, 1992.

Reference to Table 8.3 shows that among the headteachers whose schools were surveyed in south-west Wales opinion was divided on the effects of this curriculum, but that the most common view was that the National Curriculum had not enabled more field visits to be justified, especially for literature and science studies. For both geography and history, however, sizeable minorities thought that additional visits were justified by the new curriculum. It would seem that, at least in south-west Wales, the effects of the National Curriculum on field visits were subject-specific. These findings were irrespective of the age ranges of pupils, further emphasizing the importance of the subject-specific impact of the new curriculum in terms of visits.

Case Study 2: Undergraduate Fieldwork

The second case study reports the findings of a questionnaire survey of 269 first-year geography undergraduates on field visits to Kidwelly Castle, the questionnaire being a development of that first used by Prentice (1991). The students were surveyed at the end of visits made in 1992 and 1993. These visits were designed to encourage them to make judgements as to the likely markets for, and success of, sustainable tourism in an area of East Dyfed not traditionally associated with tourism. They were primed in advance, through lectures and written materials, to make appraisals of likely markets and the adequacy of tourism 'products'. As no student was reading, or had read, a historical geography course, substantial awareness of the historical and geographical significance of the castle could not be presumed; many of the students were not of local origin, although studying in Wales. The students could be expected to reflect many of the characteristics of the generally interested, highly educated, visitor profile typical of heritage attractions (Prentice, 1993a).

Little has been written on what geography undergraduates see as the purposes of field visits. This is a serious omission, as perceptions of this kind affect behaviours. The sample was asked to rank six purposes of field visits, using 1 as the most, and 6 as the least important. These purposes are ordered by the average (median and modal) rankings given to each by the students:

	Median ranking	Modal ranking
to relate concepts to reality	2	1
to stimulate enquiry	2	2
to find out about Wales	3	3
to help students to get to know each other	4	4
to get away from the university for a while	4	5
to relax	5	6

The questionnaires were completed anonymously, and the students were explicitly told to be honest in their replies. The findings suggest that the students saw field visits as an important part of their learning process, principally to relate concepts to reality and to stimulate enquiry. On the basis of these findings it would be wrong for educationalists to dismiss such visits as relaxation or 'get away from the lecture room' sessions. The students, clearly, did expect to learn from their visit.

Questions about the learning techniques used showed that thorough reading of the display boards, thorough note-taking while on site and thorough preparatory reading were very much minority activities. This was despite the students' declared purposes for field visits, and the fact that they had been given set texts to read in advance and tasks to undertake when on site. Only one in seven students had either read the castle's display boards thoroughly (14.1 per cent) or had read thoroughly the recommended texts (14.3 per cent). Most students had only read the display boards casually (63.9 per cent); and most had not in fact read the recommended preparatory texts (54.1 per cent); 3.3 per cent had made thorough notes when on site; 62.5 per cent had not. Such poor learning strategies not only contradict what the students had been asked to do, but also confound the students' collective view of the purposes of field visits.

As expected, there was an association between thoroughness in on-site study techniques and other indicators of student interest (Table 8.4). Students who had made notes were much more likely to have read the display boards. Likewise, students who had read the preparatory texts were three times more likely to have made notes on site. In other words, one study technique was not generally used as a substitute for another; rather it was used to reinforce study by some students. Many students largely ignored all of the techniques.

Students' interest in built heritage was assessed by using opinion scales to measure both general and specific study interests. The statements used related to built heritage, to environmentally sensitive tourism, and to economic development. The general statements of interest will be considered first. Few students found castles boring, but few were enthusiasts for Welsh history (Table 8.5). Similarly, few classed visits to historic sites as major leisure activities. This generalist interest was also shown in holiday preferences: most preferred beach- to heritage-based holidays. Students proved to have interests

Table 8.4 Undergraduates' joint use or avoidance of study techniques when on a field visit

Made notes?	Read display boards?				
	thorough	casual	seen, not read	not seen	N
Some	24.8%	66.3%	5.0%	4.0%	101
None	7.7%	62.5%	14.3%	15.5%	168

Two-sample chi-square = 25.67; significant at 0.00001

Preparatory texts read?	Read display boards?				
	thorough	casual	seen, not read	not seen	N
Thoroughly	28.9%	55.3%	7.9%	7.9%	38
Casually	10.7%	76.2%	4.8%	8.3%	84
Not read	11.1%	60.4%	14.6%	13.9%	144

Two-sample chi-square = 17.49; significant at 0.00764

Preparatory texts read?	Made notes?		
	some	none	N
Thoroughly	68.4%	31.6%	38
Casually	50.0%	50.0%	84
Not read	22.2%	77.8%	144

Two-sample chi-square = 35.41; significant at 0.00001

Source: Sample survey of undergraduates on field visits at Kidwelly Castle, 1992 and 1993.

similar to those of the more general public (Prentice, 1993a). On the whole, the students were unemotional about the castle (Prentice, 1993b), but had more strongly held environmental concerns.

When asked about their study interests, the comparative unimportance of built heritage was again found. Fewer than one in five considered historical geography to be one of their main interests (Table 8.5); it was not a component of their university curriculum. By contrast, four out of ten saw economic development as a main study interest. Tourism and leisure was an ambiguous interest. In summary, built heritage, and its tourism applications, was not a common study interest of the sample.

The students were unenthusiastic about the presentation of the castle. A guidebook priced £2.00 (which very few students purchased) was available, and display boards were mounted on the walls. Between 1992 and 1993 the number of these boards was reduced, first through damage and then by fencing off one section of wall. Although the boards contained graphics as well as text, the castle was presented in a traditional manner, which elsewhere has been shown to be of limited effectiveness (Prentice, 1993a). Such a style of presentation remains commonplace at built heritage attractions despite advances in presentational techniques.

Fewer than a quarter of the students thought that the information provided

Table 8.5 Student interest in built heritage and like topics*

	Strongly agree	Agree	NSF†	Disagree	Strongly disagree	N
General interests						
'Castles bore me'	4.1%	6.7%	29.4%	43.1%	16.7%	269
'I am an enthusiast for Welsh history'	6.3%	8.9%	29.0%	29.0%	26.8%	269
'Visits to historic sites are a main leisure activity of mine'	1.5%	9.3%	34.6%	31.6%	23.0%	269
'On holiday I generally prefer to sit on the beach than to visit historic sites'	26.2%	30.7%	18.7%	19.1%	5.2%	267
'Environmental matters do not concern me'	2.2%	2.6%	7.8%	39.4%	48.0%	269
Study interests						
'Historical geography is one of my main interests in geography'	2.6%	14.1%	36.1%	34.2%	13.0%	269
'Economic development is one of my main interests in geography'	6.7%	32.7%	35.7%	18.2%	6.7%	269
'I intend to read the Leisure and Tourism course in geography in Year 3'	6.0%	24.1%	44.4%	13.2%	12.4%	266

* The statements were arranged in a different order on the questionnaire, intermingling general and study interest statements.
† NSF = no strong feelings.
Source: Sample survey of undergraduates on field visits at Kidwelly Castle, 1992 and 1993.

at the castle made their visit enjoyable (Table 8.6). Only about one in ten thought that they had been informed about the castle's history, and only around one in five about the role of geography in the castle's location. Such information could reasonably be expected to be readily provided by site managers to visitors at such an attraction.

Nor did most of the students feel that the castle's presentation helped to create a feeling for its past: indeed, nearly half disagreed with this, one in ten strongly (Table 8.6). Three-quarters of the students questioned felt that the information provided compared unfavourably with sites elsewhere, emphasizing the importance of visitors' comparative experience in assessing interpretative effectiveness. Fewer than one in five students said that they would recommend a friend to visit the castle to learn about castles in Wales. Such a profile of dissatisfaction with the presentation is hardly conducive to the encouragement of interest in built heritage. For these students, at least, the site managers appear to have failed in a principal mission: to inform the castle's visitors of the significance of built heritage. This dissatisfaction concurs

Table 8.6 Quality of students' visits

	Strongly agree	Agree	NSF*	Disagree	Strongly disagree	N
'The information presented to visitors at this castle helps to make one's visit enjoyable'	1.9%	20.4%	33.8%	34.2%	9.7%	269
'I left this castle having felt informed about its history'	1.5%	9.7%	17.8%	51.3%	19.7%	269
'I left this castle having felt informed about the role of geography in its location'	1.1%	19.8%	24.3%	40.7%	14.2%	268
'The presentation of this castle to visitors helps to create a feeling for its past'	1.1%	28.3%	23.4%	35.7%	11.5%	269
'In terms of the information provided for visitors this castle compares favourably with other historic sites I have visited'	0.4%	6.3%	16.4%	51.1%	25.7%	268
'I would recommend a friend to visit this castle to learn about castles in Wales'	1.9%	17.1%	30.5%	35.3%	15.2%	269

* No strong feelings.
Source: Sample survey of undergraduates on field visits at Kidwelly Castle, 1992 and 1993.

with the students' recommendation on the length of stay necessary to see the castle fully: only one in five recommended a stay of over an hour.

The combination of generally poor study techniques and an uninspired visit led to poor on-site learning of the messages presented about the castle through interpretative media. The students were set recognition-test questions relating to on-site interpretation. These questions were used by Prentice (1991), but modified to include five responses per question. Students were told not to guess, but instead to indicate no choice if they did not know an answer. The presentation of five choices was used to counter the effects of guessing (Prentice and Prentice, 1989) and in terms of the on-site messages there was only one correct answer.

Those who answered the test questions were then asked if they had prior knowledge. For all but one question the frequency of prior knowledge was minimal (Table 8.7); the exception was that about a quarter claimed prior knowledge of the castle's concentric plan and its significance. For only two questions did prior knowledge affect choice of answer. In both cases, students admitting prior knowledge were more likely than others to be wrong (although in one case this effect may have resulted from sampling error as it is not significant at the 0.05 convention). These differences were statistically significant by the two-sample chi-square test at 0.03 and 0.08 respectively.

In five of the nine test questions, more students who chose an answer made an incorrect, rather than a correct, choice (Table 8.8). The analysis of the

Table 8.7 Prior knowledge admitted by students

	Of the students making a choice from the answers available to a test question, the proportion claiming prior knowledge of the answer selected (%)
'What are the origins of Kidwelly as a settlement?'	10.5
'In the twelfth century what was the settlement function of Kidwelly?'	14.4
'Where was the original town of Kidwelly located?'	9.5
'What was the significance of the castle's concentric plan?'	24.0
'On whose orders was Kidwelly Castle first constructed?'	9.2
'What particular topographical significance had the castle's site?'	15.7
'In which century was the first castle at Kidwelly built?'	10.4
'Why was the castle first founded at Kidwelly?'	10.2
'From what era does the present castle at Kidwelly first date?'	8.2

Source: Sample survey of undergraduates on field visits at Kidwelly Castle, 1992 and 1993.

Table 8.8 Students' knowledge of test information when leaving the site (%)

	Selecting correct response	Selecting incorrect response	No choice made
'What are the origins of Kidwelly as a settlement?'	27.1	15.7	57.2
'In the twelfth century what was the settlement function of Kidwelly?'	15.2	19.7	65.1
'Where was the original town of Kidwelly located?'	22.3	13.4	64.3
'What was the significance of the castle's concentric plan?'	1.9	49.0	49.1
'On whose orders was Kidwelly Castle first constructed?'	27.9	13.0	59.1
'What particular topographical significance had the castle's site?'	15.6	34.6	49.8
'In which century was the first castle at Kidwelly built?'	26.8	24.1	49.1
'Why was the castle first founded at Kidwelly?'	15.2	19.7	65.1
'From what era does the present castle at Kidwelly first date?'	13.8	26.3	59.9

Source: Sample survey of undergraduates on field visits at Kidwelly Castle, 1992 and 1993.

extent of prior knowledge suggests that much on-site 'learning' is incorrect or not relevant. Presumably, imagination fills the gaps left by poor study techniques and interpretative provisions not found inspiring. In particular, one of the most distinctive architectural features of the castle, its concentric plan, was not understood at all. Almost all students who chose an answer to this test question chose an incorrect answer, most thinking that the concentric design was to prevent attackers easily reaching the inner ward if the outer wall had been breached. The significance of increased fire power, the correct answer, was almost universally missed. Perhaps too many heroic movies had been seen, with fights at successive castle walls during the storming of fortresses? At present, our ability to explain these misconceptions is minimal and has not been properly addressed in higher education. Such appraisals have largely been restricted to museum studies of general-interest visitors (MacDonald, 1992).

In this case study, more of the minority who chose a response to the test question, 'Why was the castle founded at Kidwelly?', incorrectly selected 'to protect the Welsh from Anglo-Norman attacks', than chose 'to protect and administer the lands of an Anglo-Norman lord'. Yet Kidwelly was a Norman castle, and was clearly interpreted as such at the site. Of the students who thought they knew the reason why a castle was built at the site, most had the completely wrong view. The majority could offer no opinion. For these students, even MacDonald's (1992) criterion, that if 'facts' cannot be adequately conveyed, general images and messages can present a *vague notion*, would seem inapplicable. Such levels of error and ignorance are an indictment of cultural understanding: the key question is, an indictment of whom?

The students' overall knowledge about the castle can be assessed by scoring the nine test questions. A mark was given for each correct answer selected, and no mark for each incorrect answer or unanswered question. As each question had five answers from which to select, correction against guessing was avoided. The composite score ranged from 0 to 9.

In fact, no student scored 8 or 9, although one in 20 scored between 5 and 7. By contrast, three out of ten (30.1 per cent) scored 0 and a further quarter (24.2 per cent) scored 1. So, on leaving the castle, most students knew nothing or next to nothing of key items of the site's interpretation. This was despite the interpretation and the pre-visit preparation.

The effects of the run-down of interpretation at the castle were varied. The students were less satisfied in 1993 than in 1992. However, the impact of the changes on study techniques has to be analysed with care. With regard to satisfaction, the students were much more likely in 1993 to disagree or strongly disagree with the statement about feeling informed about the castle's history (a difference valid statistically at 0.01).[5] They were also more likely to disagree or strongly disagree with the statement that the information provided to them at the site had added to their enjoyment (a difference valid at 0.01).[6] This effect was not found for the statement about being informed about the castle's geography, a difference that may have resulted from the information on tourism geography given to the students prior to their visit remaining the same. As a summary of satisfaction, in 1993 the students were more likely than in 1992 to disagree that they would recommend a friend to visit the castle (a difference valid only at 0.08, and thus possibly resultant of sampling error).

When we look at the second possible impact of the run-down of interpretation, that on study techniques, the situation is less clear. In 1993 the students were found to be less likely to have read the display boards or to have made notes at the castle (differences significant at 0.01 and 0.01 respectively).[7] This could be an indication that the reduced interpretative provision at the castle had in fact reduced the students' appetite for study. However, the 1993 groups were also less likely than those of 1992 to have, by their own admission, prepared prior to their visit (a difference significant at 0.01).[8] It would be unwise to assert that the reduction in on-site study resulted from the interpretative run-down at the castle. Less studying could equally have resulted from a less motivated cohort of students, and such effects are generally multi-causal (Prentice, 1993a, 1993b).

The difference in preparatory study was quite marked between the years. For example, whereas 67.9 per cent of the students in the 1992 groups claimed to have done some preparatory reading, only 24.4 per cent of the 1993 group had done so, despite receiving similar instructions.

This ambiguity carried forward into assessment of the effect of this run-down on the students' overall knowledge, as measured by the recognition tests when leaving the site. Scores were greatly reduced in 1993 (a difference significant at 0.01).[9] In particular, in 1993 44.9 per cent of the students failed to make one correct choice, compared to 15 per cent in 1992. The preparatory material was the same in both years. However, if the failure of the 1993 groups to prepare was indicative of a generally more casual approach to study, it would again be wrong to attribute this lack of knowledge to the interpretative run-down at the castle.

Earlier in this discussion a range of field objectives as seen by the students was reviewed. Strangely, the students' ratings of these general objectives had little impact on either their study behaviour on the field visit to the castle, or on their scores in the recognition tests. Only in one case was an effect found between ratings of objectives and scores gained; in 1992, students who gave a higher rating to 'relating concepts to reality' tended to score more highly on the recognition tests (a difference significant at 0.01).[10] There was also a weak tendency for students rating this objective more highly to read the display boards thoroughly (significant at 0.05). However, it is safe to conclude that these general ratings of objectives, and the students' behaviours and achievements on the field task surveyed, were generally independent. This would suggest that care should be taken not to infer too much from students' general views about field visits.

Conclusions

This chapter has illustrated, by means of two case studies, several important aspects of educational markets for heritage attractions. First, the issue of effectiveness of interpretation has been addressed, through indicators of both output and outcome. Secondly, the diversity of the market faced by attraction managers has been indicated – by the case studies *per se*, by the differing age ranges to which the cases applied, and by the subject-specificity revealed by the first case study. Thirdly, the analysis of outcomes, and of visits defined as demand, has indicated the multi-attribute nature of causation which needs to be considered when issues of effectiveness are addressed. Fourthly, the pertinence of the National Curriculum has been shown for attraction managers in England and Wales, where this curriculum applies. While two case studies cannot be used to reach definitive conclusions, they clearly raise questions for further research by academics, schoolteachers and attraction managers.

Perhaps the major conclusion to be reached concerns the lack of current understanding of educational markets by heritage managers. At best, products and services are drawn up in line with current 'good practice', rather than specifically evaluated for their effectiveness. Equally, best practice may not always pertain. The lack of attention to effectiveness means that much recent investment is probably underachieving through sub-optimal design. Given that the case study of outcomes found that most of the students lacked correct notions of the importance of the attraction to the historical struggle between the English and the Welsh, it may be suggested that some of the strategies being adopted by heritage managers are substan:ial failures.

It may possibly be argued, in defence of heritage attraction management, that educational markets (at least those for formal education) are secondary markets, useful principally to generate out-of-season revenue. Although true, such a defence is inadequate as it ignores the longer-term objectives of interesting pupils and students in built heritage through formal education. Such effects are outside the scope of this chapter, but it should be noted that today's pupils will in future years be taxpayers and consumers. Equally, such an argument ignores the need to design services and products for market *segments* (groups of like consumers) rather than for an amorphous 'average' consumer group. The educational market provides segments, like the other markets available to heritage managers. The advantage of the National Curriculum is that by concentrating attention on key Attainment Targets, the issue of testing the effectiveness of interpretative provision becomes explicit. This has implications for other segments of the heritage market.

The diversity of the educational market may be thought to counter the opportunity for product and service developments. One, or indeed several, educational products will not suffice, and opportunities for economies of scale in production are reduced. Instead, a specifically tailored service, designed, if appropriate, for the National Curriculum, is necessary. If other sectors, not directly influenced by this curriculum are targeted, increased diversity of provision is needed. Attraction managements may well seek to develop the National Curriculum-determined educational market, rather than other educational sectors. This is where most expansion in educational provision by attraction managers in England and Wales can be expected in the medium term.

Notes

1. Quoted in *Welcome*, the magazine of the Friends of Historic Scotland, Winter 1992.
2. The chi-square coefficients are 'rounded' in the text and footnotes, but not in the tables.
3. Actually significant at the 0.0004 level.
4. Actually significant at the 0.0005 level.
5. Actually significant at the 0.00001 level.
6. Actually significant at the 0.001 level.
7. Actually significant respectively at the 0.0008 and 0.00001 levels.
8. Actually significant at the 0.00001 level.
9. Actually significant at the 0.00001 level.
10. Actually significant at the 0.006 level.

References

Bailey, P. (1989) Geography: new subject, new curricular contributions. In P. Wiegand and M. Rayner (eds) *Curriculum Progress 5 to 16*. Lewes: Falmer, pp. 175–189.

Central Regional Council and Countryside Commission for Scotland (1984) *Strategy for Interpretation in Central Region*. Stirling: Central Regional Council; Perth: Countryside Commission for Scotland.

Cooper, C. P. and Latham, J. (1988a) The pattern of educational visits in England. *Leisure Studies*, 7, 255–266.

Cooper, C. P. and Latham, J. (1988b) English educational tourism. *Tourism Management*, 9, 331–334.

Cooper, H. (1992) *The Teaching of History. Implementing the National Curriculum*. London: David Fulton.

Copeland, T. (1991) *A Teacher's Guide to Maths and the Historic Environment*. London: English Heritage.

Countryside Commission for Scotland (1982) *Family Days on the Farm*. Final Report. Perth: Countryside Commission for Scotland.

Dearing, R. (1993) *The National Curriculum and Its Assessment*. Final Report. London: School Curriculum and Assessment Authority.

DES: Department of Education and Science (1985a) *History in the Primary and Secondary Years*. London: HMSO.

DES: Department of Education and Science (1985b) *The Curriculum from 5 to 16*. London: HMSO.

DES: Department of Education and Science (1991a) *History in the National Curriculum (England)*. London: HMSO.

DES: Department of Education and Science (1991b) *Geography in the National Curriculum (England)*. London: HMSO.

Durbin, G., Morris, S. and Wilkinson, S. (1990) *A Teacher's Guide to Learning from Objects*. London: English Heritage.

Fairclough, J. and Redsell, P. (1985) *Living History. A Guide to Reconstructing the Past with Children*. London: English Heritage.

Geographical Association (1992) *Geography in the National Curriculum. Place. A Practical Guide to Teaching about Places*. Sheffield: Geographical Association.

Hill, C. and Morris, J. (1991) *Practical Guides. History. Teaching within the National Curriculum*. Leamington Spa: Scholastic.

Keith, C. (1991) *A Teacher's Guide to Using Listed Buildings*. London: English Heritage.

MacDonald, S. (1992) Cultural imagining among museum visitors. *Museum Management and Curatorship*, 11, 401–409.

Mason, P. (1992) *Learn to Travel. Activities on Travel and Tourism for the Primary School*. Slough: World Wildlife Fund UK.

Naish, M. (ed.) (1992) *Primary Schools, Geography and the National Curriculum in England. Monitoring the Implementation of Geography in the Primary Curriculum*. Sheffield: Geographical Association.

National Curriculum History Working Group (1990) *Final Report*. London: Department of Education and Science and the Welsh Office.

National Trust (1990) *Cross-currents. A Coastal Studies Handbook for Teachers*. London: National Trust.

National Trust (1991a) *The National Trust and Education*. London: National Trust.

National Trust (1991b) *Fountains Abbey. A Resource Book for Teachers*. Ripon: National Trust.

National Trust (1991c) *Directory for Schools Visits. The National Trust East Anglia*. Bury St Edmunds: National Trust.

National Trust (1992) *Rural Landscapes. A Resource Book for Teachers*. London: National Trust.

National Trust and Buckinghamshire LEA (1991) *Working with the National Trust. Educational Resources in Buckinghamshire*. High Wycombe: National Trust and Buckinghamshire LEA.

Nichol, J. (1984) *Teaching History. A Teaching Skills Workbook*. Basingstoke: Macmillan Education.

Pluckrose, H. (1991) *Children Learning History*. Oxford: Basil Blackwell.

Prentice, M. M. and Prentice, R. C. (1989) The heritage market of historic sites as educational resources. In D. T. Herbert, R. C. Prentice and C. J. Thomas (eds) *Heritage Sites: Strategies for Marketing and Development*. Aldershot: Avebury, pp. 143–190.

Prentice, R. C. (1991) Measuring the educational effectiveness of on-site interpretation designed for tourists. *Area*, 23, 297–308.

Prentice, R. C. (1993a) *Tourism and Heritage Attractions*. London: Routledge.

Prentice, R. C. (1993b) Evaluating interpretation by considering the consumer. *Interpretation Journal*, 53, 9–11.

Relph, E. (1976) *Place and Placelessness*. London: Pion.

Ritchie, W. K. (1982) *Educational Guide to the National Trust for Scotland*. Edinburgh: BP Educational Service and the National Trust for Scotland.

Tann, C. S. (ed.) (1988) *Developing Topic Work in the Primary School*. London: Falmer.

Taylor's Tea & Coffee Ltd (1992) *Discovering the Moors and Dales with Yorkshire Tea and the National Trust*. Harrogate: Taylor's Tea & Coffee Ltd.

Turner, E. and Stronach, I. (1993) *Arts and Education. Perceptions of Policy, Provision and Practice*. Edinburgh: Scottish Arts Council.

Wiegand, P. (1992) *Places in the Primary School*. London: Falmer.

9

Heritage as Business

Peter Johnson and Barry Thomas

This chapter considers the characteristics and determinants of the supply of and demand for heritage, and the way in which these two forces interact. It also examines some of the social welfare and policy implications which arise from the special characteristics of heritage supply and demand. The focus is wider than the commercial management of heritage by self-financing privately owned operations. The reason for this is that much of the management and 'consumption' of heritage is publicly financed, and many of the organizations involved are publicly owned. Furthermore, even in the private sector there is often extensive government regulation of activities, for example through planning controls, and public financial support, via special tax concessions, grants or loans. Much of this public involvement arises because of the distinctive economic features of heritage, which make any analysis based solely on private market transactions very restricted.

The chapter first examines the notion of heritage. Particular attention is paid to those features which are especially relevant for economic analysis. Estimates of the scale of the heritage sector are then provided. Consideration of these estimates is followed by an examination of the supply of, and demand for, heritage, and the 'market' within which these forces interact. The final section outlines the social welfare and policy implications that arise from the analysis.

Heritage: What Is It?

The term 'heritage' is used in a very wide variety of contexts. In recent years it has been increasingly employed to describe virtually anything by which some kind of link, however tenuous or false, may be forged with the past. The term may be employed to enhance the status of an attraction and thus to boost visitor numbers: Hewison (1989, p. 6) provides the example of the brightly painted collection of rockets and bombs in Woomera, Australia, which is described as a heritage centre. Official approval of a stretched definition of heritage in the UK was given by the formation, in April 1992, of the Department of National Heritage, which includes within its responsibilities the promotion of tourism, the National Lottery, press regulation and the safety of sports grounds (Department of National Heritage, 1993, p. 3).[1]

The more traditional uses of the term relate to the natural world (for example, mountains and rivers), buildings and monuments, the arts, and social customs and traditions. All these expressions of heritage relate in some way to the inheritance of present-day society. In order to keep the discussion to manageable proportions, attention is focused exclusively on *sites of significant historical value*. Such sites may consist of buildings and monuments – what might broadly be termed 'the built heritage' – although of course some, such as battlefields, may consist of little more than the relevant piece of land. There is some justification for separating out historical sites from the rest of heritage. For example, these sites, unlike art or museum exhibits, are not geographically mobile, and this often has implications for the way in which they are managed. Buildings may, however, sometimes be reconstructed elsewhere.

Although this chapter has a relatively narrow focus, the exclusion of other forms of heritage from consideration here is less of a restriction than may at first appear, as much of the discussion has a relevance beyond historical sites. It should also be recognized that historical sites and other forms of heritage may compete with each other, or be complementary as far as visitor demand is concerned.

The definition of heritage adopted here does of course beg many questions. For example, what is the appropriate test of 'significant historical value'? Who decides? The historian's or archaeologist's view of what qualifies for such a description may differ from that of others who may be less well informed about the site, or who may wish to use it for other purposes. Too much energy should not be expended on definitional issues. There are in any case many grey areas, and the available data come from a variety of sources, all of which use different definitions.

Heritage, as defined here, may be subject to a production process, by which the raw material – for example the original building or land – undergoes, to a greater or lesser degree, some form of transformation which adds value. Production may be for private consumption only: for example, the owner of a stately home may upgrade the living quarters; alternatively, transformation may be aimed at consumption by the public at large. The management of a castle which is open to the public may add visitor facilities, such as an information centre, a café or a souvenir shop. Other complementary attractions, perhaps not of a heritage kind, may also be developed. Possibilities include the provision of interpretive activities, such as dramatic re-enactments and so on. Sometimes buildings may be moved from their original locations. Many open-air museums consist – in part or in whole – of buildings which have been moved from the site where they were initially built (see, for example, Johnson and Thomas, 1992, pp. 16–37). Transfers of this kind transform the nature of heritage by making it more accessible, and by placing it in a different surrounding. Transformation also occurs where replicas are used either as a substitute for, or as additions to the original items or buildings. Some productive activity may be directed simply at maintenance, for example the replacement of timbers, or repointing.

The previous paragraph suggests that heritage production may be classified into two broad types. First, productive activity may be directed towards *increasing* or *maintaining the stock*. Unearthing a hitherto unknown archaeological site or putting a new roof on a castle are examples of such activity. Secondly, production may be aimed at the *provision of services* at a site such as the activities of interpreters and guides. In practice of course these two types of production are interwoven: the stock will typically affect the flow of services derived from that stock; and it will sometimes be difficult to decide into which category a particular activity falls.

Heritage production has generated much debate about the appropriateness of the scale and nature of the transformation process. Worries about the possible loss of authenticity, often resulting from attempts to meet the requirements of the market-place, have frequently been voiced. Hewison (1989, p. 21) has recently expressed such worries:

> History is gradually being bent into something called Heritage. . . . Heritage is gradually effacing History, by substituting an image of the past for its reality. . . . At a time when the country is obsessed by the past, we have a fading sense of continuity and change, which is being replaced by a fragmented and piecemeal idea of the past, constructed out of costume dramas on television, re-enactment of civil war battles and misleading celebrations of events such as the Glorious Revolution.

Rumble (1989) has expressed a rather less pessimistic view. Whatever stand is taken on these issues, it is clear that *some* form of heritage production is inevitable, if sites are not to become derelict. Even basic maintenance, however, raises important issues: the mixing of modern materials with old ones may change the character of a building.

One of the implications of heritage production aimed at increasing and maintaining the stock is that, contrary to what might be considered obvious, the stock of heritage is not fixed. Of course there will only ever be one Tower of London or Stonehenge. But the uniqueness of these sites does not mean that the *overall* stock of heritage cannot be changed. Nor does it mean that no changes can be made to the sites themselves. Indeed, both the Tower and Stonehenge are constantly evolving as repairs and improvements (in the eyes of some) are made.

The possibilities for changing the stock of heritage raises the question of how far the sites that make it up represent a 'renewable' or 'non-renewable' resource. (There is an extensive literature on both types of resource.) There are clearly renewable elements: Durham Cathedral, for example, has recently had extensive roof and window repairs, and indeed much of its present structure does not go back to the eleventh-century origins of the building. On the other hand if the Cathedral were to be destroyed by fire, it would not be possible to reconstruct a building which has genuine Norman roots. In this sense the Cathedral is a non-renewable resource. But even here it should be noted that while an original Norman Cathedral could not be built, the possibility for a new Cathedral which in some sense 'goes back' to the eleventh century remains. Much depends on precisely how the resource is specified.

The Scale of Heritage

The scale of heritage, as defined in this chapter, may be, and often is, measured in a number of ways, three of which are identified below. First, the heritage *stock* may be evaluated. Such an assessment which by definition relates to a particular point in time, may be carried out using a variety of physical measures, such as the land area involved, or the number of sites. Some data are available on the latter measure.

In England in 1992, 440 000 buildings were listed under the Planning Listed Buildings and Conservation Areas Act 1990 as being of special architectural or historic interest (Department of National Heritage, 1993, p. 55). Just over 6000 of these buildings were listed as Grade 1, i.e. of exceptional interest (Eckstein, 1992, p. 37). The figure of 440 000 may in fact be an underestimate of the number of separate buildings since it treats collections of related buildings, such as a crescent, as one entry only. The number of separate buildings is probably around 500 000 (National Audit Office, 1992, para. 2.5). It is worth noting that the number of listed buildings has grown by over 11 per cent since 1986, and that de-listing as well as new listing occurs (Eckstein, 1992, p. 37). Listing (de-listing) does not of course necessarily imply a growth (reduction) in the heritage stock, although they are likely to be highly correlated. There are about 51 000 listed buildings in Scotland and Wales. In both countries the number of listings also grew considerably in the 1980s. In addition to listed buildings, England has 13 500 scheduled monuments of national importance. The equivalent figure for Scotland and Wales is around 300 (Department of National Heritage, 1993, p. 55; Eckstein, 1992, pp. 54–55).

Most listed buildings and scheduled monuments are privately owned so their care and preservation depend on the efforts of owners and voluntary and private sector organizations. In England the government is responsible for the custody and management of around 400 of the country's most outstanding heritage properties (Committee of Public Accounts, 1993, paras 1 and 2).

Only a small proportion of the total number of sites is open to the public. About 1900 historic properties were known to be open in this way in the summer of 1992. Just under 44 per cent of these were in private ownership and 59 per cent made some form of admission charge (Eckstein, 1992).

Figures on the total number of sites make no allowance for the varying characteristics of these sites. On almost any criterion, some sites are 'worth' more than others. One possible way round this aggregation problem is to provide a monetary valuation. But such valuation, while providing a common unit of account for aggregating disparate sites, raises huge problems. How is such valuation to be arrived at? One possibility would be to take a narrow market-based approach and to ask: 'What would this site fetch on the open market?' While such an approach might be widely acceptable for (say) a habitable house which is of limited historical interest – though even here great care would have to be taken over the interpretation of the estimate – it would be regarded as verging on the silly for a site such as Durham Cathedral, since a market transaction would be unlikely to reflect the wide range of benefits received or likely to be received by individuals and groups in both current and future generations, many of whom might not in any case have the means to express a vote in the market-place. The very notion of a monetary valuation derived from market transactions would be widely regarded as wholly inappropriate in the case of the Cathedral. Monetary valuations which seek to capture the wider benefits might be possible, but they are costly to obtain and may still be objected to on the grounds of principle. Some of these issues are further considered towards the end of this chapter.

A second measure of the scale of heritage (as defined here) is the *cost of the productive activity involved*, whether it is aimed at increasing or maintaining the stock, or providing current services. Productive activity is most easily measured in terms of expenditure. Even the use of expenditure data, however, raises definitional issues: much relevant expenditure, for example on transport infrastructure which improves access to a site, may also serve other purposes. It should also be noted that expenditure data may not capture all the costs. Congestion and noise experienced by residents who live near to a site are not 'paid for' in terms of a conventional market transaction, but are real enough.

Unfortunately very few data on heritage production costs are available. Nevertheless, it is possible to give some idea of *public* expenditure on heritage (most of this goes on improving the stock rather than on providing services). Expenditure estimates for the Department of National Heritage for 1992–93 compared with the out-turn for 1987–88 are given in Table 9.1. Two limitations of the table should be noted: some of the expenditure, for example on armour, is outside the scope of this chapter's definition of heritage; and some of the expenditure is for purchase rather than production. Nevertheless the figures do provide an indication of the scale of public funding of heritage. Over half of the 1992–93 allocation went to English Heritage. Of this £102.3 million, a third (£34.1 million) was accounted for by grants to historic buildings. On the assumption that English Heritage provides 40 per cent of

Table 9.1 Expenditure on heritage in England by the Department of National Heritage (£m)

	1987/88 out-turn	1992/93 estimated
English Heritage	64.8	102.3
Royal Commission on Historical Monuments of England	3.6	12.3
National Heritage Memorial Fund	23.0	12.0
Royal armouries	3.0	5.4
Royal parks	16.3	22.4
Occupied royal palaces, other historic buildings and state ceremonial	15.6	30.6
Historical Royal Palaces agency	7.0	9.0
Other bodies	2.2	2.8
Total	135.5	196.8

Source: Department of National Heritage (1993, p. 53). For details of the role of each of the agencies see National Audit Office (1992, p. 5).

the total cost of an improvement or repair, about £86 million was spent on the buildings involved. However, although these buildings are likely to be among the more important, they nevertheless represent only a very small proportion of the total number of historic buildings in England.[2] Unfortunately no cost estimates of improvements and repairs to buildings in which English Heritage is not involved are available. Similarly, data on the (current) production cost of heritage services are unavailable.

The absence of good cost estimates makes efficient resource allocation difficult. Given the limited resources available at the level both of the individual and of society, choices have to be made over how much heritage production there is to be, and what form it should take. Without cost data, these choices must inevitably become dependent on informed guesswork.

The final measure of heritage scale outlined here relates to *the consumption of heritage*. Such consumption may take many different forms. At one level, the occupant of a stately home not open to the public may derive enjoyment from his/her residence. At another level, members of the public may visit or view a site, to derive some other enjoyment from its presence. It may be possible to go some way towards placing monetary values on such consumption, but such calculations present formidable problems, and at best are only likely to give partial results. Readily available measures have severe limitations. For example, some data may be available on entrance fees, but at many sites no admissions charge is payable or, if it is, it does not fully reflect the value placed by visitors on the site. Furthermore, there are many forms of consumption that do not involve actual entry.

Physical measures of consumption include those based on statistics such as numbers of visitors, but again these have obvious limitations. Nevertheless, in the UK, visitor numbers are the most readily available measure. It is estimated (Eckstein, 1992, p. 29) that just over 67 million people visited historic properties in the UK in 1990, 58 million in England. (The 58 million

176 Peter Johnson and Barry Thomas

in England represented a 7 per cent increase over 1985.) Visitor numbers are heavily concentrated in a few of these properties: the top 17 each attracted over 500 000 visitors in 1990, 32 per cent (21.3 million) of the total. Eight of these seventeen were churches or cathedrals.

Although there is evidence of a growing interest, measured by the increase in visitor numbers, in historic sites generally, there have also been some changes in the ranking of different sites (Eckstein, 1992, p. 28). Such changes may be evidence of a product life cycle (Johnson and Thomas, 1991).

Supply

It is helpful to maintain the broad distinction made earlier between the heritage stock and the flow of services that comes from that stock. The heritage stock, for the purposes of this chapter, consists of all known sites of significant historical interest. It has already been suggested that this stock may be changed. This may be attempted in one of two basic ways. First, efforts may be made to *widen* the stock. New sites may be discovered, and sites that were not previously regarded as having significant historical interest may, by various means, be invested with that status.[3] The provision of new wall plaques commemorating some historical event or personage not previously celebrated is one such mechanism. This may mean that sites which are progressively more marginal, in historical terms, are added to the stock. However, it is not necessarily inevitable that the more recent additions will be of lower historical significance. Major finds may still be made, and in any event there are likely to be changes over time in society's perceptions of what is historically valuable.

Secondly, the *deepening* of the heritage stock may be possible, by enhancing, in some way, existing sites through the kind of transformation discussed earlier. For example a visitor centre may be added, or additional buildings may be constructed. It should be stressed again that the scale and nature of such transformation is always likely to remain a matter of fierce debate. Some observers argue that certain kinds of transformation, far from enhancing the historical significance of a site, actually detract from that significance.

With the passage of time, of course, the stock of heritage will inevitably change, as more sites are chosen for conservation and/or preservation, and as others disappear. The net change will depend in part on the resources devoted to maintaining and enhancing the existing stock. Changes in the supply of heritage *services* will of course be affected by any changes in stock. But it may also be achieved by other means. In the following discussion attention is focused on those sites that are open to the public.

For a given stock, it may be possible to increase visitor throughput, by, for example, extending opening hours or by increasing the speed at which visitors view the site. It may also be possible, by organizational changes, for example over routing, to process more visitors in a given time. A word of caution is in order here. The quality of visitor experience is unlikely to be independent of visitor numbers, or indeed of a site's organization and the arrangements made for visitors. A castle that seeks to ease congestion by forcing its visitors round at a faster pace, or in a way that is otherwise less congenial, may not cause the total flow of services (measured in constant quality terms) to increase with visitor numbers.

Another way to increase the flow of services from a given heritage stock is by increasing the amount of added value generated by that stock. Visitors may for example receive more interpretation, through more staff, or from visitor aids, such as information boards or audiovisual equipment.[4] There is however likely to be a limit to the extent to which heritage services may be derived from a given stock. Capacity limits often determined by legislation (e.g. on fire regulations) impose a ceiling on visitor numbers.

As indicated earlier, the stock of, and flow of, services from heritage are related. The scale of the available stock affects the services that can be generated. Conversely the scale of heritage services provided may affect the stock. This latter effect may be felt in a variety of ways. Increases in services may lead to the depreciation of the stock as it gets worn out. The stock may then cease to be available for future generations of customers, unless some action constraining consumption activity – such as stopping visitors from using a staircase – is taken. (It should be noted that some of the services derived from the stock may not lead to depreciation. The enjoyment of the view of, say, Edinburgh Castle, does not itself lead to degradation of the castle.) Consumption of heritage services may, however, have an indirect positive effect on the heritage stock, by providing signals that more is required. It may also be that the provision of services may generate financial resources which can then be ploughed back to enhance the improvement of the stock.

It would be useful, for policy purposes, to know how the supply of both the stock of heritage and the services derived from that stock respond to different stimuli. Unfortunately little empirical evidence on the various elasticities of supply (of either stock or services) is available, although it would probably be fair to say that a given percentage increase in heritage services is likely to be achievable more rapidly than the same increase in stock simply because the production lags are shorter. For both stock and services the responsiveness of supply to a particular stimulus is likely to be lower, the shorter the time period under consideration.

There is one other feature of the supply of heritage services that deserves mention here. For a given stock, the marginal cost, at least up to capacity limits, of providing more services may be very low. This means that for the private owner of a heritage site who is providing services for visitors, it will be worthwhile to continue offering these services as long as marginal costs are covered by receipts. This may mean, however, that the capital costs of maintaining the stock are not met, even though all visitors pay (at least) the addition to total cost that their visit generates. This problem, well known to students of nationalized industries, means that if the site is to remain open to visitors willing to meet marginal costs then some form of public subsidy may be necessary.

Demand

The demand for heritage may come from many sources. It is worth categorizing these because the purpose for which heritage is demanded, and hence the determinants of demand, are likely to differ for different types of 'buyer'. Individuals are one obvious category. 'Individuals' here include not only persons and households, but also private sector corporations. A second source of demand is government, both central and local. It is common to treat this category as synonymous with 'society' though in doing so it is assumed that government, as the institution appointed to reflect society's wishes, does in fact do so. In addition to the private and social demands there may be a third category which straddles both, such as groups formed as guardians and watchdogs of heritage, like local civic trusts, preservation societies, and the National Trust. Some of these may be groups of private individuals and some may be quasi-governmental organizations.

There are several reasons why heritage is demanded. In the first place is the demand to *use* the heritage. This may be demand by those who wish to view or visit the site – the tourist demand – or it may be the demand to use the heritage building, for example as a place to live in or for offices or for some other functional purpose. Secondly there may be *option demand* on the part of those potential visitors or users who demand heritage because they wish to retain the option of visiting or using it. They may receive benefits from the fact that the opportunity exists for them to visit the site, but because they do not actually do so they do not express their demand through payment in the market. Thirdly, by similar reasoning, is *existence demand*. Existence value is a value placed on heritage which is not directly related to any actual or potential use of the heritage. It is 'demand' based on the notion that there is some intrinsic value which is independent of exchange value (though such an idea raises important issues about how the strength of such existence demand might be measured). Existence value may relate to the present – there is satisfaction merely from knowing that heritage exists now – but it may also be part of a desire to pass on to future generations the heritage that we have acquired from previous generations. Thus a fourth kind of demand is *bequest demand*.

It is possible, and in some cases very likely, that these kinds of demand overlap. For example, an owner of a stately home may have a strong use value, reflecting a wish to use it as a place to live in, and may also have a bequest value, reflecting a wish to pass it on to his or her heirs. Given the variety of sources of demand, it is not surprising that there are several factors which determine the level of demand for heritage buildings. The factors that determine the government's wish to preserve historic buildings may be very different from the factors influencing the number of visits by leisure day trippers. So far as the latter category is concerned, theory suggests that two key determinants of demand are real personal disposable income and the price.

A limited amount of work has been carried out which tries to identify demand functions for historic houses. Incomes of visitors seem to be far more important than prices in determining the variations in the size of visitor flows. Aylen (1978), following Snaith (1974, 1975), found that real personal disposable income was of 'overwhelming importance' in his study of eleven historic houses and gardens open to the public in Surrey, whereas real admission price was not significant or wrongly signed. This view of the importance of income was supported by Darnell *et al.* (1990) in their study of the demand for Beamish museum.[5] They found income elasticity to be over 4 but price elasticity to be about 0.5. On a more casual basis, well over half of the historic houses which were surveyed for the English Tourist Board cited the economic recession of the early 1990s as a negative factor influencing visitor flows (see English Tourist Board, 1993, p. 36, Table 8). A positive factor offsetting this decline in income was improved marketing and promotion, but there seems little dispute that income is very significant in determining visitor flows. The distribution of income may also be relevant. So far as the future is concerned the trend is likely to be one of real income growth, especially among those groups who are most likely to visit heritage properties. By the end of the century, it is estimated that one in four Europeans will be over 55 years of age, and the retirement age will fall. 'This group of potential visitors are, and are likely to be, relatively affluent with a high percentage of available leisure time' (English Tourist Board/Employment Department Group, 1991, p. 3), and they are likely to be more interested in heritage tourism than many other groups. Prentice (1993, p. 227) for example notes that 'heritage tourism is socially selective', with a disproportionate number of non-manual and, in particular, professional and senior managerial households. The growth in heritage demand, resting on a positive income elasticity of demand, may however be offset by an increasing real price of leisure (see Throsby and Withers, 1979, p. 31, for such an argument in relation to the performing arts).

The seeming inelasticity of demand with respect to price may be a short-run phenomenon, attributable to the fact that visiting heritage sites may be an 'acquired skill' (to use Throsby and Withers's phrase (1979, p. 28) in relation to art appreciation) such that when price is increased people do not lightly discard the skill and when prices fall it takes time to acquire the skill. If there is some specialist heritage interest which entails the acquisition of historical knowledge this argument may carry over from the performing arts. There is, however, little evidence that most heritage tourists are 'heritage enthusiasts'.[6] Prentice (1993, p. 225) argues that:

the prevalent characteristic of heritage tourists . . . is that many are seeking generalist recreation: heritage enthusiasts or specialists are not the dominant market segment of such tourists, despite such an assumption being implied in the manner in which many established heritage attractions had until the 1980s been presented.

In the longer term the price elasticity will depend on the existence of substitutes. Some very casual evidence which suggests that demand may in fact be price sensitive is provided by the Employment Committee (1990a, para. 39) which noted that 'tourists appeared willing to spend money in hotels but not on high admission charges to historic houses',[7] though information on levels does not of course tell us about elasticities.

The Market for Heritage

A market is a coordinating mechanism which brings together buyers and sellers. In the absence of market failure it produces an equilibrium which is satisfactory to both – the amount of heritage that people wish to 'buy' is identical to that which people wish to 'sell' – and this outcome is socially optimal in the sense that the benefits to society (including future generations), net of the resource costs of supplying and maintaining the heritage property, are maximized. Key elements of the market mechanism which are necessary to ensure such an equilibrium are that there are rational well-informed individuals who are free to act in their own interests, and who operate in a competitive environment with no externalities and with flexible prices. Any imbalance between supply and demand is eliminated by an automatic market clearing process – typically by price adjustments.

It is not at all obvious that a market, as just described, exists (or ought to exist) in the case of heritage and whether, to the extent that it does exist, the optimal amount of conservation occurs. There are clearly some special features of heritage. First, externalities are prominent (see the section on Policy Issues below). Secondly, on the one hand, there are varied ownership patterns (collective, in trust, private) and different objective functions of owners (not-for-profit, profit maximization), and on the other hand there are different sources of demand (use for visiting, use for living in, option, existence), so that the market is rather complex. Sometimes supply and demand are fused as when owners occupy their buildings as living accommodation, and in some cases, such as option demand, there is no market expression of such preferences and consequently no supply response through the market. In other cases, however, such as the supply of historic properties for tourists, there is a market with supply and demand interacting in a setting where there are elements of competition. It was argued in the section on Supply above that supply can be responsive to demand and associated possibilities for raising revenue. Additional properties can be opened up for tourists or existing ones withdrawn. There are, however, some constraints on the process of supply adjustment. The National Trust, for example, has 'the unique power to declare its land and properties inalienable, i.e. they can never be sold or mortgaged. Nor can they be compulsorily acquired without the special sanction of parliament' (Lees and Coyne, 1979, p. 36). This might provide a ratchet on supply and limit reductions. It is also the case, however, that some decisions to reduce supply are irrevocable. As Aylen (1978, p. 410) comments: 'Once demolished, an historic building cannot be resupplied. Like the supply of wilderness areas or, possibly, rare plants or animal species, reductions in the stock of historic buildings are irreversible.'

Some competitive elements do exist in the case of properties open to visitors. There is little overt price competition but there are some serious checks on ability to raise prices. Some suppliers may not be profit-maximizers but, like the National Trust, set prices to maximize visitor numbers (subject to capacity constraints,[8] the need to limit wear and tear, and to cover operating costs), and other suppliers such as some local authorities may not charge admission prices. These pricing strategies limit the ability of private sector owners to raise prices. Price competition will be stronger where there are substitutes and the question arises as to how far historic houses are substitutes for one and other. It may be argued, as Aylen (1978, p. 427) does, that 'historic buildings have intrinsically unique characteristics which, for connoisseurs at least, make them complementary to existing sites'. Aylen goes on to argue that tastes for historic buildings may adapt to the supply of facilities. This complementarity is, however, almost certainly confined to a small segment of visitors. The fact that many visitors to historic properties are seeking generalist recreation means that such properties will be substitutes and will also compete with a far wider range of attractions and leisure opportunities.

A certain amount of non-price competition and some product differentiation is possible because many potential visitors 'look to a visit to an historic property as much for its entertainment value as for its educational value' (Eckstein, 1992, p. 33) and the facilities offered by historic properties have increased significantly (see Table 9.2). Some historic properties have entered into joint ventures with nearby hotels (Employment Committee, 1990a, para. 39).

Table 9.2 Facilities of historic properties open to the public in England[*]

	1979 %	1992 %
Guided tours	29	36
Tea	24	30
Lunch	7	14
Museums or exhibitions	60	65
Literary associations	5	4
Garden	40	39
Park	22	19
Activities (sports, concerts, etc.)	10	25

[*] Excluding cathedrals and churches in use.
Source: Eckstein (1992, p. 33) based on English Tourism Board, *English Heritage Monitor*.

Policy Issues

The previous section showed that although a market exists for the services of heritage properties – especially for heritage tourism – it falls a long way short of the ideal concept of a market which would deliver a socially optimal outcome in terms of the amount of society's scarce resources which should be allocated to the 'production' of heritage. (Production in this context is the creation of value by conservation, renovation, providing access, marketing and all the other activities which are associated with heritage supply.) Market failure provides a potential justification for state intervention and it is not surprising to find that most governments have a presence in the heritage business.

The case for government intervention

There are obvious externalities in the case of heritage properties; social benefits exceed private benefits and this provides a major reason for government intervention. Free market solutions, which cannot take account of external benefits,[9] may not safeguard properties whose net social benefits are substantial. One particular form of external benefit which is not captured in the market calculation is that accruing to future generations. Present efforts to conserve the stock of heritage properties will be of benefit to future generations in the same way as the present generation benefits (or, in the case of destruction, loses) from past efforts.

A slightly different issue, though one which is closely related to externalities, is the 'public good' nature of heritage property. Whereas the interior of a property is clearly a private good (one person's consumption precludes consumption by another, and people can be excluded from consumption) the exterior is a public good (one person's consumption does not reduce its availability to anyone else, and people cannot be excluded from consumption). The view of York Minster, the ambience of the city of Bath, and the chimes of Big Ben are clear examples of public good aspects of heritage. Even the images of historic buildings are often treated as public property and appropriated by others – the image of the Cathedral is often used by anyone promoting events or business in Durham, and, as Thomas (1992) notes, Magdalen Bridge in Oxford is frequently used by marketeers.

This latter point, though in itself trivial, highlights the important issue of property rights in heritage. These can be well defined in legal terms so far as buildings are concerned but if heritage is a common property resource belonging to all members of society then markets which are essentially the interplay of private interests cannot guarantee optimal outcomes. Where heritage property is regarded as belonging to all generations then the present generation simply acts as trustees.

A further argument which has been used to justify government intervention is the role of historic houses in promoting tourism and employment. One estimate suggests that 70 per cent of overseas visitors come to Britain to see its historic towns, cities, and heritage properties (Employment Committee, 1990a, para. 37) and some estimates of employment indicate that total employment, including indirect, might be as much as double the direct employment (Employment Committee, 1990b, pp. 147–148). The government is sometimes urged to support the heritage industry on this ground of economic development, though there is nothing special about heritage as an engine of development and the relevant issue is whether the incomes and jobs created directly and indirectly from government support for heritage are greater than the benefits that could be obtained from the same level of support given to any other industry. Any comparison would have to take account of other benefits, such as cultural enrichment, which might derive from such support.

The market failure arguments only justify government support if government failure does not outweigh the market failure. To achieve a socially optimal allocation of resources to heritage there must be confidence that governments can identify the optimal levels, that they have the means to ensure such outcomes, and that they will actually take appropriate action. The problems in identifying the optimal level and the means of achieving this are now considered.

How much heritage?

This issue is looked at from the perspective of how much conservation there should be. It is clear that there may be some non-economic considerations. Buildings which have architectural or historical significance are sometimes protected on aesthetic or cultural grounds. Moreover, as noted above, the present generation's ownership may be viewed as trusteeship for future generations. In this case a policy implication is that the present generation has no rights to touch the buildings, or perhaps has a duty to maintain the stock and pass it on. Such views are not helpful as a guide to practical policy. In reality choices do have to be made about the use of resources and it is not feasible to conserve all buildings of every age because the opportunity cost would be too high. If it were accepted that some buildings will deteriorate it may be that there is some obligation to pass on a stock of equal value. All this entails assigning values to the heritage stock and making choices.

The socially optimal amount of conservation is that which maximizes net social benefits, that is, total social benefits minus total social opportunity costs. The costs are relatively easy to identify in the case of conservation. Benefits are more difficult to value. Heritage value is unlikely to be accurately measured by markets. Market prices do not measure consumer surplus,[10] though this is true of all goods and the total use value can be estimated if the size of the consumer surplus can be established. But in the case of heritage properties there is the further problem that their value as measured in the market-place derives from their use and not their cultural quality. In Lichfield's (1988, p. 169) words:

> former cotton mills have significant cultural value as industrial archaeology but may have no market value as property. . . . And the point is further emphasized in considering . . . the negative market value of a ruined castle, which must be kept that way because of its considerable heritage value, and thereby involves the government in considerable sums in maintenance and management, so producing negative exchange values.

The problem of intangibles sometimes leads to the view that 'there is no price you can put on irreplaceable historical evidence. This is a moral not a financial question.'[11] It remains, however, an unavoidable task to attempt to put value on heritage properties (including option, existence and bequest values) if the socially optimal amount of resources is to be devoted to conservation.

There have been some attempts at such valuation but these are few and far between because of the formidable problems. Environmental economists have developed a number of techniques for measuring value as the sum of market value (price, if any, multiplied by quantity) plus consumer surplus. Each of these has some important limitations,[12] but in the absence of anything better they must be regarded seriously. The contingent valuation method has been employed for example by Thomas (1992) in a study of Magdalen Bridge, Oxford, and by Navrud *et al.* (1992) in a study of Nidaros Cathedral in Trondheim. These studies were concerned to estimate willingness to pay (WTP) by users (visitors). In the cases of Thomas and of Navrud *et al.* the attempt was made to explore WTP for renewal or preservation. The travel cost method has been used by Aylen (1978) in his social cost-benefit analysis of the restoration of Barlaston Hall, Staffordshire. These methods cannot of course assess option, existence or bequest values. These are not fully revealed in measures of WTP of visitors because non-visitors may well have preferences which should be counted. One possible way of assessing such preferences is charity. If there is, for instance, an appeal to restore an historic building it may be that donations measure the option value of individual risk-averse consumers: the donations are like a risk premium paid by consumers attempting to insure against the possibility of not being able to visit the restored building in future. If the unrestored building is in danger of collapse or demolition consumers are faced with an irreversible supply and they would not be able to express their revised preferences later.[13]

The various difficulties in assessing value, which have been described, mean that precise identification of the optimal level of conservation is often not possible, but there does seem wide agreement on two matters. First, the market and decisions of private owners are likely to yield a socially sub-optimal amount of conservation and, secondly, the departure from the optimum is almost certainly great enough to warrant government intervention – that is, it is not likely to be wholly offset by any government failure.

Methods of government intervention

There are several ways in which governments can intervene in the heritage market: attempts to influence ownership, quantities and prices will be considered here. One way of internalizing the externalities is to take heritage properties into public ownership. In the case of major heritage sites or properties this sometimes happens, but more frequently 'there is in respect of certain parts of the heritage a form of ownership which transcends that of the proprietor protected in law. . . . [The government] can be said to create in the heritage a "heritage tenure", that is rights without necessarily assuming ownership' (Lichfield, 1988, p. 65).

It is this assumption of rights that leads to direct intervention to control quantities through listing and scheduling. Resource constraints prevent the government from protecting all possible candidates in the stock of heritage properties, and selection is necessary. In terms of the efficient allocation of resources the selection should be based on an explicit assessment of the social benefits and social opportunity costs arising from a protection decision. It has been argued above, however, that it is formidably difficult to express cultural values in money terms. The criterion used by the Department of National Heritage for selection under the Planning (Listed Buildings and Conservation Areas) Act 1990 and earlier legislation is 'special architectural or historic interest'. Under the Ancient Monuments and Archaeological Areas Act 1979, they similarly maintain a schedule of monuments; 'of national importance' (National Audit Office, 1992, p. 7).[14] The designation of special interest or importance is decided on the basis of judgements by 'experts' – persons who are knowledgeable and interested – and on advice from English Heritage. Their standpoint is that of, for example, an architectural historian rather than an economist concerned to measure net social benefits. One of the difficulties of using such criteria is that they will not necessarily result in standardized assessment since the people who actually undertake the listing may interpret centrally specified criteria differently and may use criteria which are not specified.[15]

The practice of listing has been used on a global scale as well as by individual countries. UNESCO's World Heritage Convention (WHC) has two main purposes: to draw up a list of World Heritage sites which UN member states pledge to protect; and to operate the World Heritage Fund which gives practical support to conservation projects at threatened sites on the list. Thirteen sites in the UK have received recognition by the WHC (see Department of the Environment, 1992, p. 73).

The Government's view is that these listing and scheduling procedures constitute: 'an effective system . . . to identify and protect the built heritage'

(Department of National Heritage, 1993, p. 55) though the lists and schedules have been severely criticized by the Committee of Public Accounts (1993, para. 9(i)) as being inadequate and out of date.

A third way of attempting to achieve a social optimum is by influencing the prices that private decision makers face. In the UK various forms of subsidy have been used to stimulate production. English Heritage have statutory powers to make loans (and to charge interest on these as they see fit) but in fact these have not been used. Grants, however, have been used, and between 1984 and 1991 about £220 million was spent by English Heritage and the National Heritage Memorial Fund on various grants, given under several Acts, intended to protect and conserve England's most important heritage buildings.[16] These grants, which are usually conditional on owners offering access to the public, are now targeted 'at historic buildings under greatest risk, for example, because they have no economic use or market value, have too low a market value to justify the costs of necessary repairs or have no conceivable commercial use' (National Audit Office, 1992, p. 19). The financial position of owners is explicitly taken into account. In addition to grant aid there are subsidies in the form of tax benefits. Various changes have been made in the legislation relating to inheritance tax in order to try and assist in preserving heritage property; in particular, provision has been made for maintenance funds to enable assets to be set aside for the support of heritage property which receive favourable tax treatment (see Emmerson, 1988). Another source of tax relief is the provision for some reconstruction work on heritage buildings to be zero-rated for Value Added Tax.

These various subsidies, designed to increase the amount of conservation of the built heritage, have to be paid for from the public purse. The use of general taxation enjoins everyone to contribute, though some individual members of society may feel that they do not benefit. Taxation according to the benefit principle might overcome this problem but this is indistinguishable from charging. The use of admission charges is in fact common[17] but it has already been argued that there are serious problems with relying on prices – there are some forms of demand not expressed through prices, there are externalities, there are some public good aspects of heritage properties which make it technically impossible to price all the attributes of the property – and these limitations mean that public subsidy is still necessary.

Conclusion

The argument in this chapter has been that the heritage business uses resources and produces an output which is valued by society. A key issue is whether the scale of this business is optimal: are we conserving too many or too few buildings and are the right ones being conserved? In principle a system of freely competitive markets can yield an optimal solution: society's scarce resources will be allocated to different activities to produce the most-valued mix of outputs. In the case of heritage there are some elements of a market – there is an identifiable demand and a variable supply – and this market appears to operate with some success for heritage tourism. This aspect of heritage is, however, part of a wider leisure market in which heritage properties compete with other attractions and the product is essentially a form of entertainment. Where the heritage product is seen more in terms of its cultural and historical attributes the market is much less satisfactory. There are sometimes confused ownership rights, as when the nation assumes rights in private properties (which can lead to conflicts between private homes and public access), there are externalities, and serious obstacles to measuring the true social value of heritage.

In these circumstances of market failure government intervention is appropriate if it can ensure that the amount of conservation is nearer to the social optimum than would be the case with private decision making. But there is still no clearly identifiable optimal level of conservation because the value of heritage is uncertain: markets do not measure it accurately and it is not feasible to undertake a social cost-benefit analysis of every heritage property. The outcomes are in practice determined in a public choice framework in which many different interest groups are represented. There is no reason to suppose that the outcomes are not the best that are attainable. Many countries have demonstrated similar levels of interest and adopted similar solutions. To the extent that such consensus exists this may be taken as an indication that the best possible solution is being achieved.

This does not imply complacency. A substantial advantage of the economic perspective on the heritage business, not always apparent in the views of others, is that it identifies two unavoidable issues to be faced if superior outcomes are to be achieved. The first is estimating net benefits of heritage. Resource costs have to be taken into account as well as the total value to society (including due consideration of intangibles). The 'save all at any cost' philosophy is unlikely to maximize welfare and indeed can block desirable developments. Prohibiting demolition may sterilize a site and prevent its development for more valuable uses. In weighing the benefits and costs it is of course necessary to allow for the asymmetry that demolition decisions are irreversible whereas preservation ones are not. The second challenge, which is a standard problem for all common property resources (see Seabright, 1993), is to decide on ownership and, if private ownership is favoured, to establish what are the most efficient incentives to induce socially optimal behaviour by private individuals. In some cases private owners, often individuals, have a genuine concern to safeguard heritage properties (even though in narrow accounting terms losses may be made) but not all private owners of heritage property, for example commercially orientated companies, might act this way. The question then is whether a trust relationship which allows individuals to act as guardians of society's welfare is more desirable than a transaction relationship.

Notes

1. The wide-ranging use of the term heritage is highlighted by its definition given by the Chairman of the National Heritage Memorial Fund. Hewison (1989) quotes him as defining heritage as 'anything you want'.
2. English Heritage (1992, p. 9) reported that 141 historic buildings and monuments grants were offered along with 226 church grant offers in 1991–92.
3. The possibility of 'manufacturing' heritage from scratch via replicas is ignored here.
4. Whether or not such aids are regarded as changing the stock depends on how the stock is defined. Such a definition is inevitably arbitrary. In the text it is assumed that the aids mentioned do not change the stock.
5. Beamish Museum is a collection of buildings, of historical interest from a social and industrial standpoint, which have been transplanted. This may not therefore be directly comparable to visiting original heritage sites.
6. The definition of heritage enthusiasts is problematic, as Prentice (1993) notes, though he explores a definition in terms of, for example, frequency of visiting heritage attractions and membership of heritage organizations.
7. The committee cites evidence (Employment Committee, 1990b, p. 148) of 'a tourist who will question an admission charge of £3 to an historic house which will provide him with more than two hours' pleasure [but who] will think nothing of paying five times that amount for a perfectly ordinary dinner in the hotel where he is staying, and probably at least 15 times that amount for his room'.
8. The notion of 'capacity' is problematic. For a discussion in the context of historic towns see Johnson and Thomas (1993).
9. Of course a 'market' also exists for charitable giving. Not all recipients of the external benefits of heritage wish to be free-riders. They may make payments for the benefits received via donations. To the extent that such giving exists, the argument in the text will need to be modified.
10. Except under the special circumstance of a perfectly discriminating monopoly.
11. This remark is by the architectural historian, Jane Fawcett, quoted in the *Independent* (1993).
12. For a review of the techniques and their limitations see Hanley (1990).
13. See Aylen (1978, pp. 430–431) for a discussion of the weaknesses and merits of using charitable giving as an expression of preferences.
14. There is no clear distinction between monuments and listed buildings, and some buildings may be both listed and scheduled.
15. Lichfield (1988, p. 81) notes that in some countries this problem is addressed by the adoption of dates: e.g. in Cyprus anything before 1850, and in Israel before 1700, receives automatic protection.
16. For details see National Audit Office (1992, p. 17).
17. About 90 per cent of historic properties monitored by the British Tourism Authority (those attracting 10 000 or more visitors per annum) impose charges; see Eckstein (1992, Table 2.5).

References

Aylen, J. (1978) The social cost-benefit analysis of historic building restoration: a case study of Barlaston Hall, Staffordshire. In M. J. Artis and A. R. Nobay (eds) *Contemporary Economic Analysis*. Harlow: Longman, pp. 409–447.

Committee of Public Accounts (1993) *Twenty-Ninth Report. Protecting and Managing England's Heritage Properly*, Hc 252, Session 1992–93. London: HMSO.

Darnell, A. C., Johnson, P. S. and Thomas, R. B. (1990) Modelling museum visitor flows: a case study of Beamish Museum. *Tourism Management*, 11, 251–257.

Department of National Heritage (1993) *Annual Report 1993*, Cm 2211. London: HMSO.

Department of the Environment (1992) *UK Environment*. London: HMSO.

Eckstein, J. (ed.) (1992) *Cultural Trends*, Vol. 15. London: Policy Studies Institute.

Emmerson, J. C. (1988) Maintenance funds for heritage property. *British Tax Review*, 11, 442–445.

Employment Committee (1990a) *Tourism*, Vol. 1. *Report*. House of Commons, Session 1989–90. London: HMSO.

Employment Committee (1990b) *Tourism*. Minutes of Evidence. House of Commons, Session 1989–90. London: HMSO.

English Heritage (1992) *Annual Report and Accounts 1991/92*. London: English Heritage.

English Tourist Board (1993) *Sightseeing in the UK, 1992*. London: ETB/BTA.

English Tourist Board/Employment Department Group (1991) *Report of the Historic Towns Working Group. Tourism and the Environment*. London: ETB/EDG.

Hanley, N. (1990) *Valuation of Environmental Effects. Final Report – Stage One*. Economists and Statistics Unit of the Industry Department for Scotland and the Scottish Development Agency. Research Paper No. 22.

Hewison, R. (1989) Heritage: an interpretation. In D. Uzzell (ed.) *Heritage Interpretation*, Vol. 1. London: Belhaven, pp. 15–23.

Independent (1993) Tourists wearing away vital pieces of history. 3 April, p. 7.

Johnson, P. S. and Thomas, R. B. (1991) The comparative analysis of tourist attractions. In C. Cooper (ed.) *Progress in Tourism, Recreation and Hospitality Management*, Vol. 3. London: Belhaven, pp. 114–129.

Johnson, P. S. and Thomas, R. B. (1992) *Tourism, Museums and the Local Economy. The Economic Impact of the North of England Open Air Museum at Beamish*. Aldershot: Edward Elgar.

Johnson, P. and Thomas, B. (1993) The notion of capacity in tourism. In C. Cooper (ed.) *Progress in Tourism, Recreation and Hospitality Management*, Vol. 5. London: Belhaven, pp. 297–308.

Lees, D. and Coyne, J. (1979) Can we afford our national heritage? *Lloyds Bank Review*, 131, 35–48.

Lichfield, N. (1988) *Economics in Urban Conservation*. Cambridge: Cambridge University Press.

National Audit Office (1992) *Protecting and Managing England's Heritage Property*, Report no. 132. London: HMSO.

Navrud, S., Pederson, P. E. and Stand, J. (1992) Valuing our cultural heritage: a contingent valuation survey. Oslo: Centre for Research in Economics and Business Administration. Quoted in Willis *et al.*, 1993.

Prentice, R. (1993) *Tourism and Heritage Attractions*. London: Routledge.

Rumble, P. (1989) Interpreting the built and historic environment. In D. L. Uzzell (ed.) *Heritage Interpretation*, Vol. 1. London: Belhaven, pp. 24–32.

Seabright, P. (1993) Managing local commons: theoretical issues and incentive design. *Journal of Economic Perspectives*, 7(4), 113–134.

Snaith, P. (1974) 'Economics of reaction planning.' Unpublished M.Phil. thesis in Economics, University of York.

Snaith, R. (1975) What price heritage? Estimating the price elasticity of demand for National Trust properties. In G. A. C. Searle (ed.) *Recreational Economics and Analysis*. Harlow: Longman, pp. 141–150.

Thomas, J. (1992) 'Tourism and the environment: an exploration of the willingness to pay of the average visitor.' Paper given to the conference on 'Tourism in Europe', Durham University.

Throsby, C. D. and Withers, G. A. (1979) *The Economics of the Performing Arts*. London: Edward Arnold.

10

Heritage as Design: a Practitioner's Perspective

Terry Stevens

'Resources Are Not; They Become'

The heterogeneity of the heritage product has been discussed by several authors (see, for example, Herbert et al., 1989; Walsh-Heron and Stevens, 1990; Prentice, 1993). Gunn (1972) concluded that 'resources are not: they become', and quoted Zimmerman, who said that:

> Neither the environment as such nor parts or features of the environment *per se* are resources [for tourism]; they become resources only if, when, and in so far as they are, or considered to be capable of serving man's needs. In other words, the word resource is an expression of appraisal and hence purely a subjective concept. (Zimmerman, 1933, p. 3)

It would appear, therefore, that a heritage attraction can be created from any historic or cultural site, event, artefact or even as a result of an association with an historic person.

The objective of those involved in the design of the heritage attraction is to utilize this diverse resource base through appropriate planning, development, management and marketing, thus creating settings which stimulate and satisfy the desires of a multi-segmented market (Gunn, 1972). Against this backcloth, it is clear that appropriate intervention and investment can create visitor attractions out of virtually any heritage resource. The interventionist requirements to convert a heritage feature into a visitor attraction include: strategic product identification and development; access and accessibility (at both the macro-and micro-levels); the marketing of the product to stimulate demand; and appropriate operational management of the visitor experience. Consequently, a fundamental prerequisite is for the attraction to be recognized as such by both visitors and managers (Walsh-Heron and Stevens, 1990).

192   *Terry Stevens*

Table 10.1   Historic properties in the United Kingdom with 50 000 or more visitors per annum, 1989

	Commercial		Free	
	Number of properties	Number of visitors (millions)	Number of properties	Number of visitors (millions)
Castles and forts	45	8.3	–	–
Cathedrals and churches	8	1.2	33	17.5
Monuments, ruins, parks, gardens	14	2.3	1	0.1
Stately homes, palaces, other houses	75	8.4	7	0.5
Historic ships	6	1.3	1	0.1
Other	11	2.1	6	0.6
Total	159	23.6	48	18.9

Source: Applied Leisure Marketing 1991, in Wooder (1991).

The past 20 years have witnessed the emergence of the heritage sector as a major component of the rapidly expanding tourist industry, a phenomenon not without its critics (Hewison, 1987). The development of visitor facilities and services at heritage sites to meet the perceived market demands has become a preoccupation for many public agencies charged with guardianship of the historic estate. Equally, the private sector has become increasingly involved in managing the traditional heritage for the day-visitor market, including archaeological sites, historic houses, gardens, religious buildings and industrial monuments. For example, the English Tourist Board (ETB) (Wooder, 1991), estimated that about 180 historic properties – one-third of the total –are controlled by the private sector, together with over 40 religious properties which attract over 50 000 visitors per annum. The private sector's involvement and share of the market continues to grow. Of the 207 private historic properties in the United Kingdom attracting over 50 000 visitors per annum in 1991, 16 had opened to the public over the past decade (see Table 10.1).

The private sector is particularly active in 'producing' simulated heritage attractions to satisfy the tourist and leisure day-visitor demand for heritage-based experiences. The development of this genre of new 'heritage experience attractions' (Wooder, 1991) often involves sensory, hands-on, visitor involvement within a re-created historical environment. A high-volume throughput is generally required in these robust environments to provide the return on investment, especially the relatively high initial capital requirements (see Table 10.2). At present the English Tourist Board acknowledges 45 such heritage experiences in the United Kingdom, focused either in historic towns which already offer a range of heritage attractions (such as York, Canterbury, Oxford and Plymouth), or in towns attempting to establish a tourism profile (Nottingham, Glasgow, Bradford, Wigan). These 45 recognized attractions have a total annual visitation in excess of 5 million, reflecting the market orientation inherent in their choice of location.

Table 10.2 Capital costs for heritage experience attractions in the United Kingdom

	Capital costs and funding	
	Total (£m)	Grants £'000
White Cliffs Experience	10.0	NK
Granada Studio Tours	8.0	750
Cadbury World	5.5	NK
Royal Britain	5.0	200
Jorvik	2.7	250
Oxford Story	2.45	550
Edinburgh Story (abandoned)	2.3	NK
Scotch Whisky Heritage Centre	2.0	NK
Knights Caverns	2.0	NK
Tales of Robin Hood	1.7	200
Canterbury Tales	1.35	225
Rob Roy & Trossachs Visitor Centre	1.2	NK
Royalty & Empire – purchased as going concern for about	0.5	NK

NK – not known.
Source: Wooder (1991).

Various surveys of international tourist arrivals around the world consistently show heritage as a primary motive for tourism. This fact has now been embraced in policy; for example the European Community's recent *Action Plan for Tourism* (1991) endorses the principle that Europe's competitive edge in the context of international tourism development will be founded upon the distinctive heritage and culture inherent in the 12 member states. Similarly, the proposed United Nations Development Programme of tourist strategy initiatives in Lesotho, Ethiopia and Nepal, together with countries covered by the Lomé IV Convention, all feature heritage as a key element of tourism development.

Significantly, therefore, the heritage and cultural distinctiveness of a country, region or place generally provide the foundation blocks upon which tourism policies are increasingly being built throughout the world. This is particularly the case in (a) those countries realigning their traditional sun/ sand/sea touristic appeal (such as Spain, Malta and Cyprus); (b) countries or regions wishing to establish a year-round tourism profile (such as Ireland or Alberta, Canada); (c) developing countries and former Eastern Bloc states wishing to restructure their economies using appropriate tourism initiatives (Fiji, Indonesia, Slovakia or Hungary).

Heritage and Economic Regeneration

In Britain the four national tourist boards have corporately recognized the economic and development potential of heritage attractions. The realization of this potential, according to the British government's Department of Employment in its document *Tourism '87* (DoE, 1987), depends upon making heritage

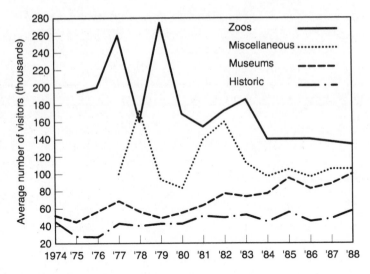

Figure 10.1   Average numbers of visitors to selected attractions, 1974–88.
Source: Anian Leisure (1989).

more accessible, through marketing and interpretation and by weaving it 'into the wider enterprise of tourism and leisure – without damaging or demeaning it' (DoE, 1987, p. 11).

Five years later, the Department of Employment consolidated the British government's view on the central position of heritage in the development of the tourism industry. Significantly, this report, *Tourism in the United Kingdom – Realising the Potential* (Employment Department Group, 1992) stressed the private sector's initiatives, contribution and opportunities in heritage attraction provision as well as public sector responsibilities. In Britain, the recently announced proposals by English Heritage to dispose of many smaller heritage sites currently in the guardianship of the state suggests an even greater role for the private sector.

The strategic interest in the contribution of heritage attractions to tourism and regional development is based upon a number of factors. First, they are indigenous, distinct and unique in their reflection of heritage. Secondly, being indigenous, heritage attractions enliven, enhance and animate naturally occurring themes and storylines from which much marketing imagery of tourist destinations is derived – for example, Robin Hood Country for Nottinghamshire; Dublin's Literary Heritage of Yeats, Behan and Joyce; and, the proposed 'Makers of Wales Campaign 1994–1997' by Cadw: Welsh Historic Monuments.

Thirdly, it is now recognized that heritage attractions provide a stable base of visitor activity suffering less from the vagaries of market demand than other types of attractions (Stevens, 1992a) (see Figure 10.1). At the same time they have innate appeal to overseas markets (Scullion, 1990) whose relatively high levels of spend helps contribute significantly to regional economies (Alberta Culture, 1989; Edwards, 1989; Johnson and Thomas, 1990).

Finally, there is growing acceptance that in this context sustainable development and commensurate sustainable tourism policies, based upon heritage attractions, can make a positive contribution to a broader environmental strategy (Rural Development Commission, 1991; Tourism Concern, 1992). In several recent studies, such as those of Malta (Horwath and Horwath, 1989), Ireland (Bord Failte, 1993), and Wales (Wales Tourist Board, 1993), heritage attractions have formed a primary area of policy development for sustainable tourism. Inskeep, in his study *Tourism Planning: An Integrated and Sustainable Development Approach* (Inskeep, 1991), drew upon numerous other examples world-wide to make this point.

Operational Standards and Management Information

Despite this advocacy and endorsement of the role of heritage attractions through policy, adoptions of systematic strategic planning approaches for the design and development of heritage attractions are relatively few and far between compared to other aspects of leisure or tourism provision. Similarly, whilst detailed design and development standards exist to guide management in sport or recreation provision, such detailed articulation for the heritage practitioner is generally absent. For example, stringent risk assessment guidance programmes have been produced for leisure centres (Safety Management Partnership, 1992); detailed standards of provision and maintenance introduced for parks (Welch, 1992); and accreditation criteria are well defined for holiday parks (Walsh-Heron, 1992). In the context of heritage attractions, there has been some work reviewing the quality of interpretive provision at heritage sites (Stevens, 1992a) together with the general development of visitor amenities within attractions generally. In the main, however, heritage by design is unable to draw upon either generic or specifically agreed principles and standards of provision. The implications of the lack of operational and strategic guidance are explored in detail later.

The early work of Miles (1977) for the Historic Houses Association and, more recently, by the Pacific Area Tourist Association (1992) went some way to redress this imbalance. Similarly, the Irish Tourist Board (Bord Failte, 1993) has attempted to establish baseline advice for those involved in heritage attraction management. In the United Kingdom, the Tourism and Environment Task Force (1991) reported on good practice in heritage site management. These sources of generic advice are, however, limited. For the practitioner, access to relevant quality information about market trends, management techniques and comparative operational data is fraught with difficulties. As a result there has emerged an over-reliance by practitioners on the use of second- or even third-hand analysis of national tourism statistics. A more recent trend has been the use of consultants to prepare market appraisals and feasibility studies for individual sites – an expensive and short-term solution.

A high proportion of attraction operators do undertake site-based market research on a regular, though somewhat idiosyncratic, basis. This generally involves using a range of formal and informal methods designed to assist their decision making at the end of the year, so shaping pricing policy, product development and promotional strategies for the next season. All too often, however, there is a tendency to use this market information rather as a drunk uses a lamp-post – for support rather than illumination. The need to adopt rigorous methodologies, to identify the right questions to be asked, with the appropriate interrogation and interpretation of the data, is widely accepted by operators but rarely implemented. Their cause is frustrated by limited resources and experience. Clear opportunities exist for researchers to work in partnership with operators to overcome these barriers and achieve more relevance of the information base. Assistance is also required to organize regionally and nationally collected aggregate tourism data and to translate it into the readily accessible information required by operators. This is an opportunity for national and local tourist boards to be more proactive in servicing their industry's needs.

Scope also exists for greater regional collaboration between the managers of attractions, perhaps involving regional tourist boards and universities, to improve this knowledge base. The work of the Cornish Association of Tourist Attractions in association with the University of Exeter and the West Country Tourist Board (Anian Leisure, 1989); and of the research unit, SEREN, at University College Swansea in association with Cadw: Welsh Historic Monuments (Herbert *et al.*, 1989) are good examples of collaboration in practice.

In the absence of such collaborative structures, individual operators rely upon a combination of (a) the purchase of secondary data from research houses such as Mintel or the Henley Centre; (b) accessing the outdated and aggregate data published by national tourist boards; (c) generalized commentary in trade magazines such as *Leisure Management* or *Park World*; and (d) relatively expensive commissioned work involving consultants.

The information imperative is becoming critical to the practitioner for a number of reasons. The first is the need for the operator initially to establish and then to demonstrate that performance targets have been achieved. Secondly, there is increasing pressure to attain short-term commercial viability with the added pressure of knowing that the revenue incomes are essential for long-term sustainability; and, finally, the requirement to prove specific, measurable outcomes of investment strategies involving regional development, sectoral, or other grant assistance. An example is the need to prove that assistance from the European Union's European Regional Development Fund creates jobs and attracts new tourists to an area (Howells, 1993).

In these demanding operational circumstances, attraction managers require clear policy objectives for their individual attractions and a strategic framework within which to identify and shape their market and develop their product. Clarity of objective is, arguably, the essential prerequisite for practitioners, especially in an environment where the claims of recreation, a relative newcomer (Miles and Seabrooke, 1993), competes with more traditional heritage values and conservation land-use systems.

The Need for Management Plans

Perhaps the greatest challenge faced by the practitioner involved in the design of heritage as a visitor attraction is the interface with those professionals whose interest is focused on the resource and its protection and for whom public access is an aberration. The legislative protection for heritage sites has a relatively long history compared to that for natural heritage. The resource being protected, or placed in guardianship, generally has rarity value, together with specific historical or cultural significance; it also has inherent archaeological or architectural quality. The day-to-day policing of the national heritage estate has, from the outset, been the responsibility of professionals whose approach invariably places preservation above amenity.

Shaping the character of the synergy between conservation and recreation at heritage properties remains an unresolved paradox that is often based upon the willingness of individuals to embrace the objectives of wise public use of the property. In England and Wales, the National Heritage Act 1983 is considered to have been a watershed in terms of the organization and management of the heritage (Stevens, 1993). The Act acknowledged public demand for greater access to historic properties with improved presentation and interpretive facilities and an outcome was the establishment of English Heritage and Cadw: Welsh Historic Monuments in 1984 (Carr, 1989) – a move designed specifically to enliven the appeal of the public heritage estate.

The Act confirmed these bodies (newly constituted as agencies) as having several purposes:

> to secure the preservation of ancient monuments and historic buildings;
> to promote and enhance the presentation of heritage under guardianship;
> to promote public enjoyment and understanding of the resource, its significance
> and the need for conservation.

There remains a prevailing emphasis within these agencies, and other heritage organizations, in favour of preservation whenever these objectives appear to be in conflict. Recreational use of heritage remains a by-product, despite its legitimate claims, due to the traditional and continuing strength within these organizations of the archaeologist, the architect, the land agent and similar heritage professionals. If those involved in the use of heritage for amenity purposes are to storm these traditional bastions of professional influence, more objective research is needed to examine the efficacy of the

Table 10.3 Recommendations of Tourism and Environment Task Force, 1991

The Working Group make the following recommendations to the Task Force:

1. that the Task Force report should take account of, and draw upon the findings of the Group as a whole.
2. that the adoption of the principles of sustainable tourism . . . is an essential prerequisite to sound management for the benefit of the visitor, the site and the local host community.
3. that the site managers and other operators are educated in conservation and visitor techniques through:

   • the production of a regularly updated directory of sources of specialist advice; and
   • the dissemination of knowledge and examples of best practice through the production and distribution of publications.

   These could be produced by the English Tourist Board in association with the relevant heritage organisations.
4. that programmes of research and development into new techniques for assessing wear and tear and for measuring capacity are continued, and that constant monitoring of the effectiveness of techniques is undertaken.
5. that the Government recognises that visitor expenditure at heritage sites, on which much overseas tourism is built, is very small and that the financial rewards of tourism go largely to those providing accommodation, transport and other services.
6. that the Government recognises that to ensure the continued preservation of heritage sites on which tourism depends, there needs to be a greater contribution from public sector funding, and in particular that the following steps are recommended:

   • the introduction of a new financial assistance scheme to encourage the development of visitor facilities and management techniques to a high standard;
   • an increase in funding through English Heritage towards essential repairs;
   • the introduction of other methods to reduce the financial burden on heritage sites, including VAT relief on repairs as already exists for alterations and continued incentives through the tax system to encourage more private money to be dedicated towards conservation and the provision of public access;
   • the development of further work towards a financial model to promote a clearer appreciation of the correlation between the total income from tourism, conservation costs and visitor numbers.

Source: Tourism and Environment Task Force (1991).

recreational management techniques and the effectiveness of interpretation and to consider which will support access to heritage amongst residents, visitors and tourists.

The recent report of the Tourism and the Environment Task Force – Heritage Sites Working Group (Tourism and Environment Task Force, 1991) recognizes the urgent need for this focused research effort if practitioners are sympathetically to manage the 'interdependence between the heritage and tourism industries . . . [recognizing] that the phenomenon we have to face is not the presence of visitors at heritage sites but rather the scale and effect of visiting' (Tourism and Environment Task Force, 1991, p. 1). The six specific recommendations of the working group confirm this need for practitioners to have access to a greater range of quality information upon which to base both their strategies and tactics in the debate with their heritage colleagues (see Table 10.3).

The resolution of site-based management issues necessitates appropriate management plans. It is interesting to note that whilst guidance appears to be readily available to assist in the production of management plans for natural sites (see, for example, Countryside Commission, 1972, 1974; UNESCO, 1975; Parcs Canada, 1982), no similar documents have been produced for heritage properties. As a result, the individual feasibility studies, development, management or marketing plans for heritage properties which do exist rarely conform to a standard approach. Comparative study and cross-fertilization of ideas in these circumstances becomes haphazard. The result is the emerging phenomenon, identified by both the West Country Tourist Board (Anian Leisure, 1989) and Bord Failte in Ireland (Ventures Consultancy, 1990), of a genuine lack of understanding of attraction management resulting in 'copy-cat attraction development'. The West Country Tourist Board's report, *Visitor Attractions in the West Country* (Anian Leisure, 1989) states:

> There is a tendency for operators to copycat individual components, even complete attractions, from perceived successful attractions . . . this smacks of desperation, lack of imagination, and the view that the secret of success lies in these features, rather than in an overall and unique visitor experience.

The report continues:

> A useful analogy to describe this process is that of someone who likes the taste of a meal, identifies the main ingredients but does not know in what proportion to use them, then wonders why the end result is not the same. (ibid., para 9.6)

This phenomenon is evident in both the public and private sectors as well as in traditional and 'manufactured' heritage provision.

Despite the development of numerous exciting, dramatic and popularist private-sector heritage experience attractions (such as Jorvik in York, England; the Geraldine Experience in Tralee, Ireland; or the Gozo Experience in Malta) heritage attraction managers maintain a cautious approach to their presentation. This is due, in part, to the continued dominance of the preservation objective, and to the limited amount of understanding of the potential of certain management techniques. Interpretation, for example, to tell the story and the significance of the site or artefact, is often ill conceived. The need for a strategic plan within which the story of individual heritage properties is identified would help resolve these problems. It is no coincidence that where a strategic planning approach to heritage presentation exists successful heritage attractions, with strong market appeal, have emerged. The recent success of Llancaiach Fawr, a fortified Civil War farmhouse near Nelson in the South Wales Valleys, was founded upon a comprehensive strategic plan for the Rhymney Valley (Touchstone, 1987). Similarly, the proposals for the development of the Hağar Qim/Mnajdra temple sites in Malta emerged from the strategic heritage plan contained within the Malta Tourism Master Plan (Horwath and Horwath, 1989). Inskeep (1991) described a number of similar actions from developing and developed countries.

A Strategic Planning Approach

The need for a strategic approach has intensified as heritage attractions have become accepted as integral components of successful national tourism development policies. Unlike other sectors of tourism development policy, these initiatives have, to date, rarely been articulated in detail at a regional or local scale. Consequently, site plans and feasibility studies tend to be developed in a piecemeal fashion, missing opportunities to achieve a cohesive approach to heritage presentation and interpretation to visitors (Jenkins, 1992).

Gunn (1972, 1988) has long been an advocate of a regional planning systems approach of the type which has been practised in North America by individual agencies concerned with specific sites, including the National Park Service (USNPS, 1990), Parcs Canada (1982) and the National Trust for Historic Preservation, for the past 30 years. The benefits of inter-agency collaboration in creating a comprehensive framework for a heritage attraction development have been identified by Capelle *et al.* (1989) and Traweek (1979). It appears, however, that despite the clear benefits of such inter-agency work, the approach has rarely been adopted.

Heritage – A Strategic Planning Approach

In Britain, the Countryside Commissions for England and Scotland experimented with a number of regional heritage interpretation planning studies in the 1970s, including studies for Nottingham (Countryside Commission, 1979) and for the Grampian Region (Countryside Commission for Scotland, 1973). This top-down imposition of strategy had a limited life span for a number of reasons. First, there needed to be more real incentives for individual attractions to participate. Secondly, whilst the plans offered a fragmented industry some cohesion, they did not give practitioners real guidance. Finally, the plans failed to proffer clear targets and objectives to facilitate performance review and within which operational design criteria could be set. The result was often a loose strategy that lacked the necessary resources, or organizational structures, to effect implementation. The recent strategic planning for heritage attraction development in Ireland has avoided these pitfalls. The result has been the successful creation of a framework plan with clear, unambiguous guidance on heritage attraction development. Bord Failte's activities provide a good case study of heritage by design at a national level. This national leadership has allowed appropriate regional programmes, led by the regional tourist organizations and Shannon Development to develop and has stimulated over 120 heritage attraction projects.

After the stagnant years for tourism in Ireland during the early 1980s the Irish government presented Bord Failte with the tasks of doubling income derived from tourism and of creating 25 000 new jobs. Bord Failte responded with *A New Framework for the Development of Irish Tourism* (Bord Failte, 1990a). This plan recognized that substantial and sustained planned investment was required in both product development and marketing. A fundamental cornerstone in the plan was the recognition of the vital contribution played by heritage and culture, particularly the heritage attraction base (Scullion, 1990). Bord Failte wished to optimize the experience of 'Irishness' for the tourist and to create a comprehensive, accessible and authentic heritage product. The key question to emerge was – 'What form of intervention and planning is required to avoid duplication and ensure complementarity?'

In order to advance these strategic considerations, the Ventures Consultancy audited the existing attraction base and produced a strategy for attraction development (Bord Failte, 1990b). This strategy focused on an interpretive planning approach to create a cohesive network of attractions each capable of contributing to the interpretation of five dominant themes and supporting storylines vital to understanding the heritage of Ireland. Over the past five years £54.6 million has been committed to the 120 heritage attractions which conform to this strategy. This investment has secured a further £50 million of private and public sector investment, has made a significant contribution to the enhancement of visitor satisfaction (MacNulty, 1992) and towards meeting job creation objectives (Browne, 1993).

The framework has allowed innovative local projects – such as the Cahersiveen Barracks, Kerry; the Middleton Distillery Centre, Cork; Boyne Valley Archaeological Park; and Ciede Fields, Connemara – to emerge and flourish. At the same time, the Framework Plan has also successfully encouraged the development of the heritage attraction management skill-base (Walsh, 1992). Bord Failte and its partners fully accept the value of the interpretive planning approach advocated by the National Park Services in North America (Capelle *et al.*, 1989), an approach which is capable of adaptation to amenity and heritage landscapes (Henderson, 1993) and will form the next stage of the strategy.

The strategic planning approach allows the site manager to locate the specific attraction in an appropriate developmental and marketing context. The strategic plan should also provide guidance that allows the manager to resolve the conflicting timescales inherent in tourism objectives (short term), those of funding (medium term) and of conservation (long term).

Whilst such strategic planning exercises provide individual site operators with an opportunity to network and derive shared benefits, site-specific, operational issues remain of primary concern. Many of these are relevant throughout the visitor attraction industry, and include:

pricing policy for admissions
seasonality and utilization of resources
revenue generation and cash flow
marketing and market research
capital acquisition and product development

health and safety
quality assurance
staffing, including recruitment and training

Management Issues and Challenges

The practitioner involved with a heritage attraction faces added complications to this management equation. These involve both perceived and real socio-economic, cultural and political factors, several of which are now discussed.

First, the role of interpretation in heritage attraction management is now widely accepted and its benefits are implied if rarely measured (Stevens, 1982; Herbert, 1989). The particular emphasis of the interpretive content tends, however, to be given less consideration than the media used. Uzzell (1989), for example, criticized the traditional blandness of interpretation at heritage properties and challenged the interpreter to face up to the 'hot' issues of site interpretation. Uzzell cited the presentation of battlefields, concentration camps and war museums as the epitome of bland practice at work in situations where issues, ethics and truth could prevail. Conceptual proposals for a new out-station of the Imperial War Museum in England, the actual provision at the Holocaust Museum, Washington, which confronts visitors with the realities of war, and l'Memorial in Normandy rise to this challenge. Elsewhere, unchallenging and 'safe' interpretation in our battlefields, castles and other heritage sites neatly sidesteps Freeman Tilden's fundamental principle of interpretation – the need to provoke the audience and stimulate a questioning attitude (Tilden, 1957).

For the practitioner, comfortable storylines that draw little critical response from their managers and/or owners provide palatable products for the visitor. The domination of this safety-first approach at a time when market evidence suggests the arrival of a more quizzical, enquiring and discerning visitor will become a major challenge for site managers. The oft-quoted tenet, 'The message not the media is important' is likely to return to centre stage. At the present the practitioner remains in danger of being seduced by technological wizardry that can trivialize themes and storylines. Sources of advice and appropriate guidance on these issues is a priority area of need if, as Cossons (1989, p. 17) has argued, 'heritage offers a commodity which has truth as a primary component'. In these circumstances the fundamental question posed by Boniface and Fowler (1993, p. 23) is, therefore, 'How does and how should the interpreter give meaning to structures, artifacts and ideas to global villagers with different backgrounds, motivations and expectations?'

The second critical operational factor to be considered by the practitioner is that of utilization. Resource utilization, a management concern throughout the attraction industry, is characterized by the problems of seasonality. This issue is partially resolved by the relatively footloose character of constructed attractions which, in theory, are capable of being located at sites selected to optimize market penetration and minimize constraints upon achieving full resource utilization. It is a fatuous, but nonetheless very real, observation that the vast majority of heritage attractions are fixed geographically and, in many ways, anchored historically. The spatial aspect, in particular, inevitably limits the market opportunities for the attraction, while the historical 'fixing' shapes the specific nature of product development.

Seasonality and the peaking of visitation leads to the inevitable under-utilization of facilities and services. Attraction managers are faced with a number of dilemmas in the quieter periods, ranging from decisions about keeping facilities open to sustaining the moral and enthusiasm of staff. Increasingly managers are seeking to achieve higher levels of utilization by extending the season and smoothing out peaks in demand. A survey of West Country attractions in 1989 revealed that for six months of the year heritage attractions operate at less than 20 per cent utilization. Although the total visitor market for heritage attractions in Britain is increasing by 5 per cent per annum, the majority of visits remain concentrated in July–September (Anian Leisure, 1989). It is not uncommon for heritage attraction owners to close for the winter season rather than face the problems of operational under-utilization. Only 56 per cent of heritage attractions in the United Kingdom remain open all year; the remainder close for at least three months.

The core catchment for the majority of attractions, including heritage attractions, is prescribed by a one-way travel time isochrone of 60 minutes on the actual day of the visit (Walsh-Heron and Stevens, 1990). This factor remains remarkably consistent throughout the entire attraction industry. Heritage attractions, as has been noted, are not always conveniently located to optimize their market potential, so are required to trade within a set market-place. On this basis few are likely to be able to fulfil their full potential to attract visitors (Herbert *et al.*, 1989) based simply upon their core product and core markets. Managers must introduce inventive schemes to stimulate broader market appeal and to add value to the experience. Events, including the use of *son et lumière*, historical re-enactments and living history presenta-tions, are increasingly regarded as a cost-effective means of achieving these objectives.

Against this background there may well be a case for innovative approaches to pricing policies; however, such innovation is not prevalent in the heritage sector (Wooder, 1991). A few attractions have adopted a more radical approach. The Tullie House Museum in Carlisle, for example, has pur-posefully adopted a radical approach to pricing for the town's residents (Johnson, 1993) to counteract inbuilt market resistance. Residents of Carlisle may purchase a lifetime season ticket allowing unlimited access to the museum for a minimal charge. Elsewhere the membership schemes of Cadw, English Heritage and the National Trust are designed to extend the scope of traditional pricing policies. Perhaps the area where help is most required by practitioners in determining pricing policy in the public sector is in countering the imposition of social-welfare policies influencing pricing schedules. This involves public sector organizations applying subsidized market prices for heritage admission charges in the belief that it has a social benefit. The Layfield Report (HMSO, 1976) on local government finance initially fuelled the debate about service provision and appropriate market pricing policy in the public sector. The 'value for money' theme was further pursued by the effectiveness and efficiency studies introduced by the Audit Commission in the 1980s and supported by central government. In the context of heritage attractions the full range of fee considerations has been explored by Marriott (1986), while others have demonstrated price relationships with customer-perceived product value of the visit or experience. Numerous surveys over recent years have demonstrated general support for the introduction of pricing – providing that product development is relevant to the market (see, for example, Schlackman Research, 1984; MORI, 1985; Prentice, 1989, 1993).

The opportunity to diversify income sources, particularly through secondary spending by visitors and by developing multiple use of the attraction's facilities, is increasingly important for attraction revenue budgets. For the heritage attraction operator such opportunities are more limited than for operators of other types of attraction. The potential is constrained by the nature of the resource and the integrity issues discussed earlier. There remains considerable scope, however, to merchandise effectively and to secure appropriate multiple use (see Table 10.4). In recent studies for the development of Celtic-themed attractions at Fishguard and at Machynlleth (Wales) as well as in 'The Tribes of Galway', Visitor Centre, Galway (Ireland), secondary sources constitute the majority of the annual revenue income. Elsewhere, the existing attraction sector is reporting a stabilization in the growth of visitor numbers and annual attendance levels but significant increased per capita spending on quality merchandise. Although this trend has been noted throughout the attraction sector, the opportunity to exploit its full potential remains to be fully recognized by the heritage sector. Some interesting initiatives do exist; for example a number of mail order and trading companies have emerged from attraction-based merchandising such as Past Times, National Trust Enterprises and the Jorvik Mail Order Service. Elsewhere sales in English local authority museums increased from £1.9 million in 1983–84 to £4.8 million in 1988–89, while the Jorvik Viking Centre in York boasts a retail sales performance of £1500 per square foot per annum – higher than the performance of many high street outlets.

Within the realm of marketing, attractions generally, and heritage attractions in particular, have tended to under-invest in marketing (Stevens, 1987; Adams, 1993). This has been the result of complacency, limited resources and a lack of appreciation of the need to promote the product (Browne, 1993). Whilst the profile of existing heritage attraction visitors is predictable and unsurprising, being heavily drawn from upper socio-economic groups within the domestic market together with overseas tourists (Prentice, 1989, 1993),

Table 10.4 Sources of revenue income at heritage sites

Direct funding	*Accommodation*
Government funding	Bed & breakfast
Local authority funding	Training courses
Grants	Residential conference
Donations	Holiday cottages
Legacies	
Membership	
'Friends of'	*Events*
Endowments	Festivals
Sponsorship/joint promotion	Craft fairs
Affinity cards	Historical re-enactments
	Plays/concerts
	Horse/dog/car shows
Admissions	Sporting activities
Site	War games
Car park	Exhibitions
Offices	
	Lease of land/building
	Land cultivation
Retail	Caravan parks
Merchandising	Golf courses
Mail order	
Farm shop	
Garden centre	*Interpretation*
Franchise reproduction	Guidebooks
Off-site shops	Publications
Bureau de change	Audio tours
Surplus plants	Audiovisuals
Speciality shops	Guided tours
	Machines/simulators
Catering	*Private hire*
Restaurants/cafés	Film sets
Banqueting	Photography
Corporate entertainment	Product launches
Conferences	Hire of artefacts

Source: Tourism and Environment Task Force (1991).

there is scope to broaden the market appeal. Promotional- and PR-based marketing strategies are the key to fulfilling this objective.

Growing demand for educationally orientated leisure and group visits, together with the general growth in special-interest tourism, provides heritage attraction managers with significant opportunities to develop niches and to extend core markets. Such market development is most likely amongst groups sympathetic with the environmental considerations implicit in heritage site management. This in turn augurs well for an ongoing consumer relationship with heritage sites and organizations through the establishment of heritage membership schemes (such as those offered by the National Trust, Cadw, English Heritage and the National Museum of Wales).

Central to the challenge of managing heritage attraction is the maintenance of high-quality recreational experiences that are founded upon the essential fabric of the heritage site, artefact, event or sense of place. A number of attraction consortia and national tourist boards have introduced quality assessment schemes for the attraction sector to assist in this process. The Association of Scottish Visitor Attractions introduced an inspection scheme in 1990 (Gaw, 1992), and the Wales Tourist Board has operated a pilot national scheme since 1992. There is considerable commonality amongst the criteria evaluated, but the schemes remain discrete and generic to all types of attraction. A heritage-specific quality assurance programme is needed. The formation of the 'Classical Sights' consortia involving heritage properties in the West Country may signal a shift in this direction.

The importance of establishing development and design standards is important (Inskeep, 1991). It has already been established that facility standards are commonplace in other spheres of leisure provision, particularly sport (Perrin, 1981), resorts (Mills, 1983) and countryside management (Van Lier, 1973). Are heritage attractions suitable candidates for a standard approach or does the sector's heterogeneity preclude this development? In the United Kingdom the application of performance indices in heritage management is implicit in the annual round of Public Expenditure Survey bids to HM Treasury by the Department of National Heritage and the Welsh and Scottish Offices. Similarly, the Countryside Commission has explored the application of performance indices to the management of national park visitor centres (Countryside Commission, 1992). Recent research suggests, however, that as long as heritage management faces the ambiguous duality of purpose and unless there is clear policy direction, effectiveness and efficient measures will be meaningless (Griffiths, 1993).

The leisure, day-trip market, within which heritage attractions operate, is increasingly competitive. The strategies deployed by attraction owners and managers to ensure their survival in this dynamic market-place, where the supply of attractions outstrips growth in demand, is more and more based on high levels of capital investment, especially in new technology but also in innovative marketing (involving pricing policies, consortia activity and event programming). The heritage attraction sector has not been immune to these developments; interactive computers and simulated dark-ride developments are becoming commonplace in the new generation of 'manufactured heritage experiences'. For example, the feasibility and conceptual studies for heritage visitor attractions in Galway and the 'Celtaith' Celtic Centre at Fishguard are based on dark-ride technologies developed in the theme park sector of the industry.

The new extension to the Imperial War Museum's out-station at Duxford, Cambridgeshire, and proposals for a Sporting Heritage Centre in Orlando, Florida, involve a 'Showscan' large-screen-format, film-based experience redolent of the new generation of 'studio' theme parks (such as MGM,

Universal Studios (USA) and Futuroscope in France. On the other hand, there is growing awareness that heritage attractions need to focus on ensuring high-quality delivery of a base product in a lively, authentic manner, founded upon a living history presentation involving interpreters and animateurs. At both scales of development, product enhancement is the main focus.

The emerging paradox is that the leisure-based attractions are now looking towards heritage as the source of themes for their thrill rides and food/ beverage areas. How far this crossover of heritage into theme parks and theme parks into heritage can evolve has been subject to recent public debate (Park World, 1993; Stevens, 1993). Heritage as the foundation for leisure attraction development is likely to become the main development trend for the next ten years.

Authenticity and the Leisure Experience

These trends clearly reflect the centrality of heritage to the leisure market-place. They raise more questions about the ethics and integrity of heritage attraction management than they answer. Heritage attraction managers have traditionally been cast in the role of balancing the demands of sympathetic resource management with demands from the market-place, while also meeting the stringent requirements of being 'guardians' of a nation's heritage. Increasing pressure from the market-place to popularize, and the further 'commodity' of heritage, need to be considered carefully. In the past the visiting public has responded positively to authenticity while accepting varying methods of presentation. Implicit is the need for heritage presentations to deal with naturally occurring storylines unique to the area or sites in a manner that fully exploits the drama and interest inherent in the theme. National or regional heritage strategies would appear to be the most appropriate mechanism to achieve this balance.

Miles *et al.* (1988) regarded heritage practitioners as having an innate 'design tradition' and an understanding of the design process. Stevens's (1983) study of heritage interpreters refuted this assumption and clearly demonstrated the transient nature of professional involvement in heritage amenity management. So it is not surprising that the heritage attraction practitioners battle to have their voice heard by the heritage cabal constituted from the ranks of professional guardians of the heritage.

This confrontational situation between amenity and conservation professionals is commonplace in northern Europe, especially in the United Kingdom. In these countries there has been a tendency to regard presentational strategies as leading to compromise of conservation efforts. In North America, however, particularly within the United States National Park Service (1990) interpretation as part of visitor management is regarded as a fundamental cornerstone of the conservation effort.

The United States National Park Service has traditionally engaged

208   *Terry Stevens*

multi-disciplinary teams (interpreters, archaeologists, architects, designers, land managers) in its master plan teams for heritage sites. Parcs Canada has always operated in a similar fashion. This integrated, holistic approach to heritage site management has not been replicated in United Kingdom agencies. Although Cadw and English Heritage now employ field specialists, rarely is there a team approach to solving site problems.

Similarly, in Southern Europe there is a tendency for heritage sites to be managed by conservation specialists. Whilst these specialists may well invite or, via aid programmes, have visitor services expertise thrust upon them, a comprehensive multi-disciplinary team approach is needed (Horwath and Horwath, 1989; Inskeep, 1991). As a result, visitor services, especially the presentation and interpretation of heritage attractions, remain wholly inadequate both from the visitor's perspective (quality of experience, employment, understanding, appreciation) and for the conservation of the heritage feature.

The successful management of heritage for amenity purposes needs a framework of strategic and site planning with clearly stated policies and objectives. This detailed planning is a time-consuming, iterative process with many stages. It is the bedrock upon which enhanced heritage attraction presentation and performance are founded. Without this planning approach practitioners are unable to construct their detailed plans, within which the principles of sustainable heritage management can be enacted and the prejudices of others adequately countered. Quality planning demands an understanding of the resource together with relevant and appropriate information available in a form which is recognizable, accessible and usable by the site managers.

References

Adams, N. (1993) *The Leisure Experience: Tourism 2000*. Cardiff: Wales Tourist Board.

Alberta Culture (1989) *The Economic Impact of Provincial Heritage: Facilities in Alberta*. Edmonton: Historical Resource Division, Alberta Culture and Multiculturalism.

Anian Leisure (1989) *Visitor Attractions in the West Country*. Exeter: West Country Tourist Board.

Boniface, P. and Fowler, P. (1993) *Heritage and Tourism in the Global Village*. New York: Routledge.

Bord Failte (1990a) *A New Framework for the Development of Irish Tourism*. Dublin: Bord Failte.

Bord Failte (1990b) *Heritage Attraction Strategy for Ireland*. Dublin: Bord Failte.

Bord Failte (1993) *Developing Sustainable Tourism: A Tourism Plan*. Dublin: Bord Failte.

Browne, S. (1993) *The Role of Heritage in Sustainable Tourism*. Paper at University College of Cork conference on 'Defining Heritage Policy', Cork.

Capelle, A., Vererka, J. and Moore, G. (1989) Interpretive planning for regional visitor experience: a concept whose time has come. In D. Uzzell (ed.) *Heritage Interpretation*: Vol. 2: *The Visitor Experience*. London: Belhaven Press, pp. 115–119.

Carr, J. (1989) Research and the heritage operator. In D. T. Herbert, R. C. Prentice and C. J. Thomas (eds) *Heritage Sites: Strategies for Marketing and Development.* Aldershot: Avebury, pp. 294–304.

Cossons, N. (1989) Plural funding and the heritage. In D. Uzzell (ed.) *Heritage Interpretation,* Vol. 2. London: Belhaven Press, pp. 16–22.

Countryside Commission (1972) *Advisory Notes on National Park Plans.* Cheltenham: Countryside Commission.

Countryside Commission (1974) *Advisory Notes on Country Park Plans.* Cheltenham: Countryside Commission.

Countryside Commission (1979) *Nottinghamshire's Heritage: A Strategy for its Interpretation.* Cheltenham: Countryside Commission Paper No. 123.

Countryside Commission (1992) *National Park Visitor Centres: Study of Good Practice.* Cheltenham: Countryside Commission.

Countryside Commission for Scotland (1973) *The Grampian Region Interpretive Strategy for Scotland.* Perth: Countryside Commission for Scotland.

Department of Employment (1987) *Tourism '87: Making the Most of Heritage.* London: HMSO.

Edwards, J. A. (1989) Historic sites and their local environments. In D. T. Herbert, R. C. Prentice and C. J. Thomas (eds) *Heritage Sites: Strategies for Marketing and Development.* Aldershot: Avebury, pp. 272–293.

Employment Department Group (1992) *Tourism in the United Kingdom – Realising the Potential.* London: HMSO.

ETB: English Tourist Board (1991) *English Heritage Monitor.* London: English Tourist Board.

European Community (1991) *Action Plan for Tourism.* Brussels: EC.

Gaw, L. (1992) *The Scottish Experience in Heritage Tourism.* Dublin: Board Failte.

Griffiths, B. (1993) 'The efficiency of national park visitor centres.' Unpublished MPhil thesis, University of Wales.

Gunn, C. (1972) *Vacationscape.* Austin: University of Texas.

Gunn, C. (1988) *Tourism Planning.* New York: Taylor and Francis.

Henderson, N. (1993) Heritage landscapes: a new approach. In R. Turner (ed.) *Sustainable Environments, Economies and Management.* London: Belhaven, pp. 296–318.

Herbert, D. T. (1989) Does interpretation help? In D. T. Herbert, R. C. Prentice and C. J. Thomas (eds) *Heritage Sites: Strategies for Marketing and Development.* Aldershot: Avebury, pp. 199–230.

Herbert, D. T., Prentice, R. C. and Thomas, C. J. (eds) (1989) *Heritage Sites: Strategies for Marketing and Development.* Aldershot: Avebury.

Hewison, R. (1987) *The Heritage Industry.* London: Methuen.

HMSO (1976) *Local Government Finance* (the Layfield Report). London: HMSO.

Horwath and Horwath (1989) *Tourism Master Plan: Maltese Islands.* Madrid: World Tourism Organization.

Howells, D. (1993) 'European structure funds for tourism.' Unpublished MSc thesis, University of Wales.

Inskeep, E. (1991) *Tourism Planning: An Integrated and Sustainable Development Approach.* New York: Van Nostrand Reinhold.

Jenkins, J. G. (1992) *Getting Yesterday Right. Interpreting the Heritage of Wales.* Cardiff: University of Wales Press.

Johnson, P. and Thomas, B. (1990) Measuring local employment impact of tourist attraction. *Regional Studies,* **24**, 395–403.

Johnson, S. (1993) Heritage attractions. In J. Buswell (ed.) *Case Studies in Leisure Management.* London: Longman, pp. 128–143.

MacNulty, P. (1992) *Visitors to Tourist Attractions in 1991*. Dublin: Bord Failte.
Marriott, K. (1986) The pricing of leisure services. *Leisure Management*, 6, 36–39.
Miles, C. W. N. (1977) *Historic Houses: Measures of Performance*. Reading: University of Reading, Historic Houses Association.
Miles, C. and Seabrooke, W. (1993) *Recreational Land Management*, 2nd edn. London: E. and F. N. Spon.
Miles, R. S., Alt, M. B., Gosling, D., Lewis, B. N. and Toft, A. F. (1988) *The Design of Educational Exhibits*. London: Unwin Hyman.
Mills, E. D. (1983) *Design for Tourism*. Cambridge: Butterworths.
MORI (1985) *Attitudes to Museums and the Armouries*. London: MORI.
Pacific Area Tourism (1992) *Tourism at Heritage Sites*. California: Pacific Area Tourist Association.
Parcs Canada (1982) *Parcs Canada Policy*. Quebec, Canada: Hull.
Park World (1993) *Theme Parks of the 21st Century*. Oldham: Worlds Fair Ltd.
Perrin, G. (1981) *Design for Sport*. London: Butterworths.
Prentice, R. C. (1989) Visitors to heritage sites. In D. T. Herbert, R. C. Prentice and C. J. Thomas (eds) *Heritage Sites: Strategies for Marketing and Development*. Aldershot: Avebury, pp. 199–230.
Prentice, R. C. (1993) *Tourism and Heritage Attraction*. London: Routledge.
Rural Development Commission (1991) *The Green Light*. London: HMSO.
Safety Management Partnership (1992) *Risk Assessment for Leisure Centres*. Swindon: Safety Management Partnership.
Schlackman Research (1984) *Research on Public Reaction to Pricing Policy among Visitors to Hampton Court and HM Tower of London*. London: DoE.
Scullion, C. (1990) Marketing heritage attractions. In *Developing Heritage Attractions*. Dublin: Bord Failte.
Stevens, T. (1982) 'Environmental interpretation in Wales.' Unpublished PhD thesis, University of Wales.
Stevens, T. (1983) *Interpretation: Who Does It, How and Why?* Manchester: Centre for Environmental Interpretation, Paper No. 2.
Stevens, T. (1987) *The Story So Far – Attractions in Wales*. Cardiff: Wales Tourist Board.
Stevens, T. (1992a) Heritage attractions and interpretation. In P. Mills (ed.) *Quality in the Leisure Industry*. London: Longman, pp. 63–71.
Stevens, T. (1992b) Visitor attractions. In J. R. Ritchie and D. Hawkin (eds) *World Travel and Tourism Review*. Vol. 2. Oxford: Commonwealth Agricultural Bureau International.
Stevens, T. (1993) Theme parks: playground or agents of social and cultural development? *American Express 1993 Annual Review of Travel*, 61–72.
Tilden, F. (1957) *Interpreting Our Heritage*. Chapel Hill: University of North Carolina Press.
Touchstone (1987) *Heritage and Tourism Strategy for the Rhymney Valley*. Ystrad Mynach: Rhymney Valley District Council.
Tourism Concern (1992) *Beyond the Green Horizon: A Discussion Paper*. Godalming: World Wildlife Fund.
Tourism and Environment Task Force (1991) *Maintaining the Balance*. London: Heritage Sites Working Group, ETB/DES, HMSO.
Traweek, D. E. (1979) A systems approach to interpretive planning. *Journal of Interpretation*, 14 (1), Association of Interpretive Naturalists, Maryland, 12–15.
UNESCO (1975) *National Park and Interpretive Plans*. Madrid: UNESCO.
USNPS: United States National Park Service (1990) *The Interpretive Challenge*. Washington: Park Service.

Uzzell, D. (ed.) (1989) *Heritage Interpretation*, Vol. 1: *The Natural and Built Environment*. London: Belhaven.

Van Lier, H. N. (1973) *Determination of Planning Capacity and Layout Criteria of Outdoor Recreation Projects*. Pudoc: Wageningen.

Ventures Consultancy (1990) *A Development and Interpretation Strategy for Heritage and Culture in Ireland*. Dublin: Bord Failte.

Wales Tourist Board (1993) *Tourism 2000: A Strategy*. Cardiff: Wales Tourist Board.

Walsh, M. E. (1992) *Education and Training for Heritage*. Dublin: Bord Failte.

Walsh-Heron, J. (1992) Caravan and camping parks. In P. Mills (ed.) *Quality in the Leisure Industry*. London: Longman, pp. 167–180.

Walsh-Heron, J. and Stevens, T. (1990) *An Introduction to the Management of Visitor Attractions and Events*. New York: Prentice-Hall.

Welch, D. (1992) Parks. In P. Mills (ed.) *Quality in the Leisure Industry*. London: Longman, pp. 153–166.

Wooder, S. (1991) *The Handbook of Tourism Products*. London: English Tourist Board.

Zimmerman, E. W. (1933) *World Resources and Industries*. New York: Harper.

11

Conclusions

David T. Herbert

One does not have to go far as a tourist in modern Britain to be faced with a wide choice of heritage attractions actively seeking visitors. As an example, the *All in One Guide to Chester* offers three museums, a Roman amphitheatre and Roman garden, in addition to a fifteenth-century cross, a late-nineteenth-century clock, a Norman castle, a Saxon church and a municipal heritage centre. All of these in addition to Chester Cathedral, the Chester Walls walk and the Chester 'Rows', or galleried streets. The whole city is in effect a heritage area and its success in attracting visitors rests upon its tangible links with the past and ways in which these combine to form an attractive and pleasant environment for locals and visitors alike. As Curphey (1994) noted, however, the influx of tourists does pose problems and Chester is one of the historic cities which is judged to have almost reached visitor capacity. In the less obviously historic places around Chester, there is again ample heritage on offer for tourists. A boat museum at Ellesmere Port, Quarry Bank Cotton Mill in Cheshire, a salt museum at Northwich, a silk museum at Macclesfield, Cheshire Workshops and Candle-makers at Tattenhall, Port Sunlight heritage centre and Jodrell Bank observatory; all of these offer examples of heritage, mostly from the industrial revolution of the eighteenth and nineteenth centuries, to interest visitors. If one looks west towards Wales, the list of possible heritage attractions is equally long. The Glodffa Ganol Slate Mine at Blaenau Ffestiniog, many castles such as those at Caernarfon, Conwy and Flint, the Daniel Owen Centre at Mold, the Franciscan Friary at Pantasaph, St Winefride's Well and Chapel at Holywell, Basingwerk Abbey at Holywell, Abakhan Fabrics and Craft Shop at Llannerch-y-Mor, a seventeenth-century warehouse which has been 'carefully restored housing a large selection of fabrics, wool, craft and gift items'. The list is formidable and continues to grow as the heritage industry capitalizes on the past and caters for the whims and fancies of modern tourists and visitors. All possible notions of heritage have appeal. Downham in Lancashire, which was used as the location for the film *Whistle Down the Wind* in 1961, still attracts visitors anxious to visit sites of the events and places occupied by the characters. Stamford, Lincolnshire, where the television series of *Middlemarch* was filmed in 1994, became an instant tourist attraction. The Isle of Wight promotes locations where Tennyson wrote 'The Charge of the Light Brigade' and another where Longfellow composed a verse. In Jamaica, Firefly, the house where Noel Coward lived, has been restored and opened to visitors for an entrance fee of $10. The moors, near the Brontë home at Haworth, Yorkshire, have signposts in both English and Japanese to guide visitors to places linked less with the authors than with the fictional characters and events of their novels.

Heritage tourism, despite its historical precedents in the archaeological sites of the ancient world and the cathedrals and palaces of Europe, is mainly a phenomenon of the latter part of the twentieth century. It is during this period that the heritage industry has flourished and the number of people visiting heritage sites has multiplied. This rapid expansion rests on a few simple premisses. The first is that more and more people are looking for places at which to spend some of their leisure time in relaxing ways. The second is the fact that many of these visitors are reasonably flexible in their choice of places; their basic needs of interest, relaxation and a change of scene can be met in a variety of locations. The third is an awareness that there is a very general, if variable in terms of its attention to detail, interest in the past and the broad idea of heritage. The fourth is the more general fact that as larger numbers of people achieve personal mobility and the means to travel, they are prepared to make trips as day visitors or tourists to locations which offer points of interest and have, preferably, a range of facilities to offer. Such trips are now part of the culture of Western society; inventories of places visited and sights seen are measures of status in that society. The camera is a crucial instrument of many such visits: witness the ubiquitous Japanese tourist, recording for personal memories but also, perhaps more significantly, compiling a record which allows the 'telling' to others at home of places visited. As the providers of the heritage industry develop attractions and equip them with facilities and presentations designed to draw visitors, they are responding to a large and growing demand from a widening range of consumers.

The essence of heritage tourism as it has developed in the 1980s in particular is attracting visitors to sites with heritage connections. The chapters in this book focus predominantly on this dimension to heritage. Themes have included the ways in which visitors are attracted to heritage sites; the manner in which a heritage site can fit into a visitor or tourist experience; the methods used by attraction managers to inform, educate or interest the visiting public; the ways in which the public respond; and the whole notion of heritage as

a business, with the range of entrepreneurial strategies and economic objectives which that involves. Embedded in this promotional thrust of heritage
tourism remain the issues of conservation and preservation. To a varying
extent, the managers of heritage attractions attach priority to these issues.
Many of the strident criticisms of the modern heritage industry arise from the
belief that they are being marginalized by the marketing priority and that,
by the same token, any regard for authenticity is being sacrificed. Peter
Larkham provides the chapter with the most explicit focus on conservation
and preservation. He shows how, for urban areas, closely worded legislation
is needed to achieve good standards of conservation and how tensions between
developers and preservers are always present. Responsibilities for conservation and preservation rest squarely in the public domain; national and local
state must define the rules and accept the roles of guardianship and custodial
care of historical heritage. There are many examples of good conservation of
the built urban environment; in the countryside too the National Parks are
playing key roles. In North America, the United States and Canadian National
Parks Services have commendable records in conservation of the natural
environment; Freeman Tilden's principles for the interpretation of natural
heritage emerged from his work with the US National Parks Service.

The issue of authenticity is closely related to those of conservation and
preservation and indeed to all aspects of heritage tourism. Frans Schouten
argues that authenticity is problematic and few could dispute that assertion.
He takes a 'liberal' view of heritage; by his definition it is not history, it is
the past processed through mythology, ideology, nationalism, local pride,
romantic ideas, or just plain marketing into a commodity. It is clear that many
visitors to heritage sites feel comfortable with that kind of definition. Most
are not seekers after truth in a highly detailed form; they accept that the record
is incomplete and that available evidence has to be interpreted and presented
to them in comprehensible ways. Some heritage attractions go beyond these
guidelines and here lies one of the critical areas of tension. Should someone
be making rules and setting standards? If we want to avoid the distortion of
history, how can the messages at heritage sites be controlled? There is a range
of heritage sites from the untouched ruin at one end, meaningful only to those
with a great deal of cultural capital and perhaps specific knowledge, to the
fabricated theme park at the other, where a recognizable heritage theme may
be presented in a place with which it has tenuous links, sometimes no link
at all, and in a manner which is far more imaginative than factual. This range
is important in understanding the nature of heritage tourism. It varies from
sites of scholarship to those of pure entertainment. The heritage managers are
catering for different types of demand and for different kinds of visitor; in a
situation of 'mass tourism' and boom in leisure-time activities, it is inevitable
that the 'plebeian' end of the market, in the eyes of the critics, is winning.

There are many critics of modern heritage tourism. What unites them is the
belief that any semblance of authenticity has been surrendered to the needs

of marketing attractions under the label of heritage, and the conviction that these developments are threats to 'real' heritage. Lowenthal (1985) regretted the gradual disappearance of the educated visitor and the fact that the 'stones and marbles' of the archaeological record have become dimly apprehended fragments of the past. Heritage managers, in his view, must cater for visitors who have the barest rudiments of history, they must service the ignorant without boring the knowledgeable and have the responsibility of protecting sites from public contamination. History must not be compartmentalized as something which belongs only in the past; it is part of a continuity and is intrinsic to our modern heritage. Hewison (1987) argued that marketing has taken over as museums are pushed into the market-place and the imperative of providing a 'pleasurable experience' has taken over. Urry (1990) stated that what was needed was a critical culture based on the understanding of history and not a set of heritage fantasies. Ashworth and Tunbridge (1990) commented on the 'bowdlerization' of history and its reduction to a few marketable products.

These are critical stances adopted by academics with a natural and genuine commitment to truth, scholarship and the custodial responsibilities attached to heritage. As such they convey a powerful message which cannot be ignored. Managers of heritage sites have always faced one major dilemma – the tension between the commitment to preserve and the pressure to make sites more accessible to a wider public. With the expansion of heritage tourism, this tension has been heightened and a further dimension of authenticity has been added or, at least, has taken a new form. The first premise to accept is that there are and will be many kinds of heritage site. Most will satisfy, to varying degrees, the acceptable limits of preservation and authenticity, but some will not. As with all other types of 'product', the types of heritage site will be recognized for what they are. Some will suit only scholars, some will suit only 'pleasure-seekers', most will have the difficult task of catering for a range of tastes. The providers in some ways hold the key, but they will respond to a perceived tourism market in predictable ways and the responsibility of defining the rules and setting the standards will rest primarily with government.

Any guidelines must revolve around a number of sets of central questions. The first set relates to preservation and conservation. Are sites of genuine heritage interest threatened? Would proposals harm heritage? What new legislation is needed to protect heritage? Do new controls need to be set to fulfil custodial and guardianship roles and to monitor the issue of authenticity? A second set of questions concerns the interests of providers and consumers within heritage tourism. What are providers seeking to achieve? What does the public want? Does a proposed development serve a useful purpose? Such a development may embellish heritage but does it do so in a harmful way? Is there a case for accurate, statutory statements to make clear what a site represents – almost an *intellectual health warning*? All of these questions are relevant but any response will clearly involve significant value judgements the bases of which will have to be explained and justified. Classifications of sites, based largely upon a judgement of authenticity, may well prove the only meaningful and practical compromise.

Adopting standards of presentation and of representation is the responsibility of the 'team' at the heritage site, which, as Terry Stevens argues, should contain a range of expertise. Alongside the market researchers and designers of facilities should be historical expertise; the aims of attracting visitors can be achieved without irresponsible creativity – people have a genuine interest in the past whether labelled as nostalgia or not. If national and regional strategies for the presentation of heritage are in place and are accompanied by quality planning, high standards can be achieved.

It has long been recognized that the claims of some heritage attractions to historical authenticity are questionable. Religious relics of the Middle Ages offer one case in point and a passage written by Proust in the early years of the twentieth century is instructive:

> the violet curtains . . . gave to this room with its lofty ceiling a quasi-historical character that might have made it a suitable place for the assassination of the Duc de Guise, and afterwards for parties of tourists personally conducted by one of Messrs Thomas Cook and Son's guides. (Proust, 1989, p. 717)

The reference to the Duc de Guise recalls a famous assassination which took place at Blois in the late sixteenth century. It was probably brought to Proust's mind by a well-known painting of the event by Delaroche. Tourism operators have always used heritage connections of this kind to promote visiting; the novelty of the 1980s has been the scale and ingenuity of the promotional activity.

One of the earliest lessons of heritage tourism in this new 'wave' is that different groups of people look for different things. The early determinants of wealth and means have largely been replaced by tastes and preferences. Very few places remain the preserve of the wealthier, more educated sections of society. It is more the nature of the attraction and the way in which it is developed which determine who the visitors will be. The task of the preservers and conservationists is to control the most vulnerable and treasured sites; what happens on sites which in their eyes have no real historical 'value' should be of no concern. Theme parks, whether based on heritage or not, whether Camelots or dinosaur parks, are simply part of the entertainment industry and belong in the same category as Blackpool Pleasure Beach, performing a valuable but non-intellectual function. The evidence of variety and differences of appeal has also been evident in natural heritage. It is the spectacular which has always captured the tourist imagination: the snow-capped mountains, majestic ranges and towering waterfalls form the best ingredients of marketing. An early depiction of spectacle is found in the writings of Charles Darwin, a true 'traveller':

the mountains rose abruptly out of the glassy expanse of the lagoon . . . there
were glimpses into the depths of the neighbouring valleys; and the lofty points
of the central mountains, towering up within sixty degrees of the zenith, hid
half the evening sky. Thus seated, it was sublime spectacle to watch the shades
of night gradually obscuring the last and highest pinnacles. (Darwin, 1968,
pp. 406, 411)

At the other end of the natural environment range is the pleasure which can
be derived from the less spectacular – the riverside bank, the secluded beach
or country lane:

The English landscape at its finest . . . possesses a quality that the landscapes
of other nations, however more superficially dramatic, inevitably fail to possess
. . . it is the very lack of obvious drama or spectacle which sets the beauty of
our land apart. What is pertinent is the calmness of that beauty, its sense of
restraint. (Ishiguro, 1989, pp. 28–29)

As Patmore (1983) has recounted, any kind of rural setting can be an attraction for urban dwellers. As long as they feel they are in the countryside, many
visitors are content even to stay in, or close to, their cars in some designated
area.

As tourists, visitors and people at leisure can draw satisfaction from many
different kinds of landscape, so can they derive pleasure from different kinds
of heritage site. The sites which were the preserve of the educated elite have
become accessible to a much wider set of visitors. Some of those who visit
a traditional site such as Tintern Abbey will be versed in its history and acutely
aware of its role in that part of the Welsh borderland; many others will not
have that knowledge but will be interested to learn a few facts, to appreciate
the solemnity of the site and the natural beauty of its setting. The large
majority of heritage sites are of this kind. They have 'modernized' in terms
of presentation and interpretation, and perhaps offer more facilities, but they
have kept close to high standards and the kind of dignity which the history
of the place deserves. A floor of the new wing of the National Gallery in
London has been designated as a 'Micro gallery', containing not paintings but
rows of touch-sensitive computer screens where visitors can call up images of
all the paintings held in the National Gallery (Graham-Dixon, 1993); the
originals of course are still near by to be viewed at first hand.

Whatever the intentions of people who go to heritage sites, whatever reason
or chance brought them there, many sites seek to inform, to educate or
to make the visit more interesting by conveying information in a variety of
legible and easily assimilated ways. Interpretation has become the *sine qua
non* of heritage sites and is itself a developed and innovative methodology.
In some ways the presence or absence of various forms of interpretive media
discriminates between types of site. The untouched are those closest to their
original residual state; the fully created are those where interpretation is in
full flood. Interpretation has many forms, is increasingly reliant upon information technology and can be enormously effective. As Duncan Light reminds

us, the keynote reference on interpretation remains that of Freeman Tilden, whose purpose was always to promote awareness, interest, understanding and eventually a sense of responsibility for heritage. It has become an instrument which can range from the sensitive to the blunt, from a subtle aid to the site to a total experience in its own right. When Eco (1986) and others speak of 'hyper-reality' and the creation of fantasy, interpretation is the means to achieve those ends. Despite these extremes, good practice abounds. The Province of Alberta in Canada, through the work of the Historical Resources Division of Alberta Culture and Multiculturalism, contains many excellent examples of sensitive and effective presentation of heritage. Its showpiece is perhaps the Royal Tyrrell Museum, which has become an international display of geological and dinosaur specimens based on local discoveries. A wide range of modern presentational techniques is used but the dedication to authenticity is complete. Similarly, the Head-Smashed-In Buffalo Jump Interpretive Center uses a range of devices and native Indian guides to convey the rich sense of the heritage of Canada. The actual site, a low cliff face, is genuine but unexceptional; it is the way in which it has been interpreted, again with close attention to authenticity, which makes the visit memorable. The Frank Slide Interpretive Center invokes the much more recent past – a landslide linked with coal-mining in the early part of the twentieth century – but again achieves high presentational standards. The lesson here is clear: attention to authentic detail and conservation are not at odds with the task of attracting visitors; these two aims can be reconciled.

Heritage has been referred to as an industry in a pejorative sense, but it can be a business in the proper sense of the word. As museums have been forced through economic circumstances to enter the market-place by charging for entry and competing for visitors, so heritage managers have some compulsion to develop their sites for similar reasons. Visitors provide the funds which facilitate the preservation and guardianship roles. Heritage as business becomes part of tourism, which is a significant component of many local economies and is often promoted in places where such economic incentives are badly needed. Areas which have lost their traditional industries, such as coal, steel-making or textiles, have turned to tourism as a substitute and heritage is often the most accessible form of tourist development. From the inner cities and former industrial docklands of major metropolitan areas to former mining valleys, the processes of change are the same. Heritage tourism, even in its more bizarre forms, such as Wild West ranches in the Rhondda, offers some economic hope to districts with very limited options. There are 'down-sides' to the success of heritage tourism, and Curphey (1994) reported that many historic towns are suffering from the influx of visitors. In Bath, local people turned hosepipes on tourists in open-top buses in protest against the noise and intrusion. A member of the English Tourist Board is quoted as saying that small historic towns are jewels in the crown of English tourism and we have to find a way of maintaining them while allowing the local people to enjoy a decent quality of life.

Heritage has wider meanings than the provision of attractions for visitors and tourists. Heritage has always been a mechanism which can be used to forge national identity; some forms of nationalism have actively promoted ideas such as common roots, past glories and shared qualities or values. The facts of heritage have been used and manipulated for political purposes. Heritage as a component of culture is one of the great bonding mechanisms which has given a territory and its people a strong sense of identity and belonging. The tie to place or territory is typical but not essential; there is an analogy with the concept of 'community', for which the coincidence with place is a normal but not necessary condition. Heritage has been used in the past to create a sense of national identity and a particular image; it is being used similarly at present. As Ashworth shows, the new concept of a wider European Union, which some political leaders in Europe wish to form, can be aided by the creation of a stronger sense of European rather than national heritage, though this would require a major promotional effort. There are many other countries in the world where this issue is of significance. Federal Canada must promote a national rather than provincial sense of identity, a task made much more difficult by the conflicting views of heritage held by French- and English-speaking Canadians. In Europe, the break-up of the USSR and Yugoslavia bears powerful testimony to the strength of a national sense of heritage, even after many decades of forced federation.

Heritage in the political sense has another dimension. It can become an instrument in the hands of image-builders to create a particular image of a nation. This can be recounted historically, as Pyrs Gruffudd has exemplified. It was in the interests of the English middle classes and the travel agencies to portray Wales as a land of mountains and simple rural people; they selected those parts of reality which suited their purposes. Duncan and Duncan (1992) noted that the 'Blue Guides' to Europe promoted the culture of nature and individualism but 'mystified' realities with their almost exclusive concern with monuments and neglect of living conditions. There are many examples: accounts of the American West which glorified the white settlers and failed to depict the deprivation of the Indians; and images of the Scottish Highlands which focused on tartans, bagpipes and deer-hunting on estates while ignoring the plight of the displaced crofters. Images can be made and unmade at the behest of those with power, resources and control of the media; heritage has been manipulated in these ways.

There are other pressing issues which have only been referred to incidentally in this book. Questions of image and heritage as a basis for national identity raise issues of acceptable and unacceptable heritage. War atrocities, crimes against humanity and disasters are all part of heritage, but what is to be preserved and what is not? Many of the symbols of Fascist activities have been swept away; it is the victims who keep the museums. Boyes (1993), writing about a new $20 million Central European Development Project to reconstruct Birkenau-Auschwitz as a museum 50 years after the end of World War II, commented that it took three years after German reunification for historians to agree on a modest tablet recording the death of 11 000 people at Buchenwald. When the Japanese Emperor visited Weimar, he was taken to a house used by Goethe, rather than to nearby Buchenwald. Cheyette (1993) reported that an estimated $300 million had been spent on three Holocaust memorials in Washington, Los Angeles and Jerusalem. Around 4 million tourists visit the best-known killing fields or memorial sites of the last world war. In Poland there is an increasing awareness of the tourist potential of this kind of heritage. Cheyette (1993) emphasized, in a review of *The Texture of Memory* by James Young, the plurality of the images of this kind of past which are shaped by radically different natural and political agendas, and thus 'interpretations' of history. There is always a down-side to human history and the new heritage industry faces ethical questions concerning what it presents and what it omits.

Clearly there are as many questions as answers concerning the phenomenon of heritage tourism. This book has tackled many of them in constructive and interpretive ways, but the research agenda remains long and demanding. There is an urgency in these matters because of the pace of change and the diversity of current activities. If the case for better understanding, good practice and high-quality planning is to pass from the realms of academic debate into the actual ways in which heritage is developed and presented, both the central issues and the practicalities need to be addressed now.

References

Ashworth, G. J. and Tunbridge, J. E. (1990) *The Tourist-Historic City*. London: Belhaven.
Boyes, R. (1993) Why Auschwitz must be saved. *The Times*, 24 November, p. 17.
Cheyette, B. (1993) Double monuments to the rhetoric of ruins. *Independent*, 24 July.
Curphey, M. (1994) Tourist trap towns are too popular for their own good. *The Times*, 25 May, p. 7.
Darwin, C. (1968) *The Voyage of the Beagle*. Geneva: Edito Service, SA. (First published 1839.)
Duncan, J. S. and Duncan, N. G. (1992) Ideology and bliss: Roland Barthes and his recent histories of landscape. In T. J. Barnes and S. S. Duncan (eds) *Writing Worlds: Discourse, Text and Metaphor in the Representation of Landscape*. London: Routledge, pp. 18–37.
Eco, U. (1986) *Travels in Hyper-Reality*. London: Picador.
Graham-Dixon, A. (1993) The virtual art gallery comes of age. *Independent*, 9 February, p. 14.
Hewison, R. (1987) *The Heritage Industry: Britain in a Climate of Decline*. London: Methuen.

Ishiguro, K. (1989) *The Remains of the Day*. London: Faber and Faber.
Lowenthal, D. (1985) *The Past Is a Foreign Country*. Cambridge: Cambridge University Press.
Patmore, J. A. (1983) *Recreation and Resources: Leisure Patterns and Leisure Places*. Oxford: Basil Blackwell.
Proust, M. (1989) *Remembrance of Things Past*. Harmondsworth: Penguin Books. (First published Paris: Gallimard, 1954.)
Urry, J. (1990) *The Tourist Gaze: Leisure and Travel in Contemporary Societies*. London: Sage.

Index